**Marian H.J. Assink,** PhD, is a teacher at the School for Higher Vocational Education at the Faculty of Health Care in Utrecht, The Netherlands. In 1988, she started studying psychology at the University of Amsterdam besides her work as a registered nurse. In 1996 she received an MA (with honors) in developmental psychology and methodology. The subject of her Master's thesis was an analysis of the structure of the life-line, as obtained by the Life-line Interview Method (LIM). After graduation she went to Davos, Switzerland, to work as a nurse in a clinic for rehabilitation. In 1999, she continued work on the Life-line Interview Method as a PhD-student at the Vrije Universiteit in Amsterdam; she obtained her doctoral degree in 2008.


**Johannes J.F. Schroots** is director of the European Research Institute on Health and Aging (ERGO) in Amsterdam. He studied psychology at the Vrije Universiteit Amsterdam, receiving an MA (*cum laude*) in experimental, industrial & organizational psychology (1969, 1970) and a PhD in social science (1979).

From 1999 until 2008, he was senior gerontology researcher at the Vrije Universiteit Amsterdam and (from 2001) executive director of ALLEA (European Federation of National Academies of Sciences and the Humanities). For the period 1990–2000, he was adjunct professor of human gerontology at the University of Amsterdam and (from 1993) chair and project leader of EuGeron (EC concerted action on Gerontology: Aging, Health and Competence) and EXCELSA/Pilot (Cross-European Longitudinal Study of Aging), respectively. From 1970 until 1990, he was coordinator of the Netherlands Institute for Preventive Medicine (NIPG/TNO) Department of Preventive Health Care for the Elderly.

His research focuses on life-course dynamics (multidisciplinary issues of development and aging) and on the longitudinal study of autobiographical memory as measured with the LIM | Life-line Interview Method.

He is a fellow of the Andrew Norman Institute for Advanced Study in Gerontology and Geriatrics at the University of Southern California, Los Angeles, CA, USA. He has edited books on aging and has published scientific articles on the psychology of aging, autobiographical memory, and life-course dynamics. He is a fellow of the Gerontological Society of America.

# The Dynamics of Autobiographical Memory

## Using the LIM | Life-line Interview Method

Marian H.J. Assink & Johannes J.F. Schroots

HOGREFE

**Library of Congress Cataloguing-in-Publication Data**
is available via the Library of CongressMarc Database
under the LC Control Number 2009927604

**Library and Archives Canada Cataloguing in Publication**

Assink, Marian
    The dynamics of autobiographical memory : using the LIM, life-line
interview method / Marian Assink & Johannes J.F. Schroots.

Accompanied by CD.
Includes bibliographical references.
ISBN 978-0-88937-370-9

    1. Autobiographical memory.  I. Schroots, J. J. F  II. Title.

BF378.A87A86 2009           153.1'3            C2009-902629-5

PUBLISHING OFFICES
**USA:**        Hogrefe Publishing, 875 Massachusetts Avenue, 7th Floor Cambridge, MA 02139
            Tel. (866) 823-4726, Fax (617) 354-6875, E-mail customerservice@hogrefe-publishing.com
**Europe:**    Hogrefe Publishing, Rohnsweg 25, 37085 Göttingen, Germany
            Tel. +49 551 49609-0, Fax +49 551 49609-88, E-mail publishing@hogrefe.com

SALES AND DISTRIBUTION
**USA:**        Hogrefe Publishing, Customer Service Department, 30 Amberwood Parkway,
            Ashland, OH 44805, Tel. (800) 228-3749, Fax (419) 281-6883, E-mail customerservice@hogrefe.com
**Europe:**    Hogrefe Publishing, Rohnsweg 25, 37085 Göttingen, Germany
            Tel. +49 551 49609-0, Fax +49 551 49609-88, E-mail publishing@hogrefe.com

OTHER OFFICES
**Canada:**     Hogrefe Publishing, 660 Eglinton Ave. East, Suite 119-514, Toronto, Ontario, M4G 2K2
**Switzerland:** Hogrefe Publishing, Länggass-Strasse 76, CH-3000 Bern 9

Hogrefe Publishing
Incorporated and registered in the Commonwealth of Massachusetts, USA, and in Göttingen, Lower Saxony,
Germany

Printed and bound in the USA
ISBN 978-0-88937-370-9

# Foreword

The study of autobiographical memory is becoming of broader interest as people are living longer and having more active lives. This book offers valuable information about the course of autobiographical memory in adults based upon longitudinal research.

The findings are based on a five-year study in which young, middle aged, and older adults were interviewed using the LIM | Life-line Interview Method three times. The research provides an important perspective on the changes in memory over adult life. Not only what is recalled but how it is evaluated by individuals is reported. The relationships between gender, age, and memory are described and discussed. Both past events and expected future events were measured, i.e., both retrospective and prospective autobiographical memory.

The method used to collect individual autobiographical memory data was the Life-line Interview Method. It results not only in chronologically ordered memories but also in data on how these are evaluated by the individuals recalling them. The method also provides individual life stories' events of the past, present, and expected future.

Those who are interested in lifespan development will find the findings significant. Young and older adults show different trends in their memories. Results of the study showed that older persons recall more past events and anticipate fewer future events. The data reveal what is described as the "bump effect," in which older adults recall a disproportionate number of events from adolescence and early adulthood. This contradicts what might be expected from classical views of lifelong memory.

The study also gives new and important findings about how age is related to positive and negative evaluations of life events. While the participants in the study reported equal numbers of negative and positive events, there were gender differences – young women were more positive about their lives than were young men. Of significance was the finding that older persons were more positive about the past than were the young. The period of life reported to be the most positive is "the period between about 20 to 40 years of age." By contrast the worst period is that of 70–80 years.

There are many other findings that are reported that will stimulate further research and lead to knowledge about lifespan developmental processes. For example, there are issues about the expression of aggression by young persons and depression by older persons. How do such behavioral predispositions relate to autobiographical memory and the ways life events are interpreted? The significance of this work will increase as the social and behavioral sciences expand their explorations of lifespan development and the ways autobiographical memory is related to individuals' behavior over the life span.

*James E. Birren*
Andrus Gerontology Center
University of Southern California
Los Angeles, CA

# Table of Contents

# Acknowledgments

The history of this study on the dynamics of autobiographical memory began in the 1980s, when the senior author developed the first experimental version of the LIM | Life-line Interview Method as part of his inquiry into metaphors of development and aging at the Andrus Gerontology Center at the University of Southern California, Los Angeles. Many versions of the LIM have followed since, but all of them were in Dutch. The final Dutch version dates from 1995, when the longitudinal study on autobiographical memory began, as part of the umbrella research project on life-course dynamics. Recently, the English version was introduced at the LIM Workshop of the International Reminiscence and Life Review Conference 2007 in San Francisco.

Many thanks are due to all those students and colleagues who in one way or another contributed to this study. In particular, we would like to thank Titia Buddingh', Sanne Janus, Liselotte Kunst, Marlies van Noppen-Schrijer, and Tinca Nijdam for collecting data and writing reports.

We also would like to thank Jim Birren, Pim Cuijpers, Douwe Draaisma, Pieter Drenth, Jaap Murre, and Willem Albert Wagenaar for their comments on the manuscript.

It is our pleasure to acknowledge the support of the University of Amsterdam, the Free University, and the ERGO foundation, which provided us with the opportunity to conduct the study.

Last, but not least, we thank the respondents who were willing to share their life story on multiple occasions.

*Marian H.J. Assink & Johannes J.F. Schroots*

# Chapter 1

# General Introduction

## 1.1 Introduction

### 1.1.1 Autobiographical memory

For more than a century psychologists have studied memory but it is only since the seventies of the last century that research on autobiographical memory started to grow substantially (Skowronski, 2005). There has been and still is considerable discussion about the position, term and definition of autobiographical memory. In this study the term 'autobiographical memory' is broadly defined as a type of episodic memory for both retrospective (memories) and prospective information (expectations) related to the self (Birren & Schroots, 2006; Schroots, van Dijkum & Assink, 2004). Autobiographical memory (AM) is studied across multiple subdisciplines. For instance, neuropsychology is concerned with aspects of anatomy and biology that mediate AM (e.g., Conway & Fthenaki, 2000); developmental psychology focuses on the development of AM (e.g., Howe & Courage, 1997); personality psychology focuses, for instance, on relations between personality traits and features of the life story (McAdams et al., 2004), and cognitive psychology investigates the accessibility of memories over the lifespan (e.g., Rubin, Rahhal & Poon, 1998). All these disciplines, however, operate rather isolated from each other and there is not yet a theoretical framework which covers the diversity of AM research (Conway & Pleydell-Pearce, 2000). As a consequence, there are many theoretical ideas instead of one dominant theory of AM and the methods used to study AM are very diverse. Skowronski (2005) assumes that the theoretical and empirical diversity contributes to the survival and progress of this area of psychology. Other researchers, however, state that a consistent method of measuring and analyzing autobiographical memories is needed in order for science to advance (Kovach, 1995; Schroots & Assink, 2004).

In the present study AM is studied from a lifespan perspective. It was not until the 1980's that lifespan psychology became subject of empirical study. For a long time, adulthood and old age were considered to be relatively stable periods without significant changes (Abeles, 1987). Only a few scientists were interested in what happened in midlife and old age (Birren & Schroots, 2001). For instance, Hall (1922) wrote a book on senescence and Bühler (1933) and Frenkel (1936) tried to reveal general developmental principles from the biographies of different individuals (McAdams, 1988). The work of Erikson (1950) gave an important impulse to the lifespan orientation in psychology (Settersten, 1999). Erikson developed a psychosocial theory of personality development across the whole lifespan consisting of eight stages in each of which a task has to be fulfilled or a crisis solved. But it was not until 1980 that the first review of lifespan developmental psychology was published by Baltes, Reese and Lipsitt. According to these authors, "Lifespan developmental psychology is concerned with the description, explanation, and modification (optimization) of developmental processes in the human life course from conception to death" (p. 66). In 1982 Schroots introduced the term 'ontogenetic psychology'. Ontogenetic psychology is concerned with the description and explanation of behavior throughout the life course from conception till death (Schroots, 1982). The term 'lifespan' is generally used by psychologists and is focused on 'intra-psychic' (or interior) phenomena and changes in these phenomena over the span of an individual's life, while the term 'life course' is mostly used by sociologists who emphasize the link between social structures and human life (Settersten, 1999).

In order to study the development of all kinds of phenomena across the lifespan most frequently cross-sectional and longitudinal studies are conducted (Sugarman, 2001). In cross-sectional studies aspects of behavior are studied in different age groups at one moment in time and the results are compared to each other. Cross-sectional studies provide data and allow inferences only about inter-individual or between-person differences. It is unclear in cross-sectional research in how far age differences equal age changes as age groups in cross-sectional research can be different from one another in many aspects besides age (e.g., Schaie & Hofer, 2001; Schroots & Birren, 1988; Sugarman 2001). In order to answer questions concerning the development of all kinds of phenomena over the lifespan and to discover the mechanisms that explain the processes within individuals, it is necessary to conduct longitudinal research where the same individuals are studied at different points in time. In principle, two repeated observations constitute a longitudinal study, but Schroots and Birren (1993) quote Deeg who considers a study to be longitudinal, "when the same persons are observed with respect to the same characteristics more often than two times and during a period long enough to enable the ascertainment of changes in these characteristics" (p. 5). Baltes and Nesselroade (1979) gave five rationales for the utility of longitudinal study of behavioral development: (1) direct identification of intra-individual change, (2) identification of inter-individual variability in intra-individual change, (3) relationships among intra-individual changes, (4) determinants of intra-individual change, and (5) inter-individual variability in determinants of intra-individual change. Hofer and Sliwinski (2006) state that these five rationales make it clear that it is necessary to measure and model change at two distinct levels of analysis: the intra-individual (or within-person) and the inter-individual (or between-person) level.

Until now little is known about changes concerning AM across the lifespan. There are a few studies in which respondents were asked to recall the same events at two different sessions (see Chapter 5) but, as far as known, there are no studies in which respondents are asked to report spontaneously events they recall from their past and expect for their future at different points in time. The present study aims to fill this gap. The study covers a period of five years in which the same respondents are measured three times. In this way it can be determined what remains stable and what changes with respect to different aspects of AM.

## 1.1.2 Life-line Interview Method

As there is not yet a comprehensive theory of AM to guide research in this area, an explorative, descriptive approach was used in this study. According to Van Zuuren (2002), an exhaustive description of the data forms the basis for gaining insight in a phenomenon and for discovering associations. In this way research contributes to the creation of hypotheses and the development of theory and is more inductive (i.e., hypotheses generating) than deductive (i.e., hypotheses testing). Qualitative research is very suitable for generating hypotheses and development of theories, as it concentrates on the entire person and his environment, and starts from the subjective experience and the meaning given to this experience. Qualitative material can provide information that may not be accessible by other methods. "Sometimes qualitative material can best reveal innermost thoughts, frames of reference, reactions to situations, and cultural conventions. In fact, language often tells more about people than they want to disclose, or than they know about themselves, and it can bring to light things a researcher might not think to ask about" (Smith, 2000, p. 313). Drenth and Heller (2004) argue that the boundary between quantitative and qualitative is often permeable and they state that a combination of different methods often gives better results than a single method.

As mentioned before there are many different methods to gather autobiographical information. In the present study a special method, the Life-line Interview Method (LIM) was used. The LIM is a semi-structured interview and combines a quantitative and a qualitative approach. "The LIM has been developed purposively to study the subjective or self-organization of past and future behavior over the course of life. With the term 'subjective' we mean the perception by the individual of his or her life, which implies some sort of retro- and prospective memory for life events, experiences, and/or expectations, as well as some sort of reflective and integrative capacity for these events" (Schroots, 2003b, p. 193). In short, in a typical LIM session, a person is first asked to place perceptions of his/her life, past as well as future, visually in a temporal framework by drawing his/her life-line. Next, the respondent is asked to label each peak and each dip by chronological age and to tell what happened at a certain moment or during an indicated period. When all peaks and dips are labeled, the respondent is asked to tell something more about each event and in this way the life story is obtained. This procedure results in a life-line, which consists of a series of chronologically ordered life events, and a life story. In this study analysis of the data will be limited to the analysis of life events.

### 1.1.3 Purpose

In the present study 98 men and women of a young, middle and older age group were asked three times in a period of five years to recall memories from their past and to report expectations they have for their future by means of the Life-line Interview Method (LIM). Until now results of the first wave of this LIM-study have been published concerning the *structure* of the LIM | *Life-line* (Schroots & Assink, 1998), the *number of events* (Schroots, van Dijkum & Assink, 2004), the *affect of events* (Assink & Schroots, 2002), the *content of events* (Schroots & Assink, 2004; Schroots & Assink, 2005) and the *number of words* respondents use to tell the LIM | *Life story* (Schroots, Kunst & Assink, 2006). From these studies different patterns emerged concerning the structure of different aspects of AM. For instance, it turned out that respondents of different age groups reported the same number of events over the total lifespan, i.e., past and future.

The studies mentioned above have got a sequel; the LIM was administered a second and third time to the same group of respondents and thus has become a longitudinal study. The main purpose, then, of this longitudinal, explorative study, which is part of the research program *Life-course Dynamics* (Schroots, 2003b) is twofold and can be summarized as follows: (1) to determine the stability and change across the lifespan of patterns which were found at the first wave, and (2) to provide a description of the stability and change of autobiographical memories and expectations over the lifespan. Autobiographical memories and expectations will be analyzed from the perspective of number, affect and content. Subsequently, the effect of age and gender on stability and change will be determined.

### 1.1.4 Overview

In the next paragraph, first, a short overview will be given of the history, position and organization of autobiographical memory. Second, different methods which are used to collect autobiographical information will be mentioned. Special attention will be given to the Life-line Interview Method. In paragraph 1.3 attention will be paid to the study of life events in the past decades and to the dimensions by which life events are classified. Life events are the building blocks of the life story and the relation between the life story and AM will be discussed. In paragraph 1.4 a description is given of the design of this study, the respondents who participated in this study, the administration of the LIM and the way in which results were analyzed. In the following four chapters the empirical results of the study are presented. LIM-results will be analyzed from the perspective of number, affect and content of events. Chapter 2 presents results concerning the (change in) number of events respondents recall from their past and expect for the future and the distribution of these events over the lifespan. The question whether respondents recall and expect mainly positive or negative events is answered in Chapter 3. Because of the enormous amount of data concerning the content of events, this subject is divided over two chapters. Chapter 4 provides a description of the content of events for the first wave resulting in a description of the model life course for men and women of a young, middle and older age group. The results of the first wave make up the base line for Chapter 5 in which the stability and change in content of memories and expectations over a period of two and five years will be analyzed. Chapter 6 includes a presentation of the main findings of this study and a general discussion about methodological issues. To conclude, Chapter 7 ends with a summary of the lifespan dynamics of autobiographical memory.

## 1.2  Autobiographical memory

### 1.2.1  History

Autobiographical memory is what is usually meant by the term *memory* in everyday usage (Rubin, 1995). The psychological study of memory started more than a century ago and is characterized by two different traditions (Baddeley, 1999). The tradition that dominated memory research for a long period was the experimental research on learning and memory which was started by Ebbinghaus (1885). Because he wanted to study memory as a pure function of learning independent of content Ebbinghaus used nonsense words as stimuli. Under controlled laboratory conditions he studied the structure, organization and accuracy of memory (Pillemer, 2003). The other direction in memory research was started by Francis Galton. As soon as 1879, he conducted what is now often considered to be the first empirical study of autobiographical memory. Galton displayed a word to himself and then allowed the word to elicit some type of association, the so called 'prompt word' technique. As psychology developed as a natural science, the direction indicated by Ebbinghaus was followed during the next 100 years and Galton's studies were not continued for the time being. In 1932, however, Bartlett criticized the Ebbinghaus approach to memory because the most central and characteristic features of human memory were excluded in these type of studies. Bartlett had his subjects learn and recall meaningful material under naturalistic conditions. But it is only since the seventies of the last century that there has been an upsurge in the interest of 'everyday memory'. From that time on research on autobiographical memory has started to grow significantly and in 1986 the first book about autobiographical memory was edited (Rubin, 1986). Draaisma (2001) wrote a fascinating book about different aspects of autobiographical memory such as first memories, déjà-vu, near-death experiences, flashbulb memories and memory feats of idiot-savants, which became very popular among the general public.

## 1.2.2 Definition

In the past decades, there has been considerable discussion about the position, term and definition of autobiographical memory. Until the 1960s it was assumed that there was not more than one kind of memory. Broadbent (1958) made a distinction between long- and short term memory and by the early 1970s this distinction was widely accepted. In the case of the psychological study of memory, there is considerable agreement now that memory can broadly be divided into: (1) sensory memory; (2) short-term or working memory; and (3) long-term memory. Sensory memory refers to the role of storage in the processes involved in perception. The sense organs have a limited ability to store information about the world in a fairly unprocessed way for less than a second. Short-term or working memory refers to the temporary storage of material necessary for performing a range of complex tasks such as comprehension, reasoning, and long-term learning. Short-term memory allows us to retain information long enough to use it and lasts approximately between 15 and 30 seconds, unless people rehearse the material. Long-term memory refers to more durable encoding and storage systems and can last a lifetime (Baddeley, 1999). Tulving (1972) divided long-term memory into episodic and semantic memory, the first referring to personally experienced events and the last to general facts, for instance, knowing how to write and read. Later, Tulving (1991) elaborated his memory theory and suggested five forms of memory: procedural, perceptual, short-term, semantic and episodic. According to Tulving (2002) episodic memory grew out of semantic memory and those two systems share many features. "Episodic memory is a recently evolved, late-developing, and early-deteriorating past-oriented memory system, more vulnerable than other memory systems to neuronal dysfunction, and probably unique to humans. Its operations require, but go beyond, the semantic memory system" (p. 5). Episodic memory requires three elements: (1) a sense of subjective time which enables one to travel back in time in one's own mind; (2) the ability to be aware of subjective time which is called 'autonoetic awareness'; and (3) a 'self' that can travel in subjective time. Tulving does not use the term 'autobiographical memory' and the question is whether episodic memory and autobiographical memory are different terms for the same memory system. According to Banaji and Crowder (1989) all episodic memory is autobiographical memory because episodic memory concerns personally experienced and therefore autobiographical information. But Brewer (1995) is convinced that 'recollective memory', a term he preferred in stead of 'autobiographical memory', is a unique form of memory. He defined an individual's autobiographical memory as "a recollection of a particular episode from an individual's past" (1986, p. 34). Baddeley states that "autobiographical memory is concerned with the capacity of people to recollect their lives" (1992, p. 26). In contrast with these researchers, Rubin (1995, p. 1) believes "that definitions should not be set a priori, but should reflect the natural cleavages that researchers found in nature!" In general, it can be said that "the term autobiographical memory has generally been used to describe any sort of research in which individuals recall episodes from their own past; the focus in most research is on the recall of specific, individual memories of particular events" (Bluck & Habermas, 2001, p. 135).

A common aspect of most definitions of autobiographical memory is that it refers to the individual's past. During the past years, however, there is an increasing interest in prospective memory, defined "as remembering at some point in the future that something has to be done, without any prompting in the form of explicit instructions to recall" (Maylor, Darby, Logie, Della Sala & Smith, 2002, p. 235). This contrasts with retrospective memory, which refers to remembering information from the past although prospective memory tasks need retrospective remembering. One has to remember that he/she should remember something (Maylor et al., 2002). This definition, which emphasizes the memory function of 'remembering to remember', covers only partly prospective *autobiographical* memory functioning. As Tulving (2002) argues, episodic memory requires a mental travel in time and it has to be realized that it is not only possible to travel backwards in the past but also to travel forwards into the future. Human beings are not only aware of what has been but also of what may come. They are aware of their continued existence in time and reflect on, worry about, and make plans for their future. Thus, when retrospective autobiographical memory – briefly summarized – relates to the retrieval of memories, experiences or past events in the present, then prospective autobiographical memory is concerned with the retrieval of expectations, anticipations or future events, which likewise are based on present memory functioning. Consequently, in this LIM-study the term 'autobiographical memory' is broadly defined as a type of episodic memory for both retrospective and prospective information related to the individual (Schroots, van Dijkum & Assink, 2004).

### 1.2.3 Organization of autobiographical knowledge

Autobiographical memory emerges at about the end of the second year of age. Before that age personal memories are not available, a phenomenon which is called 'childhood amnesia'. Children develop a sense of *me* at that time and begin to organize events that they experience as 'things that happened to me' (Howe & Courage, 1997). Conway and Pleydell-Pearce (2000) provided an integrative, hierarchical model – which still has to be tested empirically – of a self-memory system (SMS) that links an autobiographical knowledge base to personal goals. According to Conway and Pleydell-Pearce (2000), the autobiographical knowledge base contains information at three different hierarchical levels of specificity: lifetime periods, general events, and event-specific knowledge. Lifetime periods are the most general memories and cover relatively large segments of autobiographical time with identifiable beginnings and endings, like 'When I studied psychology'. General events are more specific and at the same time more heterogeneous than lifetime periods. They encompass both repeated events and single events, like 'Every morning I went to college by bicycle'. Event-specific knowledge contains event details unique to a single event, like 'That morning, I had an accident'. Event-specific knowledge is embedded in a general event which in its turn is embedded in a lifetime period. According to Conway and Pleydell-Pearce (2000) one's goals function as control processes in the SMS and modulate the construction of memories. Autobiographical memories are encoded and later retrieved in ways that serve the self's goal agendas. As such, current goals influence the way autobiographical information is absorbed and organized in the first place, and goals generate retrieval models to guide the search process later. The autobiographical knowledge base also helps to ground the personal goals. People formulate goals for the future that are reasonably in line with the information encoded as lifetime periods, general events, and event-specific knowledge.

### 1.2.4 Methods

Many different methods are used to obtain autobiographical data. As already mentioned Galton (1879), who conducted the first empirical study on autobiographical memory, used the so called 'prompt word' technique by displaying a word to himself and then allowed the word to elicit some type of association. Crovitz and Schiffman (1974) modified Galton's word technique. They gave subjects a list of words and asked them to think of a specific memory they associated with that word. This 'word-cue' method has become with some variations one of the major methods used by psychologists to study autobiographical memory (for an overview see Conway & Haque, 1999; Fromholt et al., 2003; Rubin, Rahhal & Poon, 1998; Rubin, Schulkind & Rahhal, 1999). In other studies participants are asked to generate spontaneously (a certain number of specific) memories (d'Argembeau, Comblain & Van der Linden, 2003; Baum & Stewart, 1990; Berntsen & Rubin, 2002; Elnick, Margrett, Fitzgerald, & Labouvie-Vief, 1999; Fitzgerald, 1988, 1992, 1995; Holmes & Conway, 1999; Rubin, Schulkind & Rahhal, 1999; Sehulster, 1996). Questionnaires are also used to sample information about major life events. For instance, Glickman, Hubbard and Valciukas (1990) used the Life Events Questionnaire. Fingerman and Perlmutter (1995) used an abbreviated version of the Major Life Events Inventory (Phinney, Chiodo & Perlmutter, 1988), which consists of a list of 50 normative and non-normative life events. Normative events are events which occur at about the same time to all individuals in a given (sub)culture or to most members of a given cohort, while non-normative events do not occur in any normative manner for most individuals (Baltes, Reese & Lipsitt, 1980). Fingerman and Perlmutter (1995) also used an anticipated future events questionnaire. This questionnaire examined the most important events participants expected to experience in the next two years.

Another method to gain knowledge about the working of autobiographical memory is by means of diary studies, in which diarists record one or more autobiographical events each day for a certain period (Burt, Kemp & Conway, 2003). For instance, Wagenaar (1986) recorded one or more events daily for six years. He recorded who, what, where, and when information about the events, and rated the events for saliency, emotional involvement, and pleasantness. Recall was cued by different combinations of the recorded aspects.

Besides these methods which ask participants to generate (a specific number of) memories from their lives, autobiographical memory is also studied by means of the life story of the individual. Robinson and Taylor (1998) asked fourteen women with a mean age of 46 years first to tell about their life experiences and how they felt they fit together and second, to review their lives once more but to focus now on the disruptions, detours, surprises, choices, and turning points, both good and bad that may have occurred. Luborsky (1990; 1998) asked respondents to describe their lives. McAdams (1997) developed an extended life-story technique in which the participant is asked, among others, to divide his life into its main chapters, to provide a plot summary for each and to identify eight key scenes or episodes that stand out in the story as especially important or self-determining events. The complete interview takes about 2–3 hours to complete. Fromholt et al. (2003) asked subjects to "Tell about the events that have been important in your life", in a 15-minute interview. Hermans (1992) used a method of self-investigation which enables a person to tell his or her life story to a psychologist in a way that results in an overview of valuations, including moral valuations, referring to the person's past, present, and future. This process reveals the affective and motivational characteristics of the storyteller and leads to changes in (a retelling of) the narrative. Mackavey, Malley and Stewart (1991) used the autobiographies of 49 eminent psychologists to analyze the content in terms of autobiographically consequential experiences (ACE).

There are also alternative methods to obtain autobiographical information. Respondents were asked to draw their life line (Brugman, 2000; Hentschel, Sumbadze & Shubladze, 2000) or story line (Gergen & Gergen, 1987; Gergen, 1988) or life graph (Back & Bourque, 1970; Back, 1982; Bourque & Back, 1977; Grob, Krings and Bangerter, 2001) or to draw their life (Whitbourne & Dannefer, 1985–1986). Timelines (Rappaport, Enrich & Wilson, 1985) were used by deVries and Watt (1996) and Elnick et al. (1999), while Martin and Smyer (1990) used a sorting task in which participants were asked to select events that occurred to them and order the events according to the global importance they had in their lives.

## 1.2.5  Life-line Interview Method

As mentioned before the Life-line Interview Method (LIM) was used in the present study to elicit autobiographical information in a systematic, standardized way. The LIM has been developed by Schroots

(1984) on the basis of several studies of metaphors of aging and the individual life course. According to Collins Cobuild English Dictionary (1995) a metaphor is "an imaginative way of describing something by referring to something else which has the qualities that you want to express". For a long period metaphors had a bad reputation in science because the positivistic view of science required a clear, unambiguous, and objective description or characterization of reality. In recent years, however, it is argued that science is in an essential way metaphorical and characteristically employs metaphors; science is based on more or less implicit metaphors. This approach is based on the constructivist view of reality in science which holds that reality or the objective world is mentally constructed on the basis of the constraining influences of the individual's knowledge and language. Theorists are guided by implicit metaphors in exploring and discovering new phenomena. For instance, the computer metaphor – the human brain is a computer – has guided research in human memory for decades and has resulted in much progress in this field. When making explicit the implicit metaphor the assumptions which arise from it can be elaborated and examined concerning their appropriateness and consequences. The explicit metaphor can provide a deeper understanding of the existing theory but can also generate or create a whole body of theoretical problems and solutions. In short, metaphor is a means of entering the unknown through the gateway of the known (liberally quoted from: Schroots, 1984; Schroots, 1991; Schroots & Birren, 2002; Schroots & ten Kate, 1989; Schroots, Birren, & Kenyon, 1991).

Frequently, individuals describe their lives as 'making a journey' which is symbolized by the 'footpath' metaphor. In this metaphor, both the temporal dimension and the affective dimension are expressed by traversing the mountains and valleys of life. When people use expressions as 'I'm feeling up' or 'I'm really low these days' to express positive and negative feelings, they make use of this footpath metaphor. The LIM is based on the 'footpath' metaphor, i.e., the graphical, two-dimensional representation of a footpath – with time on the horizontal dimension and affect on the vertical dimension – which symbolizes the course of human life with its ups and downs of important life events. The basic pattern of the LIM, as most metaphors of life, is the branching or bifurcation point. Such branching points may be defined as those changes in the life of the individual that direct the life path in a distinctive direction, and that are separated in time from each other by one or more affective or critical events or experiences (Birren & Deutchman, 1991). This bifurcation or branching behavior of the individual at the biological, psychological or social level of functioning is the core of the Branching Theory of Aging, an aspect theory of gerodynamics, which studies the dynamics of development and aging over the lifespan. Metaphorically speaking, bifurcation means that the fluctuating individual passes a critical point – the bifurcation, branching, choice, turning or transformation point – and can branch off into higher- and/or lower-order structures or processes. Higher- and lower-order structures can be translated in terms of mortality, morbidity and quality of life. For example, traumatic life events and a healthy lifestyle may result in lower and higher order structures, respectively, and consequently in higher and lower probabilities of dying. Thus defined, the LIM|Life-line may be conceived of as a series of branching points from birth to death which forms the basic structure of the LIM|Life story (liberally quoted from: Schroots 1988, 1995, 1996; Schroots & Birren, 1988; Schroots & Birren, 2002; Schroots & Yates, 1999).

The LIM has special characteristics which makes the method very suitable for gathering autobiographical information. First of all, most people are familiar with the graphical representation of time by a straight line and with hills and valley's representing the ups and downs in life, and they do not need much thinking before drawing their life-line.

Second, the LIM claims to elicit autobiographical information at the affective level of the behavioral organization of the individual. Because of the hills and the dips in the life-line, the respondent automatically reveals the accompanying affect of the events, while the faults of more cognitively-oriented techniques like questionnaires, open interviews and (auto)biographies, which appeal primarily to the rational verbal capacities of the individual, are avoided. In actual practice most of the interviewed only after the drawing of the life-line fully realize what they are revealing and some of them want to 'correct' the original line in order to present themselves in a more positive way. For instance, a woman had drawn a very deep dip in her childhood. When she realized this, she wanted to make the dip less deep because "she did not want to look pitiful". For some persons it is very painful to be confronted with the visualized truth of their life. They cannot ignore or deny the line they have drawn.

A third, special aspect of the LIM is its self-pacing quality. The life-line is drawn and the life story is told at the person's own pace. The LIM allows each individual to set his or her own tempo, an advantage over standardized questionnaires especially for older people. In addition, the nondirective atmosphere of the interview enhances disclosure of an individual's most sincere opinions, beliefs, and attitudes. The LIM is tailored to the unique qualities of individuals.

A final advantage of the LIM is the quality of self-structuring. The respondent and not the research-er, categorizes and structures the data in terms of number of events, age, and affect. The self-structuring quality makes it also possible to analyze the interview data in terms of patterned structures (branching points) which reflect the events, experiences, or happenings in the life of the individual. Organizing unstructured interview data into meaningful categories in such a way that they can be analyzed statisti-cally tends to be a great problem. Thanks to the design of the LIM the subject himself structures the data in terms of number of events, age at which the event occurred or is expected to occur, and affect by which the event is accompanied, which facilitates analyzing these data. This inherent structure has a validity of its own since it represents the facts of an individual's life as he or she sees it; it is the subjec-tive truth of his life (liberally quoted from: Schroots, 1984; Schroots & Birren, 2002; Schroots & ten Kate, 1989).

## 1.3   Life events

### 1.3.1   Overview

According to Sugarman (2001) life events are bench marks in the human life cycle. They are the mile-stones or transition points that give "shape and direction to the various aspects of a person's life" (Dan-ish, Smyer & Nowak, 1980, p. 342). Elder (1998) speaks about central concepts in the study of the life course. McAdams (1996) uses the term 'nuclear episodes' to refer to particular scenes in the adult life story as high points, low points, beginning points, ending points and turning points. Grob et al. (2001) use the word 'life marker' which they define as an important event that affects the life significantly, or that has a formative influence on life, or that turns life in a particular direction. Birren and Hedlund (1987) speak about major branching points. Other terms are: bifurcation points, turning points, transi-tions or transformations (Schroots & Birren, 2002), which are defined as those changes in the life of the individual that direct the life path in a distinctive direction, and that are separated in time from each other by one or more affective or critical events or experiences (Birren & Deutchman, 1991).

During the past decades many studies have been conducted with regard to life events, especially on the role of 'critical' or 'stressful' events on the onset of illness or distress, starting with Holmes and Rahe (1967) and their Social Readjustment Rating Scale. Although this scale includes positive as well as negative events, the assigned fixed weightings to different events ignore individual differences in their impact and meaning for different respondents. Many researchers have tried to improve Holmes and Rahe's scale by expanding the scope of items, rewording existing items that are ambiguous, alter-ing scaling procedures or by focusing on everyday hassles instead of major life events, e.g., the Life Events Inventory (Cochrane & Robertson, 1973), the Life Experiences Survey (Sarason, Johnson & Siegel, 1978) and the Life Events Questionnaire (Chiriboga, 1984). In spite of these improvements, many problems remain associated with the use of questionnaires. First of all, the investigator deter-mines which events are considered as important life events by selecting a set of life events out of all possible life events, with negative events being over-represented. Second, not all events are equally important for all respondents but weighting procedures of events are lacking or vary between studies. Third, the reliability of recall of events, especially over longer periods of time, is often problematic and it is difficult to obtain life events in a systematic, temporal coherence. Fourth, only the past is investigated; expectations for the future are not included in these questionnaires. From the foregoing Settersten (1999) concludes that "We must better examine the degree to which the impact of life events varies as a function of the life stage of the individual and as a function of experiences in the lives of others to whom the individual is tied" (p. 146).

## 1.3.2 Life story

Life events are embedded in the total life story. As Bluck (2001) states, life events are the building blocks of life stories. DeVries and Watt (1996) note that the story of a life is given substance, size and shape by the events it embodies. According to Conway and Pleydell-Pearce (2000) nearly all researchers in the area of autobiographical memory research assume that there is an important and strong relation between the self and autobiographical memory. "Autobiographical memory is of fundamental significance for the self, for emotions, and for the experience of personhood, that is, for the experience of enduring as an individual, in a culture, over time" (p. 261). According to some theorists autobiographical memory is a part of the self (Conway & Tacchi, 1996; Howe & Courage, 1997; Robinson, 1986). The source of information about the self lies in autobiography, "the story of an individual's life told or written by himself or herself that is based on the recall of memories, events, experiences, and relationships with other persons" (Birren & Schroots, 2006, p. 478). Although autobiographical memory and narratives are closely related to each other, memory researchers and narrative researchers have gone their separate ways for the most part using different theories and methods and having their own traditions (Robinson & Taylor, 1998).

The roots for the narrative approach lie in the 1930s. Then, personality psychology was born (Allport, 1937) which emphasized biography, myth, narrative, and the intensive exploration of the single case in the study of human lives (McAdams, 1988). Murray (1938) had his subjects tell a story in response to a picture cue. Charlotte Bühler (1933) and Else Frenkel (1936) collected and analyzed autobiographical accounts written by 400 European men and women. They were more concerned with general principles in all lives than with the uniqueness of any single life and used these autobiographical data to generate hypotheses and theories (McAdams, 1988).

After the Second World War Erikson wrote psychobiographies about important historical persons, for instance Luther (1958) and Gandhi (1969) on the basis of the stage theory of life he had created (1950). Erikson considers development as a function of both individual and cultural factors. As the individual develops, he has to adapt to new demands society places on him. Erikson distinguishes eight stages in life and in each stage a psychosocial task is met. The first stage concerns 'basic trust versus basic mistrust' (ca. 0–1 yrs); during the first year of life the child learns whether he can trust or mistrust the predictability of the environment. In the second stage (ca. 1–6 yrs) the crisis concerns 'autonomy versus shame and doubt'; the child has to attain self-control without loss of self-esteem and without feeling ashamed. In the third stage (ca. 6–10 yrs) the crisis 'initiative versus guilt' has to be solved; on one hand the child can develop a free sense of enterprise while on the other hand, with the development of conscience, the child can feel guilty about his thoughts and actions. In the fourth stage (ca. 10–14 yrs) the crisis 'industry versus inferiority' is central; when the child does not learn industry and does not become competent he can develop a sense of inadequacy and inferiority. The fifth stage (ca. 14–20 yrs) is 'identity versus role confusion'; when the adolescent does not succeed to develop a sense of ego identity, he will be uncertain about who he is and what he will become. In young adulthood (ca. 20–35 yrs) the crisis 'intimacy versus isolation' has to be solved; when the individual has developed a separate identity he will be able to involve himself in intimate relationships instead of being isolated. In the seventh stage (ca. 35–65 yrs) the crisis is between 'generativity versus stagnation'. Generativity refers to establishing and guiding the next generation. At last the person arrives at the final stage of 'ego integrity versus despair and disgust'. When an individual succeeds to fulfill this task, he will accept his life for what it has been and will not look back with feelings of despair.

Integration in later life is facilitated by the process of life review. The concept of life review was introduced by Butler (1963) who saw reminiscence in the aged as part of a normal life review process to put one's life in order by the realization of approaching death. Later, it was recognized that life review is not limited to old age but takes place in all stages of life. Reminiscence means literally the recall of memories without a specific purpose, while life review entails the recall, evaluation, and synthesis of positive and negative memories in a more systematic way (Webster & Haight, 1995). Reminiscence and life review are used for different goals such as enhancing self-esteem, improving social skills, attaining social integration, acquiring ego-integrity (Scherder, Schroots & Kerkhof, 2002) and also as a therapeutic tool for treatment of depressions for elderly (Bohlmeijer, Smit & Cuijpers, 2003). In a meta-analysis of studies which used reminiscence or life review as a method of intervention for depressive symptoms on elderly, results indicated that both reminiscence and life review are effective treatments for (severe) depressive symptoms (Bohlmeijer et al., 2003). Serrano, Latorre, Gatz and Montanes (2004) also found that at post test older adults who had received life review treatment based on autobiographical retrieval practice reported fewer depressive symptoms, less hopelessness, improved life satisfaction, and retrieval of more specific events than a non-treatment control group. Watt and Cappeliez (1995) identified two types of reminiscence which are supposed to be effective in the treatment of depression of elderly; (1) integrative reminiscence which focuses on a constructive reappraisal of the past resulting in positive beliefs about the self and attributions about one's role in negative events, and (2) instrumental reminiscence which focuses on memories of past problem-solving experiences and coping activities resulting, ideally, in the use of adaptive coping appraisals and strategies to cope more adequately with experiences of stress.

However, during the period in which psychology was dominated by behaviorism, the use of autobiographical data was of little scientific significance (McAdams, 2001). But since the mid-1980s, personality psychology has witnessed a strong upsurge of interest in personal narratives and life stories (Schroots & Birren, 2002). McAdams (1996; 2001) has delineated a conceptual framework that integrates the life story as an aspect of personality. McAdams makes a distinction between the I (self-as-knower) and the Me (self-as-known) features of personality; the I is viewed as the active subject who creates the self, while the Me is viewed as the object of knowledge, the self. The person can be described on three relatively independent, non-overlapping levels. The first level is the trait level; traits are described as those relatively nonconditional, decontextualized, generally linear, and implicitly comparative dimensions of personality which are rather stable over the lifespan. McCrae and Costa (1990) distinguished five personality traits, known as 'the big five': neuroticism, agreeableness, consciousness, extraversion, and openness. The second level of personality is called 'personal concerns' and relates to all kinds of constructs that are contextualized in time, place and role, for instance, personal strivings, defense mechanisms, goals, coping strategies and so on. The third level has to do with the meaning of life. Beyond traits and adaptations, many people seek an integrative frame for their own lives that gives them a sense that the various pieces of who they are come together into some kind of sensible whole. According to a number of theorists, this kind of integration of the self into an identity is accomplished through the construction and revision of a 'life story' (see McAdams, 1999). The third level of personality, then, is the level of identity which is expressed in the life story. The life story gives unity, meaning and purpose to a life. A life story can be defined as an internalized and evolving narrative of the self that integrates the reconstructed past, perceived present and anticipated future in order to provide a life with a sense of unity and purpose (McAdams, 1999). In sum, in the theoretical concept of McAdams (2001) the personality is viewed as a unique pattern of traits, characteristic adaptations and stories. It has to be remarked that identity and self are not the same. Children have a sense of 'self' but identity develops from the late teenage years through the mid-20s when, according to Erikson (1950), the integration of selfhood becomes a psychosocial problem for them. From that time on, individuals begin to 'work on' their identity. A life story is a psychosocial construction and not simply an objective account of 'what really happened' in the past (Gergen, 1988; McAdams, 1996). Life story data are viewed as temporary constructions of what seems most appropriate from the perspective of the narrator at that time (Gergen, 1988; McAdams, 1996); a life story is only one version of life and is subject to continuous changes.

During life many events occur but not all events individuals have experienced and which they remember are included in the story of one's life (Bluck & Habermas, 2000). Only memories that are highly self-relevant when they are encoded, that have an emotional impact, or that provide a motivational explanation for later development and/or maintain significance at the time of retrieval are likely to be included in a life story (Conway & Holmes, 2004). Bluck and Habermas (2000) consider only those memories truly autobiographical that are linked to the self through emotional or motivational significance for one's life. Another aspect of autobiographical memories is that these memories are not merely incidents but are given structure and meaning in the context of the whole life by their inclusion in a more flowing life story (Kenyon & Randall, 1999).

### 1.3.3 Categorization
#### Classifying life events
In order to make life events data more manageable, they have to be classified into categories. Life-event taxonomies classify life events according to different dimensions (Sugarman, 2001). Reese and Smyer (1983) identified 35 variables used to describe life events which can be grouped into three main dimensions: (a) 'event' dimensions which describe objective characteristics of the events themselves such as age relatedness, duration, type and prevalence; (b) 'perception' dimensions which concern the subjective impression or evaluation of the events such as control, desirability and meaning; (c) 'effect' dimensions which refer to the outcomes or consequences of the events such as impact and direction of impact (Brim & Ryff, 1980). Several life-event taxonomies utilize only one dimension, for instance Holmes and Rahe's (1967) Social Readjustment Rating Scale. Respondents are asked to indicate which of forty-three events, rank ordered according to their estimated stressfulness, they have experienced within (usually) the last 12 months. The sum of the stress ratings for these events is determined and it is assumed that the greater the amount of stress experienced by individuals, the higher the likelihood these individuals will suffer stress-related health problems. A three-dimensional taxonomy of life events was compiled by Brim and Ryff (1980) on the basis of the likelihood, i.e. the probability that an event will take place, age-relatedness, i.e. the correlation of the event with chronological age, and prevalence of events, i.e. whether the event is experienced by many or few people. For each dimension a distinction was made between a 'high' and a 'low' category. For instance, Marriage is an event that has a strong correlation with age, is experienced by many individuals and has a high probability of occurrence. A two-dimensional taxonomy comprising 4 event 'types' and 14 event 'contexts' was proposed by Reese and Smyer (1983) resulting in 56 cells. The 4 event types were social-cultural, personal-sociological, biological and physical-environmental. The event contexts were grouped into 5 categories: family, self, social relations, work and miscellaneous. An event such as Marriage is classified into the context 'Love and marriage' which belongs to the category 'Family' and to the event type 'Personal-sociological'. Baltes, Reese and Lipsitt (1980) distinguished three types of events or influences over the lifespan: normative age-graded, normative history-graded and non-normative life events. Normative age-graded events occur at about the same time to all individuals in a given (sub)culture, for instance, going to school at age four in The Netherlands. Normative history-graded events occur to most members of a given cohort in similar ways, for instance, the Second World War. Non-normative events do not occur in any normative age-graded or history-graded manner for most individuals, for instance, having a severe accident. Studies in the field of autobiographical memory all use different category lists to classify events which makes it rather difficult to compare results (Schroots & Assink, 2004).

#### Classifying LIM events
The data obtained by a LIM-interview are three-fold: a life-line, a series of temporally ordered life events and a life story. Each of these three types of data can be analyzed at different levels of complexity and requires its own specific method of analysis. For instance, concerning the life-line a factor analysis can be conducted on different measures of the life-line (mean height of line, height of line at different points in life, slope of line at different points in life, number of peaks, and age at last peak)

**Table 1.1**   Coding list of (sub)categories with typical examples of LIM life events.

| (Sub)Category | Examples |
| --- | --- |
| *Relations* | |
| Begin | meeting partner, in love |
| Commitment | marriage, family life |
| End | divorce |
| Problems | relational problems |
| Others | marriage problems children |
| Rest | close friendship |
| *School* | |
| Starting | school, college |
| Finishing | graduating, diploma |
| Problems | flunking, program problems |
| Others | graduation (grand)child, partner |
| Rest | student life, boarding school |
| *Work* | |
| Beginning | first job |
| Changing | other job, promotion |
| Stopping | retirement, family care |
| Problems | layoff, bankruptcy |
| Others | disability partner |
| Rest | unemployment, job hopping |
| *Health* | |
| Physical | illness, disease, surgery |
| Mental | depression, nervous breakdown |
| Others | illness partner |
| Rest | menopause, pregnancy |
| *Growth* | |
| Individual | self-development, self-management |
| Problems | identity problems, midlife crisis |
| Others | growth (problems) others |
| Rest | happy childhood |
| *Home* | |
| Moving | relocation |
| Leaving | (go and) live on one's own |
| Others | leaving home others |
| Rest | second home |
| *Birth* | |
| Child | child(ren) |
| Grandchild | grandchild(ren) |
| Family | brother/sister |
| Rest | birth others |
| *Death* | |
| Parents | father, mother |
| Partner | partner, spouse |
| Family | brother/sister, child, grandparents |
| Rest | death others |
| *Other* | |
| War | war, liberation |
| Travel | travel, trip, journey |
| Rest | finances, leisure |

resulting in different typologies of the life-line (Schroots & Assink, 1998). The average life-line, based on the height of the line at different points in life can be determined for the past and future of different subgroups (Assink, 1996). Life events can be analyzed on the level of categories or subcategories (Schroots & Assink, 2005). Concerning the life story, the number of words the respondent needs to tell the story of his life can be counted (Schroots, Kunst, & Assink, 2006) and affective sequences of transitions in life can be determined (Kunst, 2004). The present study is restricted to the analysis at the second level, the event level. Thanks to the special characteristics of the LIM, the subject himself structures the data which facilitates analyzing.

### LIM-category list

A special category-list was constructed in order to classify LIM-events. According to Holsti (1968) categories should be uni-dimensional, exhaustive, mutually exclusive, and independent (i.e., an entry in one category does not affect an entry in another category). The LIM-category list, that was partly empirical based – i.e. coders identified categories on the basis of the material to be analyzed (Smith, 2000) – was constructed in the following way.

First, all information concerning a specific event – a peak or dip on the life-line – was put together. In this way different units of text were created in chronological order; each unit included the age at which the event happened or was expected to happen, a short description of the event and an explanation of the event. To each identified unit a catchword was connected which describes in one or a few words, preferably in words used by the respondent, the most important theme in the unit. In a pilot study two independent coders identified these catchwords and solved disagreements by discussion.

Next, the collection of catchwords was classified into categories by two coders. Groups of catchwords which had about the same meaning were combined into a category and received a covering name. In this way, nine categories were generated (Relations, School, Work, Health, Growth, Home, Birth, Death, Other) which – with the exception of the Other category – represent the most important life-themes and which are also in line with the work of Birren and Deutschman (1991), Sugarman (1986), deVries and Watt (1996), and Zautra, Affleck and Tennen (1994).

Within each category, subcategories were developed on the basis of a combination of frequency by which an event was reported and a systematic structure by which the category list was constructed. For instance, in some categories there is a Beginning (Begin Relations), a Course (Commitment), Problems (Problems Relations) and an End (End Relations). The subcategory 'Others' (Relations Others) was added to most categories, while a 'Rest' subcategory (Relations Rest) was added standard to all categories.

In the final analysis, the coding list contains 40 subcategories divided over 9 categories. An advantage of this comprehensive category list is that (sub)categories can be taken together, for instance, in order to make comparisons with results of other studies more meaningful. Table 1.1 contains a list of the (sub)categories with some typical examples (Schroots & Birren, 2002; Schroots & Assink, 2005).

## 1.4  Method

### 1.4.1  Design

To study the dynamics of autobiographical memory across the life course a longitudinal research design was employed. The study started in 1995. About two years later the LIM was administered a second time and five years after the first wave a third time.

Longitudinal as well as cross-sectional studies provide information about changes over the lifespan and both have their pros and contras. One of the major problems when interpreting results of cross-sectional and longitudinal studies is the Age-Period-Cohort (APC) effect. Each measurement taken on a subject at a particular time-point is influenced by three factors: (a) Age: time from date of birth to date of measurement, (b) Period: time or moment at which the measurement is taken, and (c) Cohort: group of individuals that share similar environmental circumstances at equivalent temporal points in their life course (Schaie & Hofer, 2001). In both cross-sectional and longitudinal research designs only one variable can be controlled which means that the other two are inevitably confounded. The time parameters Age and Cohort are confounded in a design with cross-sectional data meaning that differences between age groups can be attributed to age as well as to cohort. The parameters Age and Period are confounded in a design with longitudinal data meaning that changes within age groups can be attributed to age as well as to time of measurement. Different designs were proposed to correct for these confounding effects (Baltes, 1968; Schaie, 1965; Schaie & Baltes, 1975). In actual practice these designs are difficult to realize because they are expensive, time consuming and many respondents and different samples are needed over a long period. For this reason and also because over a period of five years no significant effect of Period is expected no specific design was used in this LIM-study to control for confounding effects of Age and Period.

Analysis of data of respondents who took part at all three waves allows assessment of intra-individual or within-person dynamics and inter-individual or between-person variability in intra-individual dynamics, i.e., the effect of age and gender on stability and change. Besides, each separate wave can be considered as a cross-sectional study. Comparison of results of these three cross-sectionals allows the measurement of change for a group of people at the aggregate level, but does not allow measurement of change at the level of the research subject (Schaie & Hofer, 2001).

## 1.4.2 Respondents

The first wave of the study (W1) started with 98 men and women drawn from three age-categories: young, middle and older adulthood. At baseline, the mean ages and the age ranges for the three groups were 23.5 (18–30), 43.3 (31–55), and 67.4 (56–84) years, respectively. The youngest group included 18 men and 16 women, the middle group 17 men and 18 women and the eldest group 12 men and 17 women. The participants were Caucasians of primarily middle to higher socioeconomic status, recruited initially from educational and health organizations in two Dutch metropolitan areas and then sampled by means of the snowball method, i.e., a method whereby participants are asked to nominate other possible participants who meet the selection criteria.

At the second wave (W2), two years later, 83 subjects participated (drop-out 15%). Attrition was due to illness (n = 2), refusal (n = 8) and not being traceable (n = 5).

Table 1.2   W1 | W2 | W3*: Number and mean age with standard deviation (SD) of men and women per age group per wave.

| | Young | | | Middle | | | Older | | |
|---|---|---|---|---|---|---|---|---|---|
| | Men | Women | Total | Men | Women | Total | Men | Women | Total |
| W1 (N = 98) | 18 | 16 | 34 | 17 | 18 | 35 | 12 | 17 | 29 |
| Mean age | 23.3 | 23.6 | 23.5 | 41.7 | 44.9 | 43.3 | 69.0 | 66.2 | 67.4 |
| SD | 3.8 | 3.5 | 3.6 | 6.8 | 6.3 | 6.6 | 7.0 | 8.5 | 7.9 |
| | | | | | | | | | |
| W2 (N = 83) | 14 | 13 | 27+ | 17 | 17 | 34 | 8 | 14 | 22 |
| Mean age | 24.9 | 24.6 | 24.7 | 43.6 | 47.2 | 45.4 | 69.2 | 68.5 | 68.7 |
| SD | 3.6 | 3.0 | 3.3 | 6.8 | 6.2 | 6.7 | 7.2 | 7.9 | 7.5 |
| | | | | | | | | | |
| W3 (N = 77) | 15 | 14 | 29+ | 15 | 15 | 30 | 8 | 10 | 18 |
| Mean age | 28.0 | 28.2 | 28.1 | 47.3 | 49.8 | 48.5 | 72.3 | 69.1 | 70.5 |
| SD | 3.9 | 3.4 | 3.6 | 6.7 | 6.4 | 6.5 | 7.3 | 6.2 | 6.7 |

* W1 | W2 | W3 = full data of Wave 1 (W1), Wave 2 (W2) and Wave 3 (W3) analyzed independently from each other.
+ At the second wave fewer respondents of the young age group participated than at the third wave due to illness and not responding

**Table 1.3** W1→W2→W3*: Number and mean age with standard deviation (SD) of men and women – who participated in all three waves – per age group per wave.

| | Young | | | Middle | | | Older | | |
|---|---|---|---|---|---|---|---|---|---|
| | **Men** | **Women** | **Total** | **Men** | **Women** | **Total** | **Men** | **Women** | **Total** |
| W1 (N = 74) | 13 | 13 | 26 | 15 | 15 | 30 | 8 | 10 | 18 |
| Mean age | 22.8 | 22.6 | 22.7 | 42.3 | 44.7 | 43.5 | 67.3 | 64.1 | 65.5 |
| SD | 3.9 | 3.0 | 3.4 | 6.7 | 6.4 | 6.6 | 7.2 | 6.1 | 6.6 |
| | | | | | | | | | |
| W2 (N = 74) | 13 | 13 | 26 | 15 | 15 | 30 | 8 | 10 | 18 |
| Mean age | 24.9 | 24.6 | 24.7 | 44.2 | 46.7 | 45.4 | 69.2 | 66.0 | 67.4 |
| SD | 3.8 | 3.0 | 3.4 | 6.7 | 6.4 | 6.5 | 7.2 | 6.1 | 6.7 |
| | | | | | | | | | |
| W3 (N = 74) | 13 | 13 | 26 | 15 | 15 | 30 | 8 | 10 | 18 |
| Mean age | 27.9 | 27.7 | 27.8 | 47.3 | 49.8 | 48.5 | 72.3 | 69.1 | 70.5 |
| SD | 3.8 | 3.0 | 3.4 | 6.7 | 6.4 | 6.5 | 7.3 | 6.2 | 6.7 |

* W1→W2→W3 = analysis of longitudinal data of 74 respondents who took part in Wave 1 (W1), Wave 2 (W2) and Wave 3 (W3).

At the third wave (W3), five years after the first wave, 77 subjects participated (total drop-out 21%). Attrition was due to death (n = 4), refusal (n = 13) and not being traceable (n = 4). The four participants who had died all belonged to the older age group.

Two-way contingency analyses were conducted to evaluate whether there was an effect of age or gender on attrition over the three waves. There was no effect of age ($\chi2$ = 1.261, df = 4, p = 0.87) or gender ($\chi2$ = 0.900, df = 2, p = 0.96) on attrition over three waves. Table 1.2 shows the number of respondents (men and women) per age group per wave and mean age with standard deviation per sub-group. The difference in average age between the different waves is not exactly two and five years as it was not possible to interview each respondent after exactly two and five years, respectively. Due to attrition of the oldest participants in the older age group, the difference in mean age between the waves is lower than two and five years in this age group.

A total of 74 subjects participated in all three waves. Table 1.3 shows the number and mean age with standard deviation of these participants per age group per wave. Henceforth, the heading 'W1 | W2 | W3' refers to a presentation of the full data of Wave 1 (W1), Wave 2 (W2) and Wave 3 (W3) which are analyzed separately and independently from each other, while the heading 'W1→W2→W3' refers to the analysis of longitudinal data of 74 respondents who participated in all three waves.

### 1.4.3 Life-line Interview Method
**Administration**

To elicit autobiographical information the LIM|Life-line Interview Method was used. As the LIM was discussed in the previous paragraphs, the description in this chapter will be limited to the practical application of the instrument. The complete manual of the LIM, however, is presented in the Supplement of this volume (Schroots, 2007).

In Figure 1.1 an example of a LIM|Life-line is presented for a 43-year old man with a description of the life events this man mentioned on his life-line including the ages at which the events took place and the affective value of the events. This example is based on various life-lines and life stories of men of the middle age group. The affect of the life events was first rated on a 5-point scale and was than rescaled on a two-point scale (positive and negative). The procedure for the rating of affect is described in Chapter 3.

A typical LIM-session, then, starts with a short introduction after which the respondent is shown a board with LIM-paper, i.e., a blank piece of paper (A4 landscape format) on which a grid is printed. The grid consists of a bottom and top line (296 mm), connected by two solid and one dotted vertical line of equal length (180 mm) at 0 mm, 180 mm and 296 mm from the origin, respectively. The horizontal axis on this paper symbolizes the time-dimension, the vertical axis the affect-dimension.

The interviewer introduces the general plan of the session by saying that he is interested in the human life course with its ups and downs, rises and declines etc., which are all completely different from one person to another. The interviewer, then, explains that he would like to hear the life story of the respondent in a special way. After giving three examples of life-lines, from simple to complex, the respondent is asked to draw his life-line in the blank LIM grid from birth dot (middle of solid line, 0 mm) to his calendar age (solid line, 180 mm) without much thought. Next, the respondent is asked to label each peak and each dip by chronological age and to tell what happened at a certain moment or during an indicated period. When all peaks and dips are labeled, the respondent is asked to tell something more about each event and in this way the life story is obtained. After the past life-line has been labeled and described in detail, the future is explored in the same manner. The respondent is asked at what age he expects to die. Then, starting from the age point where the past life-line has stopped, the respondent is asked to continue the line until the dotted age-line (296 mm) of expected death is reached and the whole procedure of labeling the peaks and dips of the future life-line, and giving an explanation of the events is repeated. The final result of a LIM-interview is a life-line and a life-story based on important life events, labeled by chronological age, for both past and future of the individual.

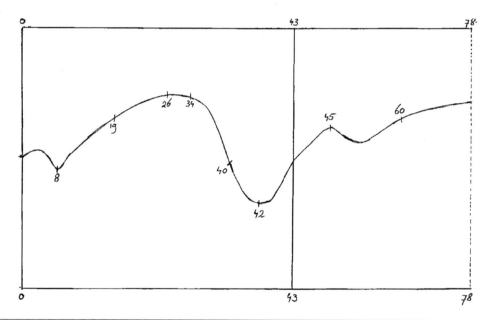

| Past | | | Future | | |
|---|---|---|---|---|---|
| Age | Event | Affect | Age | Event | Affect |
| 8 | Moving to another city | − | 45 | Get promotion | + |
| 19 | Going to university | + | 60 | Early retirement | + |
| 26 | Meeting wife | + | | | |
| 34 | Birth first child | + | | | |
| 40 | Conflict at work | − | | | |
| 42 | Father dies | − | | | |

**Figure 1.1.** Top: LIM|Life-line of a 43-year-old man with age (in years) on the horizontal axis and affect on the vertical axis. Below: overview of the series of life events with age and affect (+ = positive, − = negative) for past and future.

## Procedure
The interviews took place at the university or at the respondents' home. After a short introduction, the LIM was administered. The interview was tape-recorded and a verbatim report of the interview was made. At the end of the interview the personal particulars of the respondents were noted and the respondent was given the opportunity to express his feelings about telling his life story. Finally, the respondent got a small reward for his participation. A LIM-interview lasted on average about 40 minutes; the drawing of past and future life-line, however, didn't take more than a few minutes. The older respondents were, the more time they needed to tell their life story. As far as possible, respondents were interviewed each wave by a different interviewer in order to reduce interviewer bias (Hoyle, Harris & Judd, 2002). Between the first and second wave, and between the second and third wave, the respondents were contacted once; they got some general information about the study and were thanked again for their participation.

## 1.4.4 Analysis
### Unit of analysis
When analyzing autobiographical texts, the first and most fundamental step should be the identification of the unit of analysis (Kovach, 1995) also named 'coding unit' or 'recording unit' (Smith, 2000). In case of the LIM|Life story the life event is the basic unit of analysis. The life stories were typed out verbatim resulting in the so called 'raw' life story. In order to reverse the 'raw' life story into chronologically ordered units, a type-instruction was developed containing specific instructions for creating the so called 'integrated' life story. All information concerning a specific event – a peak or dip on the life-line – was put together. In this way different units of text were created in chronological order; each unit included the age at which the event happened or was expected to happen, a short description of the event and an explanation of the event. All irrelevant text such as remarks of the interviewer and standard sentences the interviewer used was left out in this final version of the life story resulting in a chronological readable story. This integrated story is the basis for all analyses. In this study analysis will be restricted to different aspects (number, affect and content) of the basic elements of the life story, the life events.

### Statistics
Simple descriptive statistics will be used to describe qualitative and quantitative variables, for instance, the percentage of events per category. When determining the distribution of (positive and negative) events over the lifespan the number of events reported in a certain period will be determined according to reported age at the time of event, and, subsequently, the number of events will be translated into percentage of events per period. Results will be presented in figures and the patterns will be inspected visually.

Univariate and multivariate analyses-of-variance will be carried out to determine the effect of age and gender on the variable(s) of interest. Multivariate analyses-of-variance for repeated measures will be conducted in order to determine the effect of time (past/future) or wave (three waves) on the variable(s) of interest.

When it is not possible to conduct statistical analyses because of small numbers or in case of categorical variables rules will be generated in order to determine whether a result will be considered noticeable.

### Organization of results
In the Results section of the following chapters, first of all, full data of each wave will be analyzed separately and independently from each other. To this type of analysis will be referred to by the heading 'W1 | W2 | W3'. Analysis of the three waves will result in a description of inter-individual differences at each wave but also in the description of different patterns. Results of the three waves will be compared to each other with respect to patterns found at each wave and it will be determined whether

patterns which are found at the first wave are also found at the second and third wave and can be considered as stable patterns. When there is a systematic, orderly change in patterns over time, the change can probably be attributed to age changes. When changes in patterns seem to be arbitrary, they are probably due to error, effect of testing, or attrition.

Second, longitudinal data of 74 respondents who took part at all three waves will be analyzed in order to study the individual stability and change of certain aspects of autobiographical memory over time and the effect of age and gender on stability and change of these aspects. This type of analysis will be referred to by the heading 'W1→W2→W3'.

For clarity reasons and because of the enormous amount of data full results will not always be presented in the Results section but they can be found in the Appendix on the cd-rom in the back of this book. To results which can be found in the Appendix will be referred by 'enclosed CD' and an 'A' before the number of the table or figure.

# Chapter 2

# Number of Events

## 2.1 Introduction

As mentioned before, various methods are used to obtain autobiographical data. In many studies on autobiographical memory subjects are asked to react to a certain number of cue-words (cf. Rubin, Rahhal & Poon, 1998) or to report a specific number of memories from their past (d'Argembeau, Comblain & Van der Linden, 2003; Berntsen & Rubin, 2002) resulting in the same number of memories for each respondent. In other studies, however, respondents are free to report as many events as they want resulting in a different number of events per respondent.

In most of these studies respondents are asked to mention only events from the past. For instance, Elnick et al. (1999) asked respondents to fill in a Life History Timeline that was divided into 5-year increments. They found an average of 7.4 events (SD = 4.3) for respondents ranging from 40 to 87 years of age (four age groups) without an effect of age or gender. Luborsky (1998) asked elderly women (M age = 84 yrs) to describe their lives and counted a mean number of eight topics per life story. Fromholt et al. (2003) found in a 15-minute free narrative of life history events a mean of 18.13 events for healthy 80-year-old respondents, 10 events for 100-year-old respondents, 8.33 events for demented respondents, and 11.87 events for depressive respondents. To their great surprise Martin and Smyer (1990) didn't find a significant difference in the number of recognized life events by older cohorts and a college cohort in a life event sorting task. Brugman (2000) asked 258 adults divided in two age groups (young ≤ 53 years; older > 53 years) to draw their lifeline and found a mean number of 14.14 events also without an effect of age or gender.

In a few studies respondents are asked to report past as well as future events. Hentschel, Sumbadze and Shubladze (2000) asked subjects with an age range from 27 to 35 years to fill in subjectively important life events on a lifeline (past and future) which resulted in an average number of 7.27 events over the whole lifespan. Newby-Clark and Ross (2003) asked students to list a maximum of ten events from their past and for their future and found that participants recalled more events (6.80) than they anticipated (5.63). Grob, Krings and Bangerter (2001) asked participants from three birth cohorts in a semi-structured 90-minute interview to mention important markers in their experienced and expected biographies and found an average number of about 20 life markers for the total life. DeVries and Watt (1996) asked respondents of three age groups to complete a questionnaire of which the primary measure was the Rappaport Time Line (TL) (Rappaport, Enrich, & Wilson, 1985) in a written session of about 90 to 120 minutes. They found an average number of 19 events for the whole lifespan with an effect of gender on the total number of events – woman identified more events (21) than men (17) did – but no effect of age; all age groups identified the same number of events over the total lifespan. However, the distribution of events over past and future differed by age group in their study; older respondents reported more events from the past than younger respondents and younger respondents reported more events in the future than older respondents. Studies by means of the Life-line Interview Method (Schroots & Assink, 1998; Schroots, van Dijkum & Assink, 2004) yielded the same results concerning the total number of events; the total number of events appeared to be the same for all age groups although the absolute number of events (7.03) (Schroots, van Dijkum & Assink, 2004) differed from the absolute number (19) found by deVries and Watt (1996). For the ratio of past and future LIM-events also an interaction effect of time and age group was found; the older the group, the greater the number of past events and in contrast, the younger the group, the greater the number of future events. Figure 2.1 shows the ratio between past (or future) events and total number of events (percents) by age group (young, middle, older) for both LIM and TL.

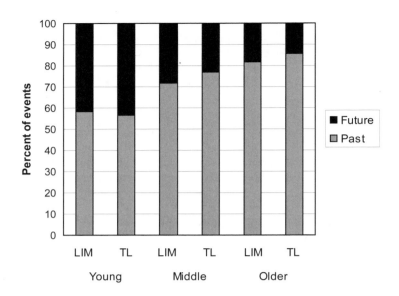

**Figure 2.1.** Ratio of past and future events (percents) for LIM (Life-line Interview Method) and TL (Time Line) by age group (Young, Middle, Older).

Given the results of these two independent studies, Schroots and Assink (1998) formulated the so called *Principle of the Constant Life Perspective*, i.e., the sum of past and future autobiographical events being constant across the lifespan.

From the above mentioned studies can be concluded that there is great variation between different studies in the absolute number of memories (and expectations) respondents recall from their past (and expect for their future) which is due to the use of different methods (Schroots & Assink, 1998, 2004). The LIM is an interview method which is administered individually. It is a rather directive, confronting method by which the life course is explored in a systematic way. An advantage of the LIM is, for instance, that most respondents of the older age group (90 percent) mention at least one event in the future while, for instance, in the Time Line study, which is administered by means of a written questionnaire, 50 percent of the oldest age group does not mention any event in the future (deVries & Watt, 1996). In the LIM-study respondents are asked to visualize their life by means of a life-line and to identify events on this line without much thinking resulting in reporting fewer events than when using a method which allows the respondent more time to identify events such as the Time Line. It is assumed, however, that LIM-events are all of 'high quality'. First of all, social desirability bias will be minimal as respondents do not realize what they are revealing when drawing the life-line. Second, when respondents get more time to generate events they will also report events of less importance. It is plausible that in case of the LIM only the most important turning points are mentioned and that the LIM gives a genuine picture of one's life with the accompanying affect closer to the personal 'truth' (Schroots & Assink, 1998, 2004).

Considerable research has been done on the distribution of reported events over the lifespan. On the basis of the forgetting curve (Ebbinghaus, 1885/1964) it is expected that people remember most events from their recent past. But in a variety of contexts it has been found that older subjects report a larger than expected number of memories (autobiographical memories, vivid memories, semantic memories) from the period of late adolescence and early adulthood. This phenomenon has been called the 'reminiscence bump' or the 'autobiographical memory bump' or simply 'bump' (cf. Fitzgerald, 1995; Fromholt & Larsen, 1992; Fromholt et al. 2003; Jansari & Parkin, 1996; Martin & Smyer, 1990; Rubin, Rahhal & Poon, 1998; Rubin & Schulkind, 1997; Schroots & Assink, 1998; Schroots & van

Dijkum, 2004; Schroots, van Dijkum & Assink, 2004; deVries & Watt, 1996). In this study the term *autobiographical memory bump* or simply *bump* will be used because reminiscence refers to life review and reflecting on one's life, while autobiographical memory bump is a more general term which refers to more comprehensive research in this field. The bump is a *universal* phenomenon. For instance, Conway and Haque (1999) found that the bump also appeared in a study in which Bangladeshi participants were asked to recall and date autobiographical memories across their lifespan.

Rubin, Rahhal and Poon (1998, p. 13–17) gave four possible theoretical accounts of the bump. The following summary of these accounts has been liberally taken from their comprehensive literature review:

(a) *Cognitive* account: Events from early adulthood are remembered best because they occur in a period of transitions from rapid change to stability. In times of rapid change many novel events are encountered, which benefit recall as follows. First, when a novel event is encountered at the end of a period of change, there is more effort after meaning, which increases the event's memorability. Second, there may be a lack of proactive interference, which is an important cause of forgetting, because the novel event is different from what has preceded it. Third, the first time that an event occurs, it should be more distinctive both because of its novelty and because more attention is paid to details that the individual will learn to ignore in later occurrences. Such distinctiveness is an aid to later memory. Rubin and colleagues also note the benefits of stability on later recall. First, events from stable periods are more likely to serve as prototypes or models for future occurrences and thus may be retrieved and rehearsed more as new events are retrospectively compared to them. Second, once a stable cognitive structure has been established, this structure will serve as a stable organization to cue events.

(b) *Cognitive abilities/Neural substrate* account. If cognitive abilities were to rise and fall as a function of age with the same time course as that for the bump, this rise and fall could account for enhanced memory in early adulthood if one assumes that people learn in proportion to their ability. In contrast, if there was a rapid, major increase in abilities followed by a period of relative stability, or slow decline, then a more complex explanation would be needed. The latter pattern is the case, both for cognitive processing speed and memory test data as for crystallized intelligence. At the neural level both patterns could exist, i.e., an aspect of neural development could either follow a course similar to the pattern of cognitive abilities, with a rapid rise and slow decline, or it could peak sharply in early adulthood.

(c) *Identity formation* account. A sense of identity develops in late adolescence. If identity is viewed as a narrative of the important aspects of one's life, and if much of identity is formed in early adulthood, there will be more events in that narrative that come from early adulthood than would be expected from a monotonic forgetting function. In addition, events from this period will be more likely to be organized and incorporated into an overall story or view of the self and thus benefit mnemonically from all the advantages of such a schematic organization as well as from increased spaced rehearsal.

(d) *Genetic fitness* account. Early adulthood could be special because it is the time of the greatest potential to reproduce. That is, the increase in memory during the bump could serve the cognitive functions needed in selecting the best mate. In addition, it might not have been as common for our ancestors to live as long as we now do, so there might have been little selection pressure for a high level of functioning beyond a certain age.

Rubin, Rahhal and Poon (1998) conclude that the first theory based on principles of cognitive psychology can account for the bump, while an account based on the pattern of cognitive abilities and their neural substrates can not explain the bump in any simple way. The last two accounts can be seen as functioning through the mechanisms of the cognitive theory. According to Schroots and Van Dijkum (2004) the four accounts "derive their interpretative power mainly from descriptive evidence but fail to give an explanation for the emergence of the bump over the lifespan" (p. 2).

Schroots and Van Dijkum (2004) developed a *dynamic model* to provide an explanation for the emergence of the bump, based on the principle of the constant life perspective, i.e., the sum of growth and decline is constant over the lifespan. From this perspective, growth is interpreted as the lifelong process of development, measured in years from birth, and decline as the lifelong process of aging, which is traditionally defined in terms of survival and measured in years of residual lifespan from chronological age to (expected) death. As the relative number of future events (expectations) decreases with age and the relative number of past events (memories) increases over time, both increase and decrease follow the same dynamic pattern of growth and decline within the constraint of the lifespan. Schroots and Van Dijkum (2004) have constructed a model which represents, both graphically and mathematically, the dynamics of autobiographical memory across the lifespan and validated this model with LIM-data of the first wave. By means of the construction, simulation and validation of this dynamic model, they have demonstrated that processes of growth and decline offer a satisfactory account for the dynamics of the autobiographical memory bump. They conclude that the neurobehavioral function of autobiographical memory is determined by two synchronic processes of ontogenetic change – development and aging – resulting in the autobiographical memory bump by relatively more intensive encoding of information between 10 and 30 years of age. For a more detailed description and explanation of the bump phenomenon, see Schroots (2008 a,b)

Besides the bump effect for middle-aged and older people, recency effects and proximity effects can be discerned when considering the distribution of autobiographical memories over the lifespan. The recency effect refers to the distribution of past events which follows a power function; recent life events are recalled more frequently than events experienced in the distant past. This effect is very clear for younger age groups. Older age groups, however, show a bimodal pattern, a bump and a recency effect. In the LIM-study respondents are also asked to generate expectations for the future which refers to prospective autobiographical memory. Prospective autobiographical memory is concerned with the retrieval of expectations, anticipations or future events. Both retrospective and prospective autobiographical memory are based on present memory functioning. The distribution for future events shows a pattern which can be compared to the power function of the recency effect; events which are expected for the near future are mentioned more often than events which are foreseen in the distant future. In analogy with the recency effect this phenomenon was called the 'proximity' effect (Schroots, van Dijkum & Assink, 2004).

In addition to the distribution of events over the lifespan the question arises from which age respondents mention their first and last event and at what age they expect to die. DeVries and Watt (1996) found in their study of three age groups (mean ages for the young, middle and older age groups were 21.2, 41.9, and 72.7 years, respectively) that women mentioned the first event at a younger age (M = 5.9 yrs) than men did (M = 8.3 yrs). For the age of the last mentioned event, which is mostly an event expected in the future, they found an effect of age; the older the age group, the later the last event was situated (M young = 57.5; M middle = 64.5; M older = 78 yrs). On the basis of objective life expectancy tables it can be hypothesised that women expect to reach a higher age than men do and that the older respondents are, the higher the subjective life expectancy.

The above mentioned phenomena of the constant life perspective, the changing ratio of past and future events, the bump, recency/proximity effects and the changing extension in time when growing older are all based on cross-sectional studies. The question is what will happen when the same subjects are interviewed for a second and third time, respectively. How robust are the patterns found in these cross-sectional studies? Is the 'principle of the constant life perspective' repeated in the other waves? Do the patterns develop in the expected direction within the same subjects over a period of five years, i.e., does the ratio of past and total number of events increase as respondents grow older and does the recency/proximity effect move in the direction of the present age? Do individuals situate the final event and the moment of expected death at a later age when growing older?

## 2.2  Method

First, full data of each wave will be analyzed separately and independently from each other (N = 98, 83 and 77 respondents, respectively). To this type of analysis will be referred by the heading 'W1 |

W2 | W3'. Besides the description of inter-individual differences at each wave, this will also result in the description of different patterns. Results of these three waves will be compared to each other with respect to patterns found at each wave and it will be determined whether patterns which are found at the first wave are also found at the second and third wave and can be considered as stable patterns.

Second, longitudinal data of 74 respondents who took part in all three waves will be analyzed in order to study the individual stability and change of certain aspects of autobiographical memory over time and the effect of age and gender on stability and change of these aspects. This type of analysis will be referred to by the heading 'W1→W2→W3'.

## 2.3 Results

### 2.3.1 Number of events
**W1 | W2 | W3**

*W1.* Initial examination of the data was in terms of the total number of life events identified by men and women of three age-groups. Overall, individuals specified an average of 7.03 events (SD = 2.73, range 3 to 14) across their entire life. There was no effect of age or gender on the total number of events. Next, a 2(Gender) x 3(Age Group) x 2(Event Time: Past and Future) analysis of variance was conducted with repeated measures on the last factor and with the number of past and future events as the dependent variable. A main effect was found for the repeated measures variable, $F (1, 92) = 142.283$, $p < .001$; life stories can be characterized by a greater number of past (M = 4.96, SD = 2.46) than future events (M = 2.07, SD = 1.30). This main effect for event time, however, was qualified by its interaction with the age group variable, $F (2, 92) = 18.429$, $p < .001$, i.e., the older the group, the greater the number of past events and in contrast, the younger the group, the greater the number of future events. In Table 2.1 the mean number of events for the young, middle and older age group for past, future and total life is shown for each wave.

**Table 2.1** W1 | W2 | W3: Number of events with Standard Deviation (between brackets) for Past, Future and Total life for three waves (W1, W2, W3) for three age groups (Young, Middle, Older).

| | Young | | | Middle | | | Older | | |
|---|---|---|---|---|---|---|---|---|---|
| | **W1** | **W2** | **W3** | **W1** | **W2** | **W3** | **W1** | **W2** | **W3** |
| Past | 3.76 (2.03) | 4.78 (2.10) | 5.24 (2.10) | 5.06 (2.15) | 5.53 (2.14) | 6.10 (2.63) | 6.24 (2.65) | 6.55 (2.35) | 7.17 (2.53) |
| Future | 2.71 (1.38) | 2.93 (1.77) | 3.10 (1.78) | 2.00 (1.11) | 1.88 (1.32) | 1.90 (1.21) | 1.41 (1.09) | 0.91 (0.81) | 1.39 (1.29) |
| Total | 6.47 (2.56) | 7.70 (2.83) | 8.34 (2.76) | 7.06 (2.62) | 7.41 (3.02) | 8.00 (2.99) | 7.66 (3.00) | 7.45 (2.60) | 8.56 (3.42) |

*W2.* At the second wave, individuals specified an average of 7.52 events (SD = 2.82; range 3 to 14) without an effect of age or gender. Again, a main effect was found for the repeated measures variable, $F (1, 77) = 200.257$, $p < .001$; participants identified a greater number of past (M = 5.55, SD = 2.26) than future events (M = 1.96, SD = 1.57). There was also an interaction effect for event time and age group variable, $F (2, 77) = 16.065$, $p < .001$. The older the group, the greater the number of past events and the younger the group, the greater the number of future events.

*W3.* At the third wave the same effects were found. Overall, individuals specified an average of 8.25 events (SD = 2.98; range 3 to 14) without an effect for age or gender. A main effect was found for time, $F (1, 71) = 164.965$, $p < .000$; more events were reported from the past (M = 6.03, SD = 2.50) than for the future (M = 2.23, SD = 1.61). An interaction effect for event time and age group was found, F (2, 71) = 10.654, p < .000. The older the group, the greater the number of past events and the younger the group, the greater the number of future events.

In sum,
- At each wave there is no effect of age or gender on the number of events respondents identify over the total lifespan;
- At each wave respondents remember more events from their past than they expect for their future;
- At each wave the older respondents are, the greater the number of past events, and the younger respondents are, the greater the number of future events.

### W1→W2→W3

A one-within, one-between MANOVA for repeated measurements was carried out with the number of events at each wave as dependent variable, and age and gender as the between-subject variable, in order to determine (1) whether there is an overall change over waves in the total number of reported events, (2) whether the change over waves in the number of events is different for the compared groups, and (3) whether there is an overall effect of gender and/or age on the total number of events. Because this analysis was conducted on 74 respondents who participated in all three waves the average value of numbers may vary slightly from the average value of numbers obtained by the cross-sectional analyses which was conducted on all participants who participated in the specific wave. The results of the MANOVA indicated a significant wave effect, F (2, 67) = 6.894, p < .01. Follow-up polynomial contrasts indicated a significant linear effect with means increasing over time, F (1, 68) = 13.959, p < .001. The average number of events in the longitudinal analysis were 7.08 (SD = 2.71), 7.61 (SD = 2.89) and 8.31 (SD = 3.00) for the first, second and third wave, respectively, without an effect of age or gender meaning that the change in number of events over three waves is the same for all subgroups. There was also no overall effect of age or gender on the total number of events over the three waves.

Next, a MANOVA for repeated measures was conducted on the number of past and future events separately. For past events, there was an effect of wave, F (2, 67) = 7.578, p = .001. In general, the number of past events increased over the three waves. For the first wave the average number of past events was 4.89 (SD = 2.44), for the second wave 5.55 (SD = 2.34) and for the third wave 6.05 (SD = 2.52). There was no interaction effect of wave and age group or gender meaning that the number of past events increased for al subgroups in the same way over the three waves. For future events, however, no effect of wave was found meaning that the same average number of future events was mentioned at the first, second and third wave. In Table 2.2 the average number of events for past, future and total life is presented per wave and per age group.

Then, the ratio of past and total number of events was determined for each participant at the three waves and a MANOVA for repeated measurements was conducted with repeated measures on the wave variable, age and gender as the between-subjects factors and the ratio of past and total number of events as the dependent variable. The results of the MANOVA indicated a significant effect of wave, F (2, 67) = 4.400, p < .05. Follow-up polynomial contrasts indicated a significant linear effect with means increasing over waves, F (1, 68) = 5.869, p < .05, meaning that over a period of five years, overall, the ratio between past and total (past + future) number of events increases. The mean ratio of past events and total number of events for the first wave was .68, for the second wave .74 and for the third wave also .74, meaning that the overall change in ratio takes place from the first to the second wave. A significant overall effect of age was found on the ratio of past and total number of events, F (2, 68) = 35.770, p < .001; the older the group, the higher the ratio of past and total number of events, which was also found in the cross-sectional analyses. For the youngest group the ratio for the first, second and third wave was .55, .62 and .63, respectively, for the middle group .70, .76 and .76, and for the oldest group .82, .87 and .85. This is shown in Figure 2.2.

**Table 2.2**  W1→W2→W3: Number of events with Standard Deviation (between brackets) for Past, Future and Total life for three waves (W1, W2, W3) for three age groups (Young, Middle, Older).

| | Young | | | Middle | | | Older | | |
|---|---|---|---|---|---|---|---|---|---|
| | **W1** | **W2** | **W3** | **W1** | **W2** | **W3** | **W1** | **W2** | **W3** |
| Past | 3.65 | 4.77 | 5.23 | 5.03 | 5.53 | 6.10 | 6.44 | 6.72 | 7.17 |
| | (1.98) | (2.14) | (2.14) | (2.24) | (2.15) | (2.63) | (2.50) | (2.54) | (2.53) |
| Future | 2.88 | 3.00 | 3.27 | 2.07 | 1.90 | 1.90 | 1.39 | 0.94 | 1.39 |
| | (1.42) | (1.77) | (1.78) | (1.11) | (1.37) | (1.21) | (1.15) | (0.80) | (1.29) |
| Total | 6.54 | 7.77 | 8.50 | 7.10 | 7.43 | 8.00 | 7.83 | 7.67 | 8.56 |
| | (2.60) | (2.86) | (2.78) | (2.72) | (3.08) | (2.99) | (2.83) | (2.72) | (3.42) |

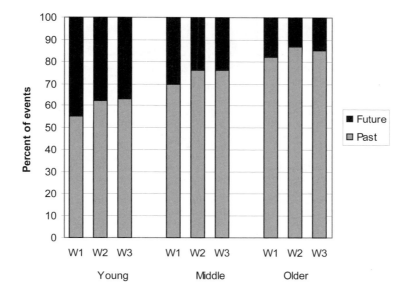

**Figure 2.2**  W1→W2→W3: Ratio of Past and Future events per age group (Young, Middle, Older) per wave (W1 = Wave 1, W2 = Wave 2, W3 = Wave 3).

Although no interaction effects of wave, age and gender were found, meaning that there is no significant difference in change in ratio of past and total number of events over waves for the different subgroups, the data suggest that the change in ratio of past and total number of events decreases as people grow older.

In sum,

- The phenomenon of the Constant Life Perspective turned out to be a robust pattern;
- The total number of reported life-events increases over the three waves which is due to an increase of the average number of past events;
- Overall, an effect of wave on the ratio of past and total number of events was found, i.e., as time passes by the proportion of past events increases whereas the proportion of future events decreases;
- There is a tendency that the change in ratio of past and total number of events is most prominent for the youngest group.

## 2.3.2 Distribution of events
### W1 | W2 | W3
According to reported age at the time of event, the number of events per five years was determined for the three age groups and subsequently, the number of events was translated into percentage of events per five years. In Figure 2.3 the percentage of events per five years per age group is shown for the first

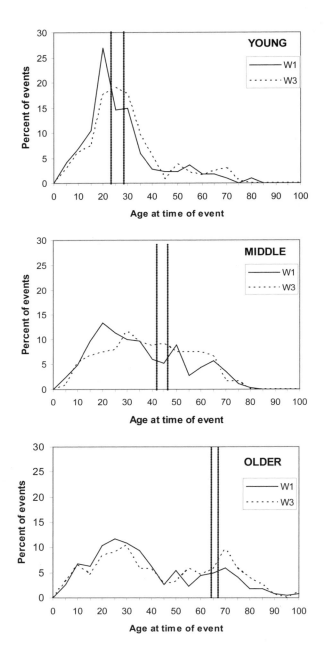

**Figure 2.3** W1 | W3: Distribution of past and future events (percents) per five years for young (M age W1 = 23.5), middle-aged (M age W1 = 43.3) and older (M age W1 = 67.4) adults as function of reported age at time of event for W1 and W3 (Vertical, dotted lines indicate the transition from past events to future events for W1 and W3).

and the third wave. For reasons of convenience the second wave is not shown. In the enclosed CD the distribution of events over the lifespan is shown for all three waves (Figure A2.3). The transition from past events to future events for the first and third wave is indicated by a vertical line.

### Age at time of event
– *Young* (M age W1 = 23.5 yrs)
At the first wave the distribution of past events shows a power function with a clear recency effect, i.e., recent life events are mentioned more frequently than events experienced in the distant past. The distribution of future events also follows roughly a power function, i.e., life events which are expected for the near future, are mentioned more often than events which are foreseen in the distant future. Earlier this was called the 'proximity' effect. The second wave shows about the same pattern with a sharp peak between 15 and 20 years of age and a recency/proximity effect between 20 to 30 years of age. At the third wave, the peak has been flattened out and the recency and proximity effect have moved in the direction of the increasing mean age or, in other words, stay centred around the present age of the respondents.
– *Middle* (M age W1 = 43.3 yrs)
The distribution of events for middle-aged adults is less clear. At the first wave a clear bump can be discerned between about 10 to 40 years of age. A recency effect is almost missing but a proximity effect can be discerned. At the second wave besides an emerging bump a small recency effect as well a small proximity effect can be discerned. The third wave shows an unclear pattern with one great 'bump'.
– *Older* (M age W1 = 67.4 yrs)
The oldest group shows at each wave a very clear pattern with a strong bump and recency and proximity effects. The bump is situated in the period of about 10 to 40 years of age. The patterns of the three waves look very much the same. However, it is noticeable that the bump is higher at the first wave than at the second and third wave while recency/proximity effects are stronger at the second and third wave.

In order to determine the location of the bump more exactly, data of all three waves were put together for the oldest group and the distribution of events over the lifespan summarized over three waves was determined per five years and per ten years. This is shown in Figure 2.4a and Figure 2.4b, respectively.

Figure 2.4a shows that, when determining the distribution of events per five years, the top of the bump is situated between 15 to 30 years of age. From Figure 2.4b can be read that the top of the bump is situated between 20 to 30 years of age when determining the distribution of events per decade fol-

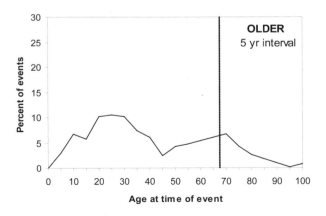

**Figure 2.4a.** Distribution of past and future events (percents) per five years for older adults (M age = 68.6 yrs) as function of reported age at time of event summarized over three waves (Vertical line indicates the transition from past events to future events).

**Figure 2.4b.** Distribution of past and future events (percents) per decade for older adults (M age = 68.6 yrs) as function of reported age at time of event summarized over three waves (Vertical line indicates the transition from past events to future events).

lowed by the period of 10 to 20 years of age. In the next chapters the period of 10 to 30 years of age will be considered the bump period when starting from decades.

### Years from time of testing
In standardized event distributions of age groups with significant age ranges (12, 24 and 28 years on the LIM for young, middle and older age groups, respectively) the mean age per age group might lead to confounding of memory effects. For instance, the age range in the older age group is 28 years. When starting from the average age of this age group (67.3 years) recency and proximity effects can be confounded; for instance, for a 56-year old respondent the period from the age of 56 is all future while for a 84-year old respondent the period of 56 till 84 is past. For a more detailed analysis of event patterns, time of testing and event time in years from time of testing might be used instead of the subject's calendar age and reported age of event. In Figure 2.5 the distributions of past and future events (percents), scaled per five years and centred on the time of testing (0 yrs at first wave) with past and future event time measured in years from time of testing, are reproduced graphically for the first and third wave for the young (top panel), middle-aged (middle panel) and older (bottom panel) age groups. For clarity reasons the pattern for the second wave is not represented but this pattern holds about the mean between the first and third wave. In the enclosed CD results are presented for all three waves (Figure A2.5). The transitions from past events to future events for the first and third wave are indicated by a vertical line. Figure 2.5 shows the following patterns per age group:
– *Young* (M age W1 = 23.5 yrs)
A power curve for the young age group with a clear recency effect, i.e., recent life events are mentioned more frequently than events experienced in the distant past. The distribution of future events shows the proximity effect, i.e., life events which are expected for the near future, are mentioned more often than events which are foreseen in the distant future. As was also shown in Figure 2.3, Figure 2.5 shows that this recency/proximity effect is clearly moving in the direction of the increasing mean age or, in other words, stays centred across the present age across the lifespan.
– *Middle* (M age W1 = 43.3 yrs)
An emerging bump and a recency effect at all three waves. This recency effect is moving with increasing age. A proximity effect can be distinguished at the second wave but is less clear at the first and third wave.
– *Older* (M age W1 = 67.4 yrs)
For the older age group there is a clear bump at all three waves and there are recency and proximity effects at the second and third wave. At the first wave there is a proximity effect. Recency and proximity effect are also moving with increasing age.

In sum, two effects seem to determine the distribution of events over the lifespan. A recency/proximity effect is moving with calendar age of the respondent, while the bump is fixed in the period of adolescence and young adulthood for middle-aged and older respondents with the top between 15 to 30 years of age when taking periods of five years as unit of time, and 20 to 30 years of age when taking decades as unit of time.

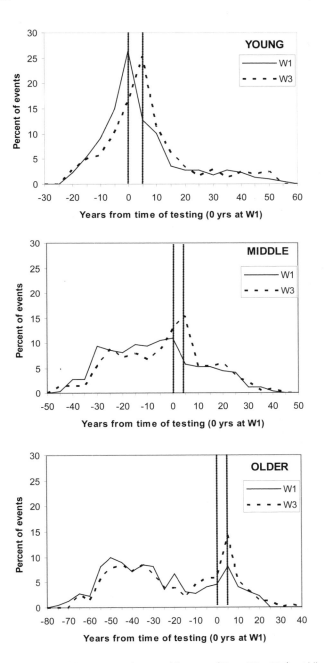

**Figure 2.5.** W1 | W3: Distribution of past and future events (percents) for young (M age W1 = 23.5), middle-aged (M age W1 = 43.3) and older (M age W1 = 67.4) adults per five years centred in years from time of testing (0 yrs at W1) for W1 and W3 (Vertical lines indicate the transition from past events to future events for W1 and W3).

### 2.3.3  Age of first and last event, and subjective life expectancy
**W1 | W2 | W3**

*W1.* The mean age for the first event was 11.5 years (SD = 6.2). There was no effect of age or gender. The mean age for the last mentioned event, which is mostly an event expected in the future, differed per age group, F (2, 92) = 29.380, p < .001; the older, the later in life the last event is situated (M young = 50.6 yrs; M middle = 60.3 yrs; M older = 74.4 yrs). For subjective life expectancy there was also an effect of age, F (2, 92) = 9.541, p < .001; the older, the higher the age of expected death (M young = 75.9 yrs; M middle = 78.4; M older = 83.9).

*W2.* The mean age for the first event was 11.4 years (SD = 6.2) without an effect of age or gender. For the age of the last mentioned event there was an effect of age, F (2, 77) = 17.967, p < .001; the older, the later in life the last event is situated (M young = 51.2; M middle = 62.2; M older = 74.7). For the age of expected death there was also an effect of age, F (2, 77) = 4.664, p < .05. The older, the higher the expected age of death (M young = 77.4; M middle = 80.5; M older = 84.1).

*W3.* The mean age for the first event was 12.4 (SD = 7.9) without an effect of age or gender. The mean age of the last mentioned event differed by age group, F (2, 71) = 18.805, p < .001, (M young = 52.6; M middle = 63.4; M older = 76.7). For the subjective life expectancy there was also an effect of age, F (2, 71) = 5.588, p < .01. The older, the later the moment of expected death (M young = 77.9; M Middle = 79.5; M older = 85.0).

In sum,
- At each wave there is no effect of age or gender on the age from which the first important event in life is reported.
- At each wave it is found that the older respondents are, the more advanced the age at which they situate the last event.
- At each wave it is found that the older respondents are, the more advanced the age of expected death.

**W1→W2→W3**

A MANOVA for repeated measurements was carried out with the age of the first mentioned event at each wave as dependent variable and age and gender as the between-subject variable. There were no effects of wave, age or gender on the age from which the first event was reported. The grand mean for the age of the first event is 11.9 years.

The effect of gender, age and wave on the age at which the last event was situated was also determined. Over a period of five years the grand mean age of the last event slightly increased but this was not statistically significant (first wave 60.5 yrs; second wave 61.3 yrs; third wave 63.6 yrs). As could be expected and became clear on basis of cross-sectional analyses, there was an overall effect of age group on the age of the last mentioned event, F (2, 68) = 28.563, p < .001, (M young = 52.4; M middle = 62.3; M older = 74.7).

Finally, the effect of gender, age and wave on the age of expected death was determined. Over a period of five years, overall, the mean age of expected death slightly increased but this was not statistically significant (first wave 79.1 yrs; second wave 80.4 yrs; third wave 80.6 yrs). An overall effect of age group on the age of expected death was found as well, F (2, 68) = 7.062, p < .01. Over three waves the average age of expected death was 77.7 years, 79.5 years and 84.5 years for the young, middle-aged and older group, respectively.

In sum, the first important event in life is situated at about 12 years of age, while the age of the last expected event as well as the age of expected death is depending on the age of the respondent; the older the respondents are, the later in life they situate the last event and the moment of expected death.

## 2.4   Discussion

In the LIM-study respondents of a young, middle and older age group were asked to report important events from their past and expectations they have for their future at three measurement points over a period of five years. In the present chapter the focus was on the number and distribution of events over the lifespan. The most important results are summarized and discussed below.

### 2.4.1  Sum of past and future events is constant

A significant outcome from the lifespan perspective is the finding that the total number of events (past + future) does not differ by age group at all three waves. Earlier, this phenomenon was called the *Principle of the Constant Life Perspective*, i.e., the sum of past and future autobiographical events is constant across the lifespan (Schroots & Assink, 1998). This principle, which was also found by deVries and Watt (1996) who made use of the Time Line (TL), seems to be very robust as it is also found in the second and third wave. DeVries and Watt (1996) concluded that "It is as if there exists a sort of finite capacity for the identification and representation of the events of a life" (p. 95). Although the number of events over the total lifespan appeared to be equal for respondents of different age groups within a specific method, the absolute number of events identified by respondents varied between different methods; the more time respondents are allowed to recall events, the more events they report.

It is noticeable that in a number of studies it was found that the number of events is also independent of age when exploring only the past (e.g., Elnick et al., 1999; Martin & Smyer, 1990; Brugman, 2000). As the LIM is administered in two parts – first, the past is explored and second the future – and as the LIM-grid is the same for all age groups as well as the time allowed to identify events in the past and in the future separately, it would be expected on the basis of results of the above mentioned studies that the number of past events in the LIM-study would be equal for all age groups as well as the number of future events. The results of the LIM-study, however, are more in accordance with reality; older respondents have experienced more events in their life than younger respondents while younger respondents will experience more events in the future than older respondents. It seems that the LIM-method of visualizing and drawing one's life evokes a rather genuine picture of one's life and of the most important events in one's past and future. The *number* and, consequently, the *'quality' of events* respondents identify over the total lifespan seem to be dependent of *the method used* and independent of age of respondent.

### 2.4.2  The ratio of past and total number of events is dependent of age

Although the total number of events over the lifespan is the same for all age groups, the ratio of past and total number of events differs by age group at all three waves. The older respondents are, the greater the number of past events (memories), and the younger respondents are, the greater the number of future events (expectations). Cross-sectional studies show that this ratio of past and total number of events is systematically changing with age. As in this longitudinal study all subjects grow older, the ratio of past and total number of events is expected to increase for the whole group. This hypothesis is (partly) confirmed; the ratio increases between the first and second wave for the whole sample and for all age groups. Between the second and third wave, however, the ratio remains the same for the total group. For the oldest group the ratio decreases slightly compared to the second wave; apparently, changes within this group are minimal and can show small fluctuations within the standard error of measurement. Overall, the younger respondents are, the greater the change in the ratio of past and total number of events.

### 2.4.3  Over waves respondents report more events

Over the three waves, the average number of reported events over the whole lifespan increased which is probably a test-retest effect. At the third wave respondents were asked at the beginning of the interview whether they remembered something of the previous interviews. Most respondents remembered they had to draw a line and had to tell something about their life but they, mostly, did not remember what they had told. Thus, vaguely, respondents know what is expected at the second and third wave and they are more or less prepared on what the interviewer asks from them. It will be easier for them, then, to retrieve memories from their past and expectations for the future and the result is that they identify more events over the total lifespan.

## 2.4.4 The distribution of events over the lifespan shows a bump, and recency and proximity effects

At first sight the patterns for the distribution of events over the lifespan look quite different for the three age groups. For the youngest age group there is a very strong recency effect and a proximity effect. This recency/proximity effect is moving with the present age as the longitudinal analysis shows. For the middle-age group the recency/proximity effect is also moving with the present age and a bump is emerging. For the oldest group bump and recency/proximity are clearly separated. Results (only past events) found by Fromholt et al. (2003) also show this 'moving' recency effect; the period of relatively low recall between the bump and the recency effect was 20 years longer for centenarians than for 80-year old participants. Generally, it is found that *the bump is very fixed in the period of about 10 to 30 years of age*. Most researchers assume that the bump appears only after middle age. However, it is salient from the results that the recency effect is much stronger for the younger age group than for the middle age and older age group. Fitzgerald (1995) suggested that for younger adults the autobiographical memory bump could be overshadowed by memories for recent events. In the Introduction of this chapter the model of Schroots and Van Dijkum (2004) was introduced; they showed that there is an autonomous process of growth and decline that produces the bump, which slowly emerges from the forgetting curve with age. Between about ten and thirty years of age information is encoded more intensively than in other periods of life. This applies also to the young age group. For this group retention and encoding curves overlap completely resulting in one big bump. As people grow older the recency effect is moving with age and bump and retention curves get more and more dissociated resulting in a bimodal distribution of bump and recency effects for older adults.

## 2.4.5 Mean age of first event is 12 years; mean age of last event is dependent of age

In this LIM-study no effect of age was found on the age from which the first important event was reported, while the age of the last expected life event changed with increasing age. This is in accordance with results reported by deVries and Watt (1996) although the absolute mean ages of first and last event were different in the two studies. In the LIM-study the average age of the first event was 12 years which is higher than the average age (5.9 years for women and 8.3 years for men) found by deVries and Watt (1996). For the last event the mean age in the LIM-study was 52.4 for the young age group, 62.3 for the middle age group and 74.7 for the older age group (over three waves) while the mean ages in the Time Line (TL) study of deVries and Watt (1996) were, respectively, 57.5, 64.5 and 78 years. These differences in average age can be due to the fact that in the TL-study more events are generated and consequently also more events at a younger and older age. The age of the subjective life expectancy also appeared to be dependent on the age of the respondent which is in accordance with life expectancy tables; as people grow older, the average life expectancy increases.

In concluding this chapter, it can be stated that:
- The sum of past and future events is independent of age of respondent and dependent of method used;
- The ratio of past and total number of events is dependent of age and increases as respondents grow older;
- The change in the ratio of past and total number of events tends to be stronger for younger age groups;
- The recency/proximity effect is moving with the present age of the subjects while the bump is fixed in the period of adolescence and young adulthood;

- It can be hypothesized that the bump and recency/proximity effects play a part in all age groups. For young adults the bump and recency/proximity effects could show a com plete overlap resulting in a high peak in adolescence and young adulthood;
- As people grow older they situate the last event and the moment of expected death further into the future.

# Chapter 3
# Affect of Events

## 3.1 Introduction

In the LIM-study respondents are asked to draw their life-line with ups and downs. The ups represent the positive events or the happy periods in life while the dips represent the negative events or the unhappy periods in life. In the previous chapter the number of events and the distribution of events over the lifespan were studied. In this chapter events will be split up according to their affective value into 'affective positive' and 'affective negative' events. Events that are considered as 'affective positive' have evoked positive emotions as joy and happiness while 'affective negative' events have evoked negative emotions as sadness, anger, depression and pain. The meaning of the terms 'emotion' and 'affect' is not univocal. Frijda (1988) defines 'emotions' as "responses to events that are important to the individual" (p. 351). Fischer (1996) uses the term 'emotion' "to indicate the bodily and psychological arousal from which we infer that an event has personally affected someone" (p. 76). In practice the terms 'emotion' and 'affect' are used more or less interchangeably (Strongman, 1996).

During several decades a great body of research has focused on the influence of mainly negative, stressful life events on measures of health and life expectancy starting with the Social Readjustment Rating Scale of Holmes and Rahe (1967). In these studies, subjects are asked to indicate on a list which, mostly negative, events they have experienced in a particular period. In the LIM-study, however, respondents are free to recall and anticipate personally important events. The question arises whether subjects are indeed focused on mainly negative memories and expectations or are more positively oriented. Results of most studies point in the direction of a more positive view on the past. For instance, Martin and Smyer (1990) asked participants to report life events that had occurred at different times of their lifespan and found that the ratio of positive and negative events was 1.6 : 1. In a study where depressed and non-depressed participants were asked to retrieve thirty memories, all participants recalled more positive than negative memories (Yang & Rehm, 1993). Using a diary self-report memory methodology Thompson (1998) found a small effect of pleasantness such that positive events were remembered slightly better than negative events. Robinson and Taylor (1998) simply asked women in the age of 40 to 55 years to describe four vivid memories and to rate these memories for pleasantness. More memories were rated as pleasant (52%) than unpleasant (39%). Walker, Skowronski and Thompson (2003) found in a review of several studies concerning the recall of positive and negative events that in all studies more pleasant than unpleasant events were yielded. They gave two explanations for these results. First, people perceive life as generally pleasant and are inclined to seek out pleasant experiences and avoid negative experiences to keep life pleasant. This is reflected in the content of autobiographical memory which is more positive than negative in all studies the authors reviewed. Second, pleasant emotions fade more slowly than unpleasant emotions implying that the memory system does not treat negative and positive affect equally. Positive emotions associated with good events tend to persist whereas negative emotions associated with bad events tend to fade away. But Baumeister et al. (2001) argue that across a broad range of psychological phenomena it is a general principle that bad is stronger than good. However, they admit that the memory literature yields several exceptions to this principle. They give two explanations for this exception. First, negative memories are suppressed or positive memories are accessed more easy in order to enhance the self. Second, non-depressed individuals recall information that matches their current mood which is mostly positive.

There are only a few studies which have examined individual conceptions of both past and future. DeVries and Watt (1996), using the Rappaport Time Line (Rappaport, Enrich, & Wilson, 1985), found that respondents of different age groups reported more positive memories from their past and expected more positive than negative events in the future but older participants expected fewer positive events for the future than younger respondents did. Newby-Clark and Ross (2003) asked 30 students to list a maximum of 10 events from their past and future and to rate the affect of these events on a 10-point rating scale. Their respondents recalled an affectively mixed past, which was still more positive than negative, whereas they anticipated an ideal positive future.

In the first wave of the LIM-study it was found that, in general, respondents reported as many positive as negative events for both the total life and for past and future separately. In other words, the general mean affect over the total lifespan and over past and future was affective neutral (Assink & Schroots, 2002; Schroots & Assink, 2004). This difference in results – life is affective positive versus life is affective neutral – is probably due to differences in methods used. The LIM method asks from participants to report events spontaneously, without much thinking. In fact, LIM-participants don't realize what they exactly are revealing when drawing the lifeline. For this reason it is assumed that the LIM is closer to the real self and the personal truth than would be the case with other methods, which allow more time to generate events and possibly also more socially desirable events, i.e., more positive than negative memories and expectations (cf. Greenwald, 1980, who uses the term 'benefectance' to describe the tendency for the self to be perceived as effective in achieving what is desired). Although, overall, respondents reported as many positive as negative events, the distribution of positive and negative events over past and future turned out to be dependent of age in the first wave of the LIM-study; the older participants were, the more positive they were about the past and the less positive about the future, and – conversely – the younger participants were, the more positive they were about the future and the less positive about the past (Assink & Schroots, 2002), as was also found by deVries and Watt (1996).

In the previous chapter the distribution of events over the lifespan was studied and three effects were observed: (1) a memory 'bump', which is situated in adolescence and young adulthood, and (2) recency and (3) proximity effects which move with the present age of the individual. The question is whether the distribution of positive and negative events follows the same pattern as was found for the distribution of events in general. There are a few studies which have examined this question. Berntsen and Rubin (2002) asked respondents of different age to report the age of, among others, their happiest, saddest, most traumatic and most important memories. For all age groups they found a clear bump in the 20s for the most important and happiest memories. For the saddest and most traumatic memories they found a monotonically decreasing retention function with some indication of a bump only for the oldest respondents. In another study Rubin and Berntsen (2003) asked respondents ranging in age from 20 to 94 years to date several memories associated with positive and negative affect. The results were in accordance with Berntsen and Rubin's (2002) earlier findings, i.e., a peak in the 20s for all age groups for memories associated with positive emotions and relatively flat curves with an increase in the most recent decades for memories associated with negative memories. An exception, however, was found for jealousy; although this is considered a negative emotion a bump was found. Rubin and Berntsen (2003) also asked respondents ranging in age from 21 to 41 years to answer the same questions for a hypothetical 70-year-old person. The patterns of the distribution of different memories of this hypothetical 70-year-old person matched the distributions of the survey data largely. Subjects were more certain in ratings at which age positive events were to be expected than at which age negative events were to be expected. The authors argue that this finding – a dissociation between emotionally positive and emotionally negative memories – is a support for the life script theory which states that there are culturally shared life scripts for positive but not for negative events.

In addition, the question can be asked which period in life individuals consider as most positive and which period as most negative. Sehulster (1996) found that people (age range: 26–67, mean age: 44 yrs) perceive the period between the ages 14 and 24 as their era; they believe that everything was better and funnier in that specific period. This implies that the most positive period in life falls within the bump period. Mehlsen, Platz and Fromholt (2003) asked individuals in the age from 62 to 77 years, to point out the most and the least satisfying decades of life. The years from 30 to 39 were most frequently chosen as the most satisfying decade, followed by the adjoining decades. A decade in old age was chosen as the least satisfying by 24 percent of the participants, while only 8.5 percent of the participants evaluated old age as the most satisfying period of life. These results are partly in contrast with results found by deVries, Blando, Southard and Bubeck (2001). They asked participants to identify what has been or is expected to be the best time of life and the worst time of life. For the best times they found a clear pattern: the times of the present including the recent past and the near future were identified as the best time, i.e., the best time was related to the age of the participant. For the worst times, no clear pattern was found. The worst time was not clearly related to age and was also more variable than the best time. Takkinen and Suutama (2004), who had older adults aged 83–87 years draw their lifeline, also found that the highest points were located in the period of 80–89 years indicating the present time while most of the lower points were located in childhood. Gergen and Gergen (1987) created lifelines on the basis of evaluations of different periods of life by a sample of men and women between 63 and 93 years of age. The years between roughly the ages of 50 till 60 were evaluated as the most positive. Assink & Schroots (2002) found that in the 'bump' period a greater percentage of events was rated positive than negative by middle-aged and older adults while in other periods of life a greater percentage of events was rated negative. Younger adults had high expectations of the near future and expected the thirties to be the time of their life containing relatively most positive events.

As far as known, no longitudinal research has been conducted concerning changes in subjective feelings about life as people grow older. Assink and Schroots (2002) determined on the basis of the affective ratings of events the mean affect for the total life and for past and future separately. Cross-sectional research of the first LIM-wave showed an interaction effect of age and gender on the mean affect for the total life, young women being more positive about life than young men, while middle-aged and older men were more positive about life than middle-aged and older women. Another finding was that respondents of older age groups were more positive about the past and less positive about the future while younger persons were more positive about the future and less positive about the past. The question is what will happen when respondents grow older. Is there a change in the direction that the past becomes more positive and the future more negative over a period of five years?

In sum, the four questions to be answered in this chapter are:
– How do people feel about their life?
– How are positive and negative LIM-events distributed over the lifespan?
– Which periods are considered the best times and which periods are considered the worst times in life?
– Which changes take place in the affect patterns over a period of five years?

For each of these questions, the role of age, gender and time (past and future) will be taken into account.

## 3.2   Method

After a chronological readable story had been created as was described in the first chapter, a coding instruction was developed in order to determine, among others, the affective value of each event on a 5-point scale ranging from very negative (–2) to very positive (+2). All events were coded independently by two coders. The affective value of each event was determined on the basis of the text belonging to the specific event. When the text was unclear concerning the affective value of the event, the life-line was consulted. Discrepancies between the two coders were resolved by discussion. The inter-rater agreement for affect was determined on the basis of 24 randomly chosen stories for each wave. At the first wave the two coders agreed on the affective value in 66 percent of all events mentioned in the 24 stories, at the second wave in 79 percent of all events and at the third wave in 77 percent of all events. When using a 3-point scale (negative, neutral and positive) the two coders agreed on the affective value in 86 percent of all events at the first wave, in 95 percent of all events at the second wave and in 93 percent of all events at the third wave. In order to determine the ratio of positive and negative events and the distribution of positive and negative events over the lifespan, events were divided into two categories: 'very negative' and 'negative' events were put together in the category 'negative' and 'very positive' and positive' events were put together in the category 'positive'. Neutral events were recoded into either 'positive' or 'negative' on the basis of common sense or by random assignment.

## 3.3　Results

### 3.3.1　Mean affect
#### W1 | W2 | W3
Per respondent the number of positive and of negative events was expressed as a percentage of the total number of events in order to control for the differences in event number. In Table 3.1 the mean percentage of positive and negative events is given for each wave for the total life and for past and future.

**Table 3.1**　W1 | W2 | W3: Mean percentage of positive and negative events for the Total life, and for Past and Future for Wave 1 (W1), Wave 2 (W2) and Wave 3 (W3).

|  | W1 | | W2 | | W3 | |
|---|---|---|---|---|---|---|
|  | Positive | Negative | Positive | Negative | Positive | Negative |
| Total life | 49.2 | 50.8 | 50.9 | 49.1 | 51.0 | 49.0 |
| Past | 46.8 | 53.2 | 49.3 | 50.7 | 47.0 | 53.0 |
| Future | 47.6 | 52.4 | 54.5 | 45.5 | 57.5 | 42.5 |

At all three waves the percentage of positive and negative events for the total life and for past and future didn't differ significantly from each other (paired t-tests, p < .05). In other words, at all three waves half of the events were positive and half were negative for the total life and for past and future.

To facilitate further analyses, i.e., to determine the effect of age, gender and wave, the mean affect for all events over the total lifespan and – separately – for past and future events was determined per respondent:

*W1.* A 2(Gender) x 3(Age group) ANOVA was conducted to evaluate the effects of gender and age group on the mean affect over the total life. Overall, participants expressed slightly negative feelings about their life (M = –0.09, SD = 0.49) but this value was not statistically significant from zero confirming the finding that half of the events were rated positive and half negative. However, an interaction effect for age and gender was found [F (2, 92) = 3.611, p < .05]. Young women are more positive about life than young men, while – conversely – middle-aged and older women feel less positive about life than men of these age groups.

In order to differentiate between past and future, a 2(Gender) x 3(Age Group) x 2(Event Time: Past and Future) analysis of variance (ANOVA) was conducted with repeated measures on the last factor and with the mean affect for past and future as the dependent variable. Generally, negative affect for the past is somewhat stronger than for the future (M past = –0.15, SD = 0.64; M future = –0.05, SD = 0.87) but this difference is not statistically significant. However, there was an interaction effect of time and age group [F (2, 88) = 3.971, p < .05]. The older people are, the more positive feelings they have about their past and the more negative they feel about their future. Conversely, the younger people are, the more negative they feel about their past and the more positive about their future.

*W2.* Again, participants expressed slightly negative feelings about their life (M = –0.04, SD = 0.56) but this value was not statistically significant from zero. Now, there was a tendency in the direction of an interaction effect for age and gender [F (2, 77) = 2.784, p = .07]. Young women are far more positive about life than young men, while for middle-aged men and women and for older men and women there is no difference in affect over the whole lifespan. Older men and women are less positive about their whole life than middle-aged men and women.

As at the first wave, participants expressed less negative affect about their future (M = 0.07, SD = 0.91) than about their past (M = – 0.04, SD = 0.60) but this difference was not significant. Again, an interaction effect of time and age group [F (2, 68) = 4.058, p <. 05] was found. Now, young and middle-aged respondents were more positive about the future than about the past while for the oldest group it is the other way around.

*W3.* Again, participants expressed slightly negative feelings about their life (M = –0.08, SD = 0.50) and this value was again not statistically significant from zero. In contrast to the first two waves, there was no effect of age or gender on the mean affective rating of the whole life.

Concerning the past and future, participants, in general, expressed less negative affect about their future (M = 0.14, SD = 0.85) than about their past (M = – 0.14, SD = 0.67) but again, this difference was not significant. Contrary to the first and second wave, no significant interaction effect of time and age group was found.

In sum:
– At all three waves respondents reported as many positive as negative events for the total life, for the past and for the future, i.e. overall the affective rating of the total life, the past and the future is neutral.
– At the first wave young women were more positive about their total life than young men, while middle-aged and older women felt less positive about life than men of these age groups. At the second wave there was a tendency of this effect but at the third wave no interaction effect of age and gender was found.
– At the first and second wave it was found that the older people are, the more positive feelings they have about their past and the more negative they feel about their future. Conversely, the younger people are, the more negative they feel about their past and the more positive about their future. At the third wave this pattern was not found.

## W1→W2→W3

A 2(Gender) x 3(Age Group) x 3(Wave) analysis of variance (ANOVA) was conducted with repeated measures on the last factor and with the mean affect for the whole life as the dependent variable. No effect of wave on the mean affect for the total life was found. As was found in the cross-sectional studies, there was an overall interaction effect of gender and age on the mean affect for the total life [F (2, 68) =

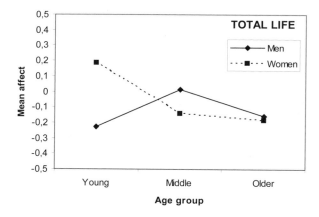

**Figure 3.1** W1→W2→W3: Grand mean affect (over three waves) for the Total life for men and women of a young (M age = 25.1), middle-aged (M age = 45.8) and older (M age = 67.8) age group.

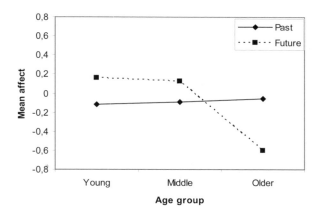

**Figure 3.2** W1→W2→W3: Grand mean affect (over three waves) for Past and Future for a young (M age = 25.1), middle-aged (M age = 45.8) and older (M age = 67.8) age group.

4.022, p < .05] over three waves. Young women are more optimistic about life than young men, while for the middle-aged group it is the other way around. For the oldest group it was found that men and women feel about the same about their whole life. This general effect over the three waves is shown in Figure 3.1.

A 2(Gender) x 3(Age Group) x 2(Time: past and future) x 3(Wave) analysis of variance (ANOVA) was conducted with repeated measures on the last two factors and with the mean affect for past and future as dependent variables. An interaction effect of time and age group was found, F (2, 56) = 6.335, p < .01; younger and middle-aged individuals are more positive about the future than about the past while for the oldest group it is the other way around. This is shown in Figure 3.2.

In sum:
- The mean affective rating of events over the total life and over past and future separately does not change over a period of five years for the total group.
- Summarized over three waves, young women are more positive about their whole life than young men, middle-aged men are more positive than middle-aged women and older men and women are about equally positive (or negative).
- Summarized over three waves, younger and middle-aged individuals are more positive about the future than about the past, while older individuals are more positive about the  past than about the future.

### 3.3.2 Percentage of intense affect
**W1 | W2 | W3**

As mentioned before, events were rated on a 5 points scale running from very positive to very negative. The question arises how often events are accompanied by an intense affect and whether there is an effect of age, gender, time or wave on the percentage of very positive and very negative events. In Table 3.2 the mean percentage of very positive and very negative events for the total life, and for past and future is presented for three waves.

*Total life.* At each wave respondents reported a greater percentage of 'very negative' events than of 'very positive' events (paired t-test; p < .05) over the total lifespan.

For the second wave an effect of gender on the percentage of 'very positive' events was found, F (1, 77) = 8.308, p < .01; women report more 'very positive' events over the total lifespan than men do (17% versus 10%).

**Table 3.2** W1 | W2 | W3: Mean percentage of very positive (pos) and very negative (neg) events for the Total life, and for Past and Future for Wave 1 (W1), Wave 2 (W2) and Wave 3 (W3).

| | W1 | | W2 | | W3 | |
|---|---|---|---|---|---|---|
| | Very Positive | Very Negative | Very Positive | Very Negative | Very Positive | Very Negative |
| Total life | 7.2 | 14.0 | 14.1 | 20.0 | 14.4 | 23.5 |
| Past | 9.2 | 16.8 | 17.3 | 24.4 | 16.6 | 29.0 |
| Future | 4.4 | 9.0 | 5.9 | 6.3 | 8.2 | 6.4 |

For the third wave an effect of age was found on the percentage of 'very positive' events, $F(2, 71) = 3.886$, $p < .05$. The older the age group, the lower the percentage of very positive events (oldest group 8%, middle group 15%, youngest group 18%).

*Past and Future.* For all three waves it was found that in the past more events are accompanied by an intense affect than in the future (paired t-test; $p < .05$) and that a greater percentage of these past events are rated as 'very negative' than as 'very positive'. For the future applies that at all three waves the percentages of 'very positive' and 'very negative' events do not differ significantly from each other.

Besides, at the second wave there is an interaction effect of age and gender on the percentage of 'very positive' events in the past, $F(2, 77) = 3.130$, $p = .05$. In general, women report more 'very positive' events from the past than men do but as women get older, the percentage of very positive events decreases while middle-aged men report more 'very positive' events from the past than young and older men (young women 34%, middle-aged women 19%, older women 14% versus young men 11%, middle-aged men 17% and older men 5%).

For the third wave there is a tendency of an effect of age, $F(2, 71) = 2.976$, $p = .06$; the older the group, the lower the percentage of very positive events in the past (young 22%; middle 17%; older 9%). There was also an effect of gender on the percentage of very negative events in the future, $F(1, 64) = 4.204$, $p < .05$; women expect more very negative events in the future than men do (10% versus 2%).

In sum:
– At each wave respondents reported a greater percentage of 'very negative' events than of 'very positive' events over the total lifespan.
– For all three waves it was found that in the past more events are accompanied by an intense affect than in the future.
– For all three waves it was found that a greater percentage of past events is rated as 'very negative' than as 'very positive'.
– For the future it was found that at all three waves the percentages of 'very positive' and 'very negative' events do not differ significantly from each other.

## W1→W2→W3

*Total life.* A MANOVA for repeated measures was conducted on the percentage of intense affect (very positive + very negative) for the total life. An effect of wave was found, $F(2, 67) = 14.364$, $p < .001$. Over waves the percentage of 'very positive' and 'very negative' events is increasing (first wave 22%, second wave 35%, third wave 37%). Analyses of the effect of wave on 'very positive' and 'very negative' events separately showed that for both 'very positive' events [$F(2, 67) = 8.227$, $p = .001$] and 'very negative' events [$F(2, 67) = 7.065$, $p < .01$] there is an effect of wave. The percentage of 'very positive' events for the first wave was 7 percent, for the second wave 15 percent and for the third wave 14 percent. For 'very negative' events these percentages were 15, 21 and 24, respectively. For 'very positive' events there is also an overall interaction effect of age and gender, $F(2, 68) = 3.431$, $p < .05$; young women mention more very positive events than young men (17 versus 9 percent), middle-aged women and middle-aged men mention about the same percentage of very positive events (11 and 13 percent) and older women mention more very positive events than older men (13 versus 4 percent) over the total lifespan over three waves..

*Past and Future.* For the past there is an effect of wave for the percentage of intense affect, $F(2, 67) = 8.419$, $p = .001$; at the first wave 28 percent of all past events were accompanied by an intense affect, at the second wave 43 percent and at the third wave 45 percent. Besides that, there was an overall effect of gender, $F(1, 68) = 4.125$, $p < .05$; women report more events which are accompanied by an intense affect from the past than men do (43 versus 33 percent). Both the percentage of 'very negative' events [$F(2, 67) = 5.275$, $p < .01$] and the percentage of 'very positive' events [$F(2, 67) = 3.412$, $p < .05$] increased over waves. The percentage of 'very negative' events in the past was for the first, second and third wave 18 percent, 25 percent and 29 percent respectively. The percentage of 'very positive' past events was 10 percent, 18 percent and 16 percent, respectively. For the percentage of 'very positive' past events there was an overall effect of gender, $F(1, 68) = 5.538$, $p < .05$; over three waves women identify a greater percentage of 'very positive' events in the past than men do (17 versus 10 percent).

For the future there was no effect of wave for the percentage of intense affect, or for the percentage of very positive or very negative events, separately. There was an overall effect of age on the percentage of 'very positive' events, $F(2, 56) = 4.431$, $p < .05$; the oldest age group expects no 'very positive' events in the future, the middle group expects four percent of all future events to be 'very positive' and the youngest group expects nine percent of all future events to be 'very positive'.

In sum:
– Over waves the percentage of events which are accompanied by an intense affect is increasing.
– For the past it is found that, overall, women recall more 'very positive' events from the past than men do.
– Overall, the older individuals are the fewer 'very positive' events they expect for the future.

### 3.3.3 Distribution of affect over the lifespan
W1 | W2 | W3

*Distribution of positive and negative events*
In order to determine whether there are differences in the patterns of the distribution of positive and negative events over the lifespan, the total number of positive events and of negative events was put at 100 percent for each age group, i.e., the area under the positive curves is 100 percent as well as the area under the negative curves. Analogue to the distribution of events over the lifespan in the previous chapter, time of testing and event time in years from time of testing were used instead of the subject's calendar age and reported age of event. The distribution of positive and negative events at the first wave is presented graphically in Figure 3.3 for young, middle-aged and older adults. The percentage of positive and negative events is scaled per five years and centred on the time of testing (0 yrs at first wave) with past and future event time measured in years from time of testing. In the enclosed CD the distribution of positive and negative events is presented for all three waves (Figure A3.3a, Figure A3.3b and Figure A3.3c for the young, middle and older age group, respectively). The transition from past events to future events is indicated by a vertical line. Figure 3.3 shows the following patterns per age group:
– *Young* (M age W1 = 23.5 yrs)
For the young age group the distribution of positive events and negative events looks similar to the pattern of the distribution of events in general. There is a very strong recency effect for positive as well as for negative events. For positive events there is also a very strong proximity effect while for negative events this effect is almost missing. From the distant past and for the distant future more negative than positive events are recalled and expected. The patterns are the same at all three waves.
– *Middle* (M age W1 = 43.3 yrs)
At the first wave a clear bump can be discerned concerning the distribution of positive memories for middle-aged adults while the distribution of negative memories follows more the classical forgetting curve. Besides, there is a proximity effect for positive expectations while for negative events this ef-

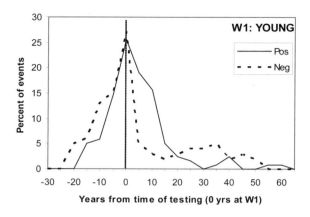

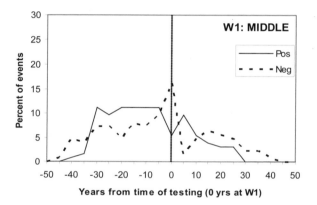

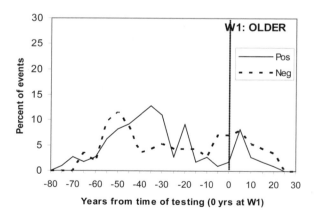

**Figure 3.3** W1: Distribution of positive and negative events for young (top panel; M age W1 = 23.5), middle-aged (middle panel: M age W1 = 43.3) and older adults (bottum panel: M age W1 = 67.4) per five years centred in years from time of testing (0 yrs) for Wave1.

fect is missing. In the distant future, however, more negative than positive events are expected. At the second and third wave there is, besides a recency effect for negative memories, also a recency effect for positive memories, although not as strong as for negative events. A bump for positive events can be distinguished but this bump is less pronounced than at the first wave.

– *Older* (M age W1 = 67.4 yrs)

At the first wave there is a very clear positive affect bump as well as a proximity effect for positive events. For negative events there is a recency and a proximity effect and there is also a small bump for negative events which starts in the same period as the bump for positive events. This negative bump starts at the point of –55 years. The first wave was administered in 1995; fifty five years before, the Second World War started. It can be assumed that the war in combination with the bump period has led to this 'negative bump'. At the second wave the same effects can be discerned. At the third wave there is also a recency effect for positive events.

In order to determine how the patterns of the distribution of positive and negative events change over time the distribution of positive events at the first and third wave are compared for three age groups as well as the distribution of negative events. For each age group the percentage of positive and negative events scaled per five years and centred on the time of testing (0 yrs at first wave, 5 yrs at third wave) with past and future event time measured in years from time of testing, is presented in Figure 3.4. In the enclosed CD results for all three waves are presented (Figure A3.4). The transition from past events to future events is indicated by a vertical line for the first and third wave. Figure 3.4 shows the following patterns per age group:

– *Young* (M age W1 = 23.5 yrs)

For the young age group the recency and proximity effect for negative events is moving with the present age. This applies also for the recency and proximity effect for positive events.

– *Middle* (M age W1 = 43.3 yrs)

At the first wave there is almost no recency effect for positive events for the middle-aged group but at the second and third wave there is a recency effect for positive events. The recency effect for negative events is moving with the present age. The bump for positive events is most pronounced at the first wave.

– *Older* (M age W1 = 67.4 yrs)

For older adults the bump for positive events is rather fixed and shows about the same pattern at all three waves. The narrow bump for negative events is also rather fixed and starts 55 years before time of testing at the first wave. The proximity effect for positive events is moving with the present age of the respondents. The recency effect for negative events also moves with the present age and is more pronounced at the second and third wave than at the first wave.

In Table 3.3 the three effects – bump, recency, proximity – which can be discerned for the distribution of positive and negative events for the young, middle and older age group for three waves is summarized. From this Table can be read that for the middle-aged and older age groups there is a bump for positive events. For older adults there is also a narrow bump for negative events. Besides, for all age groups there are recency effects for negative events and proximity effects for positive events. For the older age group there is also a proximity effect for negative events at the first wave.

*Distribution of 'very positive' and 'very negative' events*

The distribution of very positive and very negative events over the lifespan was determined in the same way as the distribution of positive and negative events. In Figure 3.5 the distribution of very positive and very negative events is presented for three age groups for the first wave. In the enclosed CD results can be found for all three waves (Figure A3.5a for the young age group, Figure A3.5b for the middle age group and Figure A3.5c for the older age group).

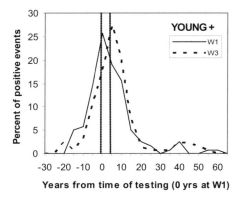

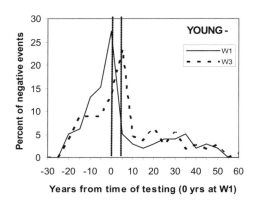

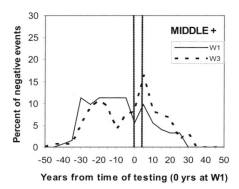

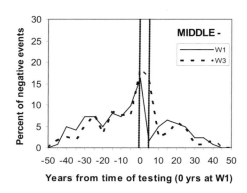

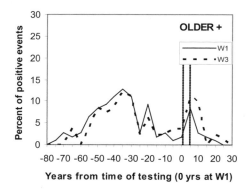

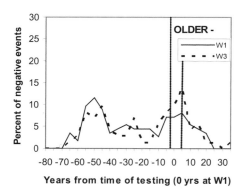

**Figure 3.4** W1 | W3: Distribution of positive events (+) (left panel) and negative events (–) (right panel) for young (top panel; M age W1 = 23.5), middle-aged (middle panel; M age W1 43.3) and older adults (bottum panel; M age W1 = 67.4) per five years centred in years from time of testing (0 yrs at W1) for Wave 1 and Wave 3 (vertical lines indicate transition from past events to future events for W1 and W3).

**Table 3.3**  W1 | W2 | W3: Bump, recency and proximity effect (*) for the distribution of positive and negative events for a young (M age W1 = 23.5), middle-aged (M age W1 = 43.3) and older (M age W1 = 67.4) age group for three waves.

**Wave 1**

|  | Young | | Middle | | Older | |
|---|---|---|---|---|---|---|
|  | Positive | Negative | Positive | Negative | Positive | Negative |
| Bump |  |  | * |  | * | * |
| Recency | * | * |  | * |  | * |
| Proximity | * |  | * |  | * | * |

**Wave 2**

|  | Young | | Middle | | Older | |
|---|---|---|---|---|---|---|
|  | Positive | Negative | Positive | Negative | Positive | Negative |
| Bump |  |  | * |  | * | * |
| Recency | * | * | * | * |  | * |
| Proximity | * |  | * |  | * |  |

**Wave 3**

|  | Young | | Middle | | Older | |
|---|---|---|---|---|---|---|
|  | Positive | Negative | Positive | Negative | Positive | Negative |
| Bump |  |  | * |  | * | * |
| Recency | * | * | * | * | * | * |
| Proximity | * |  | * |  | * |  |

The transition from past events to future events is indicated by a vertical line. Figure 3.5 shows the following patterns per age group:

— *Young* (M age W1 = 23.5 yrs)

At all three waves there is a recency effect for very positive as well as for very negative events. In the near future more very positive events are expected than very negative events but this effect is not very strong.

— *Middle* (M age W1 = 43.3 yrs)

For very negative events there is a clear recency effect at all three waves. For very positive events there is a recency effect at the third wave. At the first wave middle-aged respondents recall most very positive events from the period of 5 till 10 years ago. For the future almost no very positive or very negative events are expected.

— *Older* (M age W1 = 67.4 yrs)

For older adults there is no clear pattern for very positive and very negative events. At each wave there is a small peak for very negative events situated 55 years ago at the first wave.

In Figure 3.6 the distribution of very positive events is given for the first and third wave for the young, middle and older age group as well as the distribution of very negative events. For each age group the percentage of very positive and very negative events is scaled per five years and centred on the time of testing (0 yrs at first wave, 5 yrs at third wave) with past and future event time measured in years from time of testing. In the enclosed CD results for all three waves are given (Figure A3.6). The transition from past events to future events is indicated by a vertical line for the first and third wave. Figure 3.6 shows the following patterns per age group:

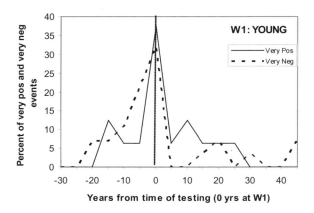

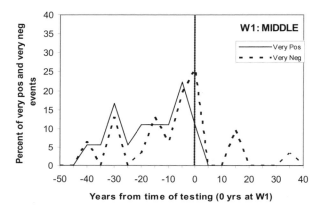

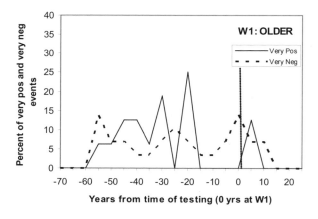

**Figure 3.5** W1: Distribution of very positive and very negative events for young (top panel; M age W1 = 23.5), middle-aged (middle panel; M age W1 = 43.3) and older adults (bottum panel; M age W1 = 67.4) per five years centred in years from time of testing (0 yrs) for W1.

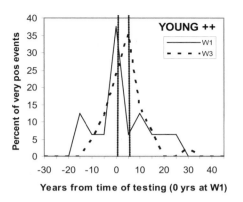

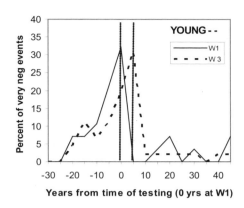

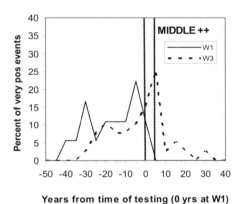

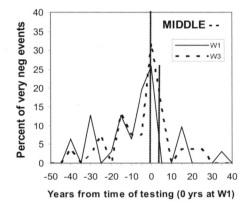

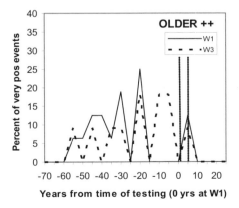

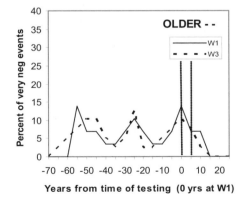

**Figure 3.6** W1 | W3: Distribution of very positive events (+ +) (left panel) and very negative events (− −) (right panel) for young (top panel; M age W1 = 23.5), middle-aged (middle panel; M age W1 = 43.3) and older adults (bottum panel; M age W1 = 67.4) per five years centred in years from time of testing (0 yrs at W1) for Wave 1 and Wave 3 (Vertical line indicates transition from past events tot future events for W1 and W3).

- *Young* (M age W1 = 23.5 yrs)

The recency effect for very positive and very negative events is moving with the present age for the young age group. There is only a small proximity effect for very positive events which is also moving with age.

- *Middle* (M age W1 = 43.3 yrs)

For middle-aged adults the recency effect for very positive events moves from the first to the third wave in the direction of the changing age. For very negative events the recency effect also moves in the direction of the present age but at the third wave respondents recall more very negative events from the period that has lasted 5 till 10 years ago than from the most recent past (0 till 5 years ago). There is no proximity effect for very positive nor for very negative events. For very positive events a small bump is emerging.

- *Older* (M age W1 = 67.4 yrs)

The distribution of very positive and very negative events over the lifespan is very irregular for older adults at all three waves but the distribution of very negative events is quite similar at all three waves.

In general, it can be concluded that:

- For all age groups there is a recency effect for negative events; more negative events are recalled from the recent past than from the distant past.
- For all age groups there is a proximity effect for positive events but not for negative events; respondents are positive about the near future. Negative events are projected in the more distant future.
- For positive events a bump can be discerned for middle-aged and older adults.
- For older adults there is a narrow bump for negative events which corresponds with the beginning of the Second World War.
- For young adults there is a strong recency effect for very negative and very positive events which is moving with the present age. For very positive events there is also a proximity effect which is also moving with the present age.
- For middle-aged respondents there is a recency effect for very negative events and very positive events which is moving with the present age. No proximity effect can be discerned. For very positive events a small bump is emerging.
- For the older age group very positive and very negative events are distributed irregular over the lifespan without a specific pattern to discern although the distribution of very negative events shows about the same pattern at all three waves.

## 3.3.4 Affect first and last event
### W1 | W2 | W3

The affect of the first mentioned event on the life-line and the last mentioned event, which is mostly situated in the future, was determined. In Table 3.4 the percentage of first events and last events that are rated very negative, negative, neutral, positive and very positive are presented for three waves.

Table 3.4   W1 | W2 | W3: Percent of first events and last events that are rated very negative, negative, neutral, positive and very positive for Wave 1 (W1), Wave 2 (W2) and Wave 3 (W3).

| | First event | | | Last event | | |
|---|---|---|---|---|---|---|
| | **W1** | **W2** | **W3** | **W1** | **W2** | **W3** |
| Very negative | 15.3 | 27.7 | 22.1 | 13.3 | 13.3 | 10.4 |
| Negative | 42.9 | 30.1 | 33.8 | 39.8 | 41.0 | 36.4 |
| Neutral | 2.0 | 1.2 | 3.9 | 13.3 | 2.4 | 5.2 |
| Positive | 31.6 | 28.9 | 29.9 | 30.6 | 41.0 | 41.6 |
| Very positive | 8.2 | 12.0 | 10.4 | 3.1 | 2.4 | 6.5 |

A 2 x 3 ANOVA was conducted to evaluate the effects of gender and age group on the mean affect of the first and last event:

*W1*. The mean rating of the *first* event is negative and differs significantly from neutral (M first wave = –0.26, t(97) = –1.975, p = .05). There is no effect of age or gender on the affective rating of the first event.

The mean rating of the *last* event is negative and differs significantly from neutral (M first wave = –0.30, t(97) = –2.587, p = .01. There is no effect of age or gender on the affective rating of the last event.

*W2*. Again, the mean rating of the *first* event differs significantly from neutral (M second wave = – 0.33, t(82) = –2.045, p < .05) and there is no effect of age or gender on the affective rating of the first event.

For the *last* event an effect of age on the affective evaluation was found, F (2, 77) = 4.009, p < .05; the middle-aged group is more positive about the last event than the young and older age group. The oldest group is most negative about the last event they expect (mean affect last event: young –0.30; middle 0.15; older –0.68).

*W3*. There is a trend that the mean affect rating of the *first* event differs negatively from neutral (M third wave = –0.27, t(76) = –1.743, p = .085). Again, there is no effect of age or gender on the affective rating of the first event.

The mean affect rating of the *last* event does not differ significantly from neutral and there is no effect of age or gender on the affect of the last event.

In sum:
– At all three waves the mean affective rating of the first event is negative or there is a tendency that the mean affective rating is negative.
– There is no clear pattern concerning the affect of the last event over three waves.

### W1→W2→W3
A MANOVA for repeated measures was conducted on the affect of the first and last event. There was no effect of wave on the affect of the first event and last event. The grand mean affect over three waves for the first event was –0.27. Overall, there was an effect of age on the affect of the last event, F (2, 68) = 4.984, p = .01 (young –0.19, middle 0.07, older –0.65). Post hoc tests showed that the difference between the middle and the older age group is statistically significant; overall, the oldest group is more negative about the last event they expect in the future than the middle-age group.

In sum:
– The mean affect of the first and last event does not change over a period of five years.
– The first important event respondents report from the past is predominantly accompanied by a negative affect.
– The grand mean of the affect of the last event respondents expect in their life is depen dent of age; older adults are most negative about this event.

## 3.3.5 Best and worst times of life
### W1 | W2 | W3
In this LIM-study the best period in life is operationalized as the period (decade) in which the proportion of positive events is highest while the worst period in life is operationalized as the period in which the proportion of negative events is highest. In order to determine these periods, the total percentage of positive and negative events for each decade was put at 100 percent. In Figure 3.7 the percentage of positive (and consequently negative) events per decade is presented for the first and third wave for three age groups for men and women separately as the best and worst times turned out to be different for men and women. Full results can be found in the enclosed CD (Figure A3.7). Results are only shown if at least three events per decade were reported. The transition from past events to future events is indicated by a vertical line for the first and third wave.

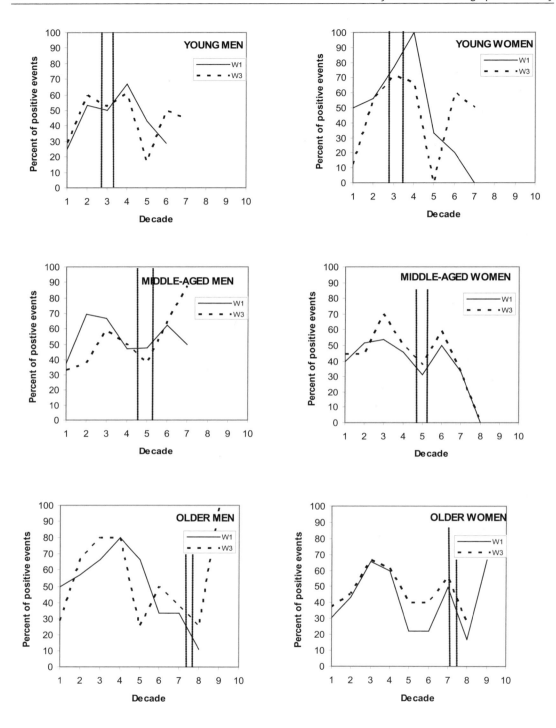

**Figure 3.7** W1 | W3: Percent of positive (and consequently negative) events per decade for men (left panel) and women (right panel) of a young (top panel), middle-aged (middle panel) and older age group (bottum panel) for W1 and W3 (Vertical lines indicate transition from past events tot future events for W1 and W3).

**Table 3.5** W1 | W2 | W3: Best and worst period (= decade with highest and lowest ratio of positive and total number of events, respectively) in life for young men and women, middle-aged men and women and older men and women for W1, W2 and W3.

| | Young | | Middle | | Older | |
|---|---|---|---|---|---|---|
| | **Men** | **Women** | **Men** | **Women** | **Men** | **Women** |
| W1: Best time | 31–40 | 31–40 | 11–20 | 21–30 | 31–40 | 21–30 / 81–90* |
| W2: Best time | 31–40 | 21–30 | 51–60 | 21–30 / 51–60* | 21–30 | 21–30 |
| W3: Best time | 31–40 | 21–30 | 61–70 | 21–30 | 81–90 | 21–30 |
| W1: Worst time | 0–10 | 61–70 | 0–10 | 71–80 | 71–80 | 71–80 |
| W2: Worst time | 51–60 | 51–60 | 0–10 | 71–80 | 71–80 | 0–10 |
| W3: Worst time | 41–50 | 41–50 | 0–10 | 71–80 | 41–50 / 71–80* | 71–80 |

* the ratio of positive (or negative) and total number of events is about the same at two decades (difference < 2 percent)

In Table 3.5 an overview is given of the best and worst times in life for men and women of three age groups for three waves:
- *Young* (M age = 25.1 yrs)

*Best period.* Young men consequently expect the period of 31 to 40 years of age to be the most positive period in life. Young women expect this period at the first wave to be the best period; they expect only positive events to happen in this decade. At the second and third wave they seem to have become more realistic. Then they mention also negative events in the period of 30 to 40 years and they consider then the period of 21 to 30 years of age to be the best period.

*Worst period.* For both young men and women the worst period in life is mostly situated somewhere in the future. Only at the first wave the worst period is situated in childhood by young men. It is salient that the affective pattern is very unstable from the age of forty for this age group.
- *Middle* (M age = 45.8 yrs)

*Best period.* For middle-aged men the best period in life is different at each wave while for middle-aged women the best period in life is consequently situated in the period of 21 to 30 years of age. At the second wave middle-aged women are also positive about the period of 51 to 60 years of age which is the near future for them.

*Worst period.* Middle-aged men as well as middle-aged women are very consequent in their feeling over the worst period in life. For middle-aged men the worst period was childhood while middle-aged women expect the period between 71 and 80 years of age to be the worst period in life. The present period is a rather negative period in life for both middle-aged men and women. The middle age group has a more consistent view of the future than the youngest age group.
- *Older* (M age = 67.8 yrs)

*Best period.* Older men are at the first wave most positive about the period of 31 to 40 years of age and at the second wave about the period of 21 to 30 years of age. At the third wave the period of 81 to 90 is considered to be the best period but in this period only few events are mentioned. At all three waves the period of about 21 to 40 years of age has been a rather positive period for older men. For older women the period of 21 to 30 was a positive period at all three waves; at the first wave the period of 81 to 90 is expected to be a very positive period; it has to be remarked that only a few events are mentioned in this period.

*Worst period.* For older men the period of 71 to 80 years is expected to be the worst period while the period of 41 to 50 belonged also to the worst period in life at the third wave. Older women also identify the period of 71 to 80 as the worst period in life at two waves; at the second wave childhood was considered the worst period. Figure 3.7 shows that for older women life was rather negative in the period of about 40 to 60 years of age but after this period life has become more positive. For older men applies that the positive bump lasts somewhat longer than for older women but after the age of 50 it is going down.

In sum:
- overall, respondents consider most frequently the period between about 20 to 30 years of age as the best period in life, followed by the period of 30 to 40 years of age,
- while the period of 70 to 80 is most frequently considered the worst period in life followed by childhood.

## 3.4  Discussion

In this chapter the affective value of events that respondents recall from their past and expect for their future was examined. The first aim of this chapter was to answer the question how men and women of different age groups feel about their life, what they recall from their past and what they expect for the future in terms of positive and negative events and whether these feelings change over a period of five years. The second aim was to determine how positive and negative events are distributed over the lifespan and in what way these patterns change over a period of five years.

### 3.4.1  Overall, life is perceived as affective neutral

In a previous study (Assink & Schroots, 2002) the first LIM-wave was analyzed with regard to the affective value of events resulting in the finding that, overall, respondents report as many positive as negative events over their total lifespan. This finding was confirmed in the second and third wave. Therefore, it is a robust finding in the LIM-study that, in general, positive and negative events over the total lifespan counterbalance each other, while in most other studies life is perceived as being more positive than negative (see Walker et al., 2003). As was discussed before, it is assumed that the LIM elicits information that is very close to the real self and that social desirability is minimized because respondents don't realize what they are revealing when drawing the LIM|Life-line. However, it can be argued that these results – as many positive events as negative events – are an artifact of the method used; participants might have automatically alternated peaks and dips, resulting in fifty percent positive and fifty percent negative events. On an individual level, however, the distributions of positive and negative events are quite different, suggesting that the overall distribution of half positive and half negative events is not an artifact of the administration of the LIM (Assink & Schroots, 2002). The conclusion seems to be warranted that taking everything into account, the ups and downs in one's life counterbalance each other at the end.

### 3.4.2  As people grow older the past is valuated more positively and the future more negatively

Although, overall, positive and negative events counterbalance each other over the total lifespan, the feelings people have about their past and future depend on age. In this LIM-study it was found that young and middle-aged individuals are more positive about the future than about the past while older individuals are more positive about the past than about the future. Similar results were obtained by other researchers. Keys and Ryff (1999), for instance, found that younger adults expect to function better in the future than they do now, while middle-aged adults believe that they will function in more or less the same way in the future as they do in the present and older adults expect to function worse in the future than in the present. But Fleeson and Heckhausen (1997) found that middle-aged respondents also expected to improve in the future. Schmotkin (1991) showed that older respondents were more satisfied with their past than with the present and future in contrast to younger adults. In addition, Staudinger, Bluck and Herzberg (2003) found that in young adulthood, past subjective well-being (SWB) was rated lower and future SWB higher than present SWB. In contrast, in later adulthood, the past was rated higher and the future lower than present SWB. Although the impact of life events on current well-being is found to be limited (Heady & Wearing, 1992; Suh, Diener & Fujita, 1996) combining results of the above mentioned studies suggests that there is a strong relation between past SWB and events recalled from the past, and between future SWB and events expected for the future.

### 3.4.3 The past evokes more intense feelings than the future

Respondents mentioned relatively more events which were accompanied by an intense affect from the past than for the future. Newby-Clark and Ross (2003) also found that for young adults unpleasant events in the past were much more negative than those in the future: " the past (…) contains much deeper valleys than the future" (p. 815). It seems to be very difficult to picture one self in the future and to assess how one will feel and react to events which are expected to happen in the future. Moreover, individuals have a culturally determined life script for the future (Bernsten & Rubin, 2002; Schroots & Assink, 2005). Expectations for the future are based on this life script and non-normative events are not included in such a life script and are not expected. Non-normative events are unanticipated, off-time events (e.g. death of a child) and require greater adjustment than anticipated on-time events (Neugarten, 1979) and, consequently, will be accompanied by a stronger affect. Individuals do not imagine this type of events to happen in the future and do not anticipate such events and, consequently, will not indicate such events on their future life-line. Life turns out to be more intense in retrospect than is expected in advance.

### 3.4.4 Extreme negative is stronger than extreme positive

Respondents remember more 'very negative' events than 'very positive' events. Although the consequences of events are not examined in this study, it can be argued that very negative events have a deeper impact and more intense and longer lasting consequences than very positive events (Baumeister et al., 2001). After a very positive event there is a short peak in happiness but then people become accustomed to the new situation and are not happier than they were before the event. After a traumatic event, however, people need much more time and it costs much more effort to adjust to the new situation. In this respect Frijda (1988) defined the 'law of hedonic asymmetry', which states that there exists misery one does not get used to, while this fact has no counterpart for positive emotions: one does get used to pleasure. Baumeister et al. (2001) give an evolutionary explanation for this phenomenon. It is adaptive for human beings to respond more strongly to bad than to good and consequently, it would be more adaptive to remember (very) bad events than (very) positive events in order to be better prepared for future bad events.

### 3.4.5 Over a period of five years there is no significant change in the mean affective rating of life

The mean affect for the total life and for past and future did not change over a period of five years although on the basis of results of the first wave – the older the more positive about the past and the more negative about the future – it could be expected that the past would be rated as more positive and the future as more negative as all respondents grow five years older. However, analysis of the three waves separately showed that at the first two waves there was an interaction effect of time (past, future) and age group; younger adults were more positive about the future while older adults were more positive about the past. At the third wave this effect was not found anymore; the three age groups seem to have grown towards one another at that time. But overall, five years turned out to be a too short period to bring about systematic changes in the affective outlook of past and future life.

### 3.4.6 Negative memories follow the forgetting curve; for positive memories there is a bump and a proximity effect

Positive and negative events did not show the same pattern in past and future. For the past the distribution of negative events follows the classical forgetting curve for all age groups while there is a bump for positive events for middle-aged and older adults and often also a recency effect for positive events. These results are in accordance with results found by Berntsen and Rubin (2002) and Rubin and Berntsen (2003) who asked participants to recall one memory which was accompanied by an extreme emotion. Despite the differences in method, they also found a bump for positive memories and a monotonically decreasing retention function for negative memories.

The difference in distribution of positive and negative events can be due to differences in encoding of positive and negative events and/or differences in retrieval. According to Berntsen and Rubin (2002) three different theoretical frameworks can explain the dissociation between emotionally positive and emotionally negative memories: a cognitive framework, a narrative/identity framework, and an account based on life scripts. The first two frameworks are based on earlier accounts of the bump (Rubin, Rahhal & Poon, 1998), whereas the life script account was introduced by Bernsten and Rubin (2002). According to a cognitive explanation events followed by relative stability are better remembered. Because negative events are mostly followed by more instability than positive events and negative events are less often rehearsed in conversations, a bump for negative events is absent. This explanation refers to the process of encoding. According to the narrative/identity account young adulthood is a critical period for the formation of an adult identity. To build up a positive enduring identity, negative memories from this period might be repressed and positive events might be stressed resulting in a bump for positive events. This explanation refers to retrieval; positive events are retrieved more easily than negative events. The explanation based on life scripts assumes that the retrieval of autobiographical memories is governed by culturally shared representations of the prototypical life cycle. A life script represents a prototypical life course consisting of a series of life events in a specific order and happening within certain age ranges in a certain culture. A life script deals with an ideal picture a person has about how life is organized in general and contains almost only positive events (Berntsen & Rubin, 2003). A distinction can be made between life-script and life-narrative. Life-narrative refers to the past and deals with personal memories. It concerns the concrete and real life as actually lived, with its ups and downs. Life script refers to expectations for the future which are based on a prototypical life course (Schroots & Assink, 2005). As was discussed before, it is assumed that the LIM|Life story is very close to the real self and reveals how the past is actually experienced by the respondent and not how the respondent thinks the past should have been. This means that an account based on life scripts can not sufficiently explain the difference in distribution of positive and negative events. Conway and Pleydell-Pearce (2000) assume that negative events are encoded in memory but that people do not like to retrieve these events. They state that "it seems then that there is a general bias against retrieving memories of intense and negative emotional experiences. This general inhibition must be supplemented by other forms of defense against reinstating intense emotions because it can be overcome and emotional memories can be intentionally retrieved" (p. 270). Baumeister et al. (2001) also concluded that "the occasional finding of greater recall for positive experiences probably reflects a selective and motivated process by which bad memories are suppressed, so it does not really indicate that the bad experiences had lesser power" (p. 356). According to Schroots and Van Dijkum (2004) the appearance of the autobiographical memory bump is due to more intensive encoding of information in the period of 10 to 30 years of age. It is possible that the encoding process is different for positive and negative affect. Positive events could be better encoded in the bump period of life while the distribution of negative events follows more the classical forgetting curve; these events are forgotten after some time. It is not clear yet which explanation for the difference in distribution of positive and negative events over the lifespan is most satisfactory.

Respondents of all age groups are positive about the near future. This effect is strongest for the young age group, which is in accordance with results found by Newby-Clark and Ross (2003) who asked thirty students to list a maximum of 10 events for the past and also for the future. They found that these students anticipated almost exclusively positive events. In the LIM-study it was found that when young adults expect negative events, they situate these events in the more distant future. The same applies for the middle-age group. Although this group expects more negative events in the future they do not expect negative events within the next five years. Only the older age group expects, besides positive events, also negative events in the near future. The same applies for very negative events; young and middle-aged respondents do not expect very negative events in the near future, older respondents do. It can be concluded that young and middle-aged adults are very optimistic about the near future and project negative events in the more distant future while older respondents seem to be more realistic and expect positive as well as negative events in the near future.

### 3.4.7 Traumatic events have the power to disturb the 'normal' pattern of distribution of events
Negative events follow the forgetting curve but traumatic events have the power to change this curve. For instance, for the oldest group there is an unexpected negative bump which covers fewer years than the positive affect bump. This bump corresponds with the beginning of the Second World War and coincides with the beginning of the bump of this age group. A comparable result was obtained by Conway and Haque (1999); they found in an older group of Bangladeshi participants, who recalled and dated autobiographical memories from their past, besides the usual memory bump a second bump in the period of 35 to 55 years of age. This second bump corresponded with the period in which there was a conflict between Pakistan and the Bengalee people. Conway and Haque (1999) argue that such traumatic events are retained in a highly available way in long term memory because they are novel and of high self relevance. These memories have been encoded so deeply that they have the force to change the 'normal' pattern of the distribution of events over the lifespan, i.e., overshadow the memory bump. In this LIM-study the negative affect bump for the Second World War is found in all three waves in the same period meaning that these events have had a very strong impact. It can be hypothesized that the impact is even stronger because the events occurred in the bump period, a period in which encoding of events is more intense. It can be concluded that major negative events can have a devastating impact on 'normal' patterns concerning autobiographical memory.

### 3.4.8 The first event recalled is accompanied by a negative affect
The average affective rating of the first event is negative, i.e. respondents report more often a negative event as first important event than a positive event. An explanation could be that life is generally perceived as being positive (Walker, Skowronski & Thompson, 2003) and a negative event, therefore, is novel and has more impact than a positive event. The affective rating of the first event shows some resemblance with the affective rating of the earliest memory. Blonsky (1929, in: Draaisma, 2001), for instance, found that a high percentage of earliest memories of students and 12-year old children referred to frightening situations. According to Draaisma (2001) events which deviate from the routine, and are novel and exceptional are encoded better than events which occur repeatedly and are common. The affect of the last event, which is mostly a future event, did not show a common pattern in each wave. In the previous chapter it was shown that the timing of this event is different for each age group. Younger respondents identify the last event at an earlier age than older respondents. It can be assumed that the type of these events is different for different age groups and, consequently, also the accompanying affect of a specific event. The results showed a tendency that for older respondents the last event is more often accompanied by a negative affect than for younger respondents. It can be concluded that the first event mentioned in the life story is mostly a negative event, while the affect of the last mentioned event in the life story is dependent of the age of the respondent; for older people the last event mentioned in the life story is often a negative event.

### 3.4.9 The best period in life is the period of 20 to 40 years of age
Most frequently the best period in life is situated in the period from 20 to 40 years of age, which is in contrast with results of deVries et al. (2001) who found that for most of the participants of three age groups the best of times is the present. In the LIM-study the near future is the best of times for young adults, while part of the bump period, which is situated in the past, is perceived the best of times by middle-aged and older adults. At the first wave young respondents, especially young women, have very

high expectations for the near future, the thirties. From an evolutionary perspective, it can be assumed that young women are looking forward to fulfill the biological task of getting children. Analysis of the content of events in this period of life can give a decisive answer whether this assumption is right. At the second and third wave the curve for young women has flattened somewhat. This could be a test-retest effect. At the second and third wave respondents can anticipate the question what they expect in their future and they will also generate negative events. Another possibility is that young women have become somewhat more realistic as they grow older.

Middle-aged men identify at each wave another period as the best period of life. The period of 10 to 30 years of age – the bump period – is, however, a positive period at all three waves. But middle-aged men also expect good periods in the future. Middle-aged women are very consequent in assessing the period of 20 to 30 years of age to be the best period. Middle-aged women also have high expectations of the period of 50 to 60 years of age which is the near future for them. The present, the period between forty and fifty years of age, is perceived as more negative than positive which is inconsistent with the findings of deVries et al. (2001) and of Mirowsky and Ross (1999). Although midlife has long been characterized as a period of crisis for men and women, little support for this assumption is found in the literature (Aldwin & Levenson, 2001). But midlife can be a time of change and it seems that in this LIM-study these changes are more often valued negatively than positively, thus supporting the midlife-crisis theory.

For older LIM-respondents there is a clear positive bump which covers a longer period for older men than for older women. An explanation for this finding could be that men in their midlife are closer and more continuously attached to career and worklife than women, an aspect of life which is supposed to have a positive impact on psychological well-being (Moen & Wethington, 1999). Generally, the period of 20 to 40 years of age is remembered as a very positive period in life which is in accordance with results found by Mehlsen et all. (2003) who found that most (older) participants in their study indicated the period from 30 to 39 years of age and adjoining decades as the best years of life. Mirowsky and Ross (1999), however, identified middle age as the best time of life because Americans in the age of 40 to 60 years old report a lower average frequency of depression than younger and older adults do. The explanation of Mirowsky and Ross (1999) for this finding is that middle-aged adults do not yet have the problems of old age while the tensions and conflicts of young adulthood have faded away. It is striking that also the period of 81 to 90 years of age is mentioned a few times as the best period in life. This can be due to the positive outlook of a few respondents of the older age group.

### 3.4.10 The worst periods in life are old age and childhood

Young adults are very inconsistent in what they consider the worst time of life. Mostly they mention a (different) decade in the future which can be due to a stereotype idea they have from middle and older age. However, childhood, the period of 0 till 10 years of age, is also mentioned as the worst time of life. Results of the three waves show that the feelings the young age group has about the future after the age of forty are very unstable and differ strongly between waves. The middle-aged and older age group are more stable in what they consider the worst time of life. For middle-aged men this was the period of 0 till 10 years while for middle-aged women the period of 70 to 80 years of age is expected to be the worst time of life. An explanation could be that middle-aged women often take care of elderly parents and, in this way, are confronted with health problems in older age, while middle aged men are more focused on their work and do not look so far ahead. Childhood and the period of 70 to 80 years of age are also mentioned by the older age group as the worst time of life. An explanation for this finding could be that in both periods, the beginning and end of life, people have less control over their life and are more dependent on other people than in other periods of life.

From the preceding it is clear that results of different studies concerning best and worst times of life are variable and inconsistent, which may be due to different operationalizations of the terms 'best time' and 'worst time'. A common standard of value by which these times can be measured and compared is missing (Mirowsky & Ross, 1999). More research is needed to get a better understanding of what individuals experience as good and bad times in their lives and especially what reasons they have to choose a certain period as a good or bad time. In the next chapters, it will become clear what type of events respondents report from the best and worst times of life.

In concluding this chapter, it can be stated that:

- In general, positive and negative events counterbalance each other over the lifespan but are differentiated by gender, age and time (past and future).
- There is a asymmetry of strong affect, i.e., very negative memories are stronger than very positive memories.
- For positive events there is a bump for middle-aged and older adults, and a proximity effect for all age groups which is moving with the present age.
- Negative events follow the forgetting curve which is moving with the present age.
- It is not clear whether the dissociation between the distribution of positive and negative affect over the lifespan can be explained by an easier retrieval of positive memories than of negative memories and/or by different encoding of positive and negative memories.
- Traumatic events have the force to change the 'normal' pattern of the distribution of events and affect over the lifespan.
- The best time of life is most consistently situated in the period of about 20 to 40 years of age and the worst time of life in old age or in childhood.

# Chapter 4
# Content of Events

## 4.1  Introduction

In the previous chapters the number and affect of events was studied. In this chapter the focus will be on the content of these events. What type of 'building blocks' (Bluck & Habermas, 2001) does the life story of memories and expectations contain? To answer this question, a thematic content analysis needs to be conducted, in which unstructured interview data will be categorized in such a way that they can be analyzed statistically. As discussed in the first chapter, many different category lists are used in the field of autobiographical and life course research and there are many different ways of analyzing and reporting results of such studies. Hence, it is difficult to compare results of studies in this field. Nevertheless, results of different studies show some similarity when comparing differences in reported life events between men and women and between age groups. For instance, deVries and Watt (1996) and Baum and Stewart (1990) found that women were mostly focused on romance and childbirth and men on work related issues. DeVries and Watt (1996) found that younger adults mentioned school related events, friendship, and sexuality, middle-aged adults mentioned childbirth and growth activities while for older participants events such as war, retirement, and health were important. Elnick et al. (1999) studied the content of events which were reported in the bump period by individuals aged 40 year and older and found that the predominant category in this period was the family/relationship domain. Rönka, Oravala and Pulkkinen (2003) asked 283 men and women at age 36 to report important turning points in their life; most turning points involved family life, for example, marriage, divorce and the birth of a child followed by turning points relating to education, work and social transitions. They also found differences between men and women. Women often mentioned events related to building a family and to changes in the health of people close to them, while men were focused on the work sphere.

In this chapter, not only the content of life events, but also the main affect of specific events will be determined. Rönka, Oravala and Pulkkinen (2003) summarized that positive turning points are usually related to the birth of a child, marriage, and success in realizing one's own goals while negative turning points are often related to a loss and include, for example, interpersonal problems and failures in regard to one's own goals. Gender, age of respondent and age at occurrence of a certain event also have an effect on the affective rating of events as the same event can be experienced in quite different ways depending on personality, life stage, earlier experiences and experiences in the lives of others to whom the individual is tied (Settersten, 1999). Neugarten (1977), for example, claims that the timing of salient events is very important. Unanticipated, off-time events (e.g. death of a child) require greater adjustment than anticipated on-time events (e.g. death of parent at old age) and, consequently, will be accompanied by a stronger affect.

After having determined of what elements the life story is composed and with what affect these elements are mainly accompanied, a modal description of the life course in terms of important life events will be given for the different subgroups on the basis of the events which are mentioned most frequently in a certain period in order to reveal the structure of the life course. There are a number of theories about the structure of the life course in terms of successive stages people go through from birth till death (cf. Erikson, 1950; Levinson, 1986; Lowenthal, Thurnher & Chiriboga, 1975). It is particularly Erikson (1950) who had great influence on the emergence of the study of the total lifespan. He viewed personality development as a function of both individual and cultural factors and – as described in the first chapter – posed eight stages of life, each with its own conflict that has to be solved. There have been efforts to found Erikson's psychosocial stages theory (1950) empirically. For instance, Stewart, Franz, and Layton (1988) and Peterson and Stewart (1990) found that young adolescents were preoccupied with the theme of identity while middle-aged adults were preoccupied with themes of intimacy and generativity. McAdams, Diamond, de St. Aubin and Mansfield (1997) and McAdams and de St. Aubin (1998) focused on the stage of 'generativity' in midlife and found that adults who scored high on generativity created prototypical commitment stories. Conway and Holmes (2004) asked older respondents to recall memories from each decade of life and classified these memories in terms of the psychosocial stages to which their content corresponded. They found that each decade was dominated by memories related to the theme relevant to that age in terms of Erikson's stage theory.

In the present study respondents of different age groups are not only asked to recall spontaneously memories from their past but also to look forward to their future. In this way the picture people have of their total life, past as well as future, at different ages will be obtained in terms of important life events. The purpose of this chapter, then, can be summarized as follows:

- To determine what type of events men and women of different age groups consider important in their past and future;
- To determine the affect of specific events, and
- To reveal the structure of the life course in terms of most important events per decade.

Because of the enormous amount of data, the analysis of the content of events is divided over two chapters. In the present chapter only data obtained at the first wave will be analyzed. The results of the first wave make up the base line for the next chapter in which the stability and change in content of memories and expectations over a period of two years and five years will be the subject of study.

## 4.2  Method

### Coding procedure

As described in the first chapter, life stories were revised in such a way that all information concerning a specific event – a peak or dip on the life-line – was put together. In this way different units of text were created in chronological order; each unit included the age at which the event happened or was expected to happen, a short description of the event and an explanation of the event. Next, a special category-list was constructed in order to classify LIM-events. The category-list consists of 40 subcategories divided over nine categories (see Chapter 1). Then, a coding instruction was developed with guidelines as to how to determine the catchword, the category of the event, the subcategory and the affective value on a 5-points scale (very negative, negative, neutral, positive and very positive). The catchword describes in one or a few words, preferably in words used by the respondent, the most important theme in the unit. Next, all life stories were coded independently by two coders on catchword. On basis of the catchword the event was classified into a category and a subcategory. The affective value of each event was determined on basis of the text belonging to the specific event on a 5-point scale which was described in the previous chapter. Disagreements between the two coders were resolved through discussion. The inter-rater agreement was determined on the basis of 24 randomly chosen stories for each wave. For the first wave the two coders agreed on category in 91 percent of all events and on subcategory in 86 percent of all events. For the second wave these percentages were respectively 90 and 82 percent and for the third wave also 90 percent and 82 percent.

### Analysis

Basically, there are two mutually exclusive ways of presenting and analyzing categorical data: (a) as number of *events* per (sub)category (cf. Elnick et al., 1999), or (b) as number of *persons* per (sub)category (cf. deVries & Watt, 1996). Both methods have their pros and cons. The disadvantage of 'number of events per (sub)category' is that outliers may affect the relative frequencies of events disproportionately as the percentages of events across categories are mutually dependent; for instance, a high percentage of events in one category results inevitably in lower percentages for other categories. A great advantage of 'number of events per (sub)category', however, is that percentages of events across (sub) categories can be added and subtracted without any problem. A disadvantage of 'number of persons per (sub)category' is that one respondent may report more than one life event per (sub)category; for instance, when 50 percent of the women mention one event in the category Work and 50 percent of the men mention each three events in the category Work, this difference between men and women can not be read from the results when reporting the number (percentage) of persons per (sub)category. Because of this disadvantage and in view of the emphasis in similar studies on the frequency distributions of life events for specific groups (age, gender), the number of events per (sub)category (Jansari & Parkin, 1996; Martin & Smyer, 1990; Rubin, 2002) was chosen to analyze and present the LIM-data.

## 4.3  Results

### 4.3.1  W1: Content of events

#### Event distribution over categories

First of all, the percentage of events per category was determined for the total group and for the past and future of young, middle-aged and older men and women. In Table 4.1 these percentages are presented. The total number of events per subgroup (column) over all categories equals 100 percent. From Table 4.1 can be read, for instance, that 27.3 percent of all events that young men report from the past belong to the category Relations. In the enclosed CD (Table A4.1a), the percentage of events per category is presented in separate columns for men and women, for three age groups and for past and future.

Next, a 2(Gender) x 3(Age Group) x 2(Event Time: Past and Future) x 9(Category) analysis of variance was conducted with repeated measures on the last two factors and with the logarithmic transformation [ln(number+1)] of the highly skewed event distribution per category as the dependent variable. When there is an overall statistically significant effect results will be mentioned for those categories for which the difference in percentage of events between subgroups is $\geq 5$ percent. The following effects, then, were found:

– *Category*. First of all, a main effect of Category was found [$F (8, 85) = 12.301$, $p <. 001$], meaning that the percentage of events per category differs significantly from each other; for example, most events are reported in the category Relations (17.6%) and fewest in the categories Birth (7.8%) and Other (5.7%). About 70 percent of all reported life-events fall within the categories Relations (17.6%), School (13.6%), Health (13.6%), Work (13.4%) and Growth (11.0%).

– *Category x Age group*. The main effect for Category, however, was qualified by its interaction with Age group [$F (16, 170) = 3.176$, $p < .001$]. The older respondents are, the fewer events they report in the category School. The young age group reports fewer events in the category Work than the middle-aged and older age group. The older age group reports more events in the categories Health and Other than the other age groups, fewer events in the category Growth than the other age groups and fewer events in the category Home than the young age group.

– *Category x Gender*. There was also an interaction effect of Category and Gender [$F (8, 85) = 2.391$, $p < .05$]. Men reported more events in the category Work while women reported more events in the categories Health and Birth.

– *Event time*. A main effect of time was found, $F (1, 92) = 132.836$, $p < .001$. Overall, respondents mention more events per category in the past than in the future.

– *Events time x Age group*. The main effect of time was qualified by its interaction with Age group [$F (2, 92) = 23.839$, $p < .001$]. The older respondents are the more events per category they report in the past and the fewer events per category they report in the future.

– *Category x Event time*. Next, an interaction effect of Category and Event time was found [$F (8, 85) = 7.400$, $p < .001$]; events in the categories Relations and Home were mentioned more often for the past than in the future and events in the categories Work, Health, Birth and Death were mentioned more often in the future than in the past, relatively.

– *Category x Event time x Age group*. Finally, an interaction effect of Event time, Category and Age group was found [$F (16, 170) = 3.350$, $p < .001$). It is not surprising that, for instance, the middle and

**Table 4.1** W1: Percent of events per category for the total group and for past (P) and future (F) of young (M age W1 = 23.5), middle-aged (M age W1 = 43.3) and older (M age W1 = 67.4) men and women (bold type means one event mentioned within category).

| Category | Young | | | | Middle | | | | Older | | | | Total |
|---|---|---|---|---|---|---|---|---|---|---|---|---|---|
| | Men | | Women | | Men | | Women | | Men | | Women | | |
| | P | F | P | F | P | F | P | F | P | F | P | F | |
| Relations | 27.3 | 12.8 | 9.7 | 13.3 | 21.3 | 9.1 | 27.8 | 5.4 | 12.2 | 13.3 | 23.4 | – | 17.6 |
| School | 16.7 | 17.0 | 22.6 | 20.0 | 22.5 | **3.0** | 15.5 | **2.7** | 13.5 | – | 4.7 | 7.7 | 13.6 |
| Work | 3.0 | 19.1 | 3.2 | 13.3 | 20.0 | 36.4 | 4.1 | 21.6 | 21.6 | **6.7** | 12.1 | 11.5 | 13.4 |
| Health | 13.6 | 4.3 | 11.3 | 13.3 | 3.8 | 12.1 | 10.3 | 27.0 | 13.5 | 26.7 | 16.8 | 42.3 | 13.6 |
| Growth | 16.7 | 14.9 | 22.6 | **2.2** | 12.5 | 12.1 | 11.3 | 16.2 | 6.8 | – | 6.5 | – | 11.0 |
| Home | 16.7 | – | 17.7 | 8.9 | 3.8 | **3.0** | 11.3 | 5.4 | 8.1 | – | 5.6 | 7.7 | 8.3 |
| Birth | – | 10.6 | 3.2 | 20.0 | 7.5 | 9.1 | 6.2 | 8.1 | **1.4** | **6.7** | 14.0 | 11.5 | 7.8 |
| Death | 1.5 | 17.0 | 3.2 | 8.9 | 7.5 | 9.1 | 11.3 | 13.5 | 9.5 | 40.0 | 5.6 | 11.5 | 9.0 |
| Other | 4.5 | 4.3 | 6.5 | – | **1.3** | 6.1 | 2.1 | – | 13.5 | **6.7** | 11.2 | 7.7 | 5.7 |

older age groups mention fewer events in the category School in the future than the younger age group, the older and middle-age group mention more events in the category Work in the past than the young age group, and the older and middle-age group mention more events in the category Birth in the past than the younger group while the younger group mentions Birth more in the future.

### Event distribution over subcategories

Next, the percentage of events per subcategory was determined for the whole group and for the past and future of young, middle-aged and older men and women. The results are presented in Table A4.2 (see CD). The total number of events per subgroup (column) over all categories equals 100 percent, while the sum percentage of subcategories within a category equals the percentage of events per category (italics). In other words, both the sum of events (percents) across categories (italics) and subcategories (regular) totals at 100 percent per subgroup. When a subcategory contains only one event the percentage is printed in a shadowed lettertype. From Table A4.2 can be read, for instance, that 10.6 percent of all events that young men report from their past belong to the subcategory Starting School and that 1.5 percent, which includes one event (shadowed lettertype) belongs to the subcategory Commitment.

Because of the small number of events per subcategory and the great number of subcategories, it is not possible to conduct statistical analyses to determine the effect of age, gender and event time on the event distribution over subcategories. The most noticeable results for the total group will be mentioned below as well as the most noticeable differences between men and women of each age group for past and future. A difference is considered to be noticeable in case the subcategory of one subgroup contains ≥ 5 percent of events than the subcategory of the other subgroup. The most noticeable results, then, are as follows:

*Total*
- Overall, the most frequently mentioned subcategories in life are, respectively, Physical Health, Commitment, Birth Child, Starting School, Moving and Finishing School.

*Young-Past* (M age W1 = 23.5 yrs)
- Young men have more memories concerning Begin Relations and Relations Others than young women have.
- Young women mention more events in the subcategory School Rest (e.g. attend boarding school) than young men.
- Young men report more Physical Health problems than young women, while young women report more Mental Health problems.
- For both young men and young women Growth Problems were important in the past.
- Moving has been experienced as an important event by both young men and young women.

*Young-Future* (M age W1 = 23.5 yrs)
- Young men less often mention Finishing School (e.g. graduating) in the future than young women.
- Young men expect more Problems Growth (e.g. midlife crisis) in the future than young women.
- Young men do not mention Home Others (e.g. children leaving home) in the future in contrast to young women.
- Young men less often mention Birth Child in the future than young women.
- Young men expect Death Parent to have a great impact while this event is not mentioned at all by young women.

*Middle-Past* (M age W1 = 43.3 yrs)
- Middle-aged men more often report Starting School than middle-aged women.
- Middle-aged men also have more memories of events concerning Beginning Work and Changing Work than middle-aged women have.

*Middle-Future* (M age W1 = 23.5 yrs)
- Middle-aged men are more focused on Changing Work and Stopping Work in the future than middle-aged women are.

– Middle-aged men are less focused on Physical Health and Growth Others (e.g. problems of children) in the future than middle-aged women are.
– Some middle-aged men expect Birth Child in the future, while middle-aged women already look forward to Birth Grandchild.
– Middle-aged men anticipate Death Parents, while middle-aged women fear Death Partner.

*Older-Past* (M age W1 = 67.4 yrs)
– For older men Finishing School was more important than for older women.
– Changing Work was also more important for older men than for older women.
– Older men report more Physical Health from their past than older women but have not been occupied with Health Others as older women have been.
– Older men almost do not mention Birth Child in contrast to older women for whom this event was very important.
– Older men more often mention Death Parents than older women do.
– For both older men and women the War was an important event in the past.

*Older Future* (M age W1 = 67.4 yrs)
– Older men mention more Relation Others (e.g. children getting married) in the future, older women more School Others (e.g. graduation grandchild).
– For both older men and older women Physical Health is expected to be important in the future, while Health Others is mentioned only by older women.
– Older men anticipate Death Partner more than older women do.

*Other salient findings:*
– For all age-groups Death Parents seems to be more important for men than for women.
– Men are less oriented on other people (Home Others, e.g. children leaving home; Growth Others, e.g. children having problems; Health Others, e.g. illness of parents) than women are.
– Middle-aged women mention Home Others in the future but older women do not mention this event in their past.

## 4.3.2 W1: Affect of events

Table A4.3 (see CD) shows the mean affect of events per subcategory, both for the total group and for the past and future of young, middle-aged and older men and women. Events were rated on a five point Likert scale, varying from very negative (–2), negative (–1) and neutral (0) to positive (+1) and very positive (+2) affect. Table A4.3 does not show the mean affect of events per category, as the affect ratings per subcategory, which are predominantly positive or negative, tend to cancel each other out and consequently contaminate the mean affect score per category. When the mean affect is based on a single event, the mean affect is printed in a shadowed lettertype, e.g., '–2' in a shadowed lettertype means that this single event was coded 'very negative'. The most noticeable results for the total group and the most noticeable differences between the mean affective rating of subcategories ($\geq$ 0.5 and $\geq$ 2 events per subcategory) for past and future for men and women of three age-groups are reported below.

*Total*
– Generally, the following life events are rated as most positive: Birth Grandchild, Individual Growth, Birth Child, Leaving Home, Commitment, Beginning Work and Changing Work.
– Events in the categories Health and Death are always rated (very) negative. Events that refer to Problems are also rated negative.
– Some events, for instance, Stopping Work, Moving, Growth Others, Home Others and Birth Family are accompanied by a (almost) neutral affect (–0.5 < mean affect < 0.5), meaning that sometimes these events are experienced as positive and sometimes as negative.

*Young-Past* (M age W1 = 23.5 yrs)
– Young men rate Individual Growth not as positive as young women do.
– Young men have experienced Moving as somewhat more negative than young women.

– Young men mention positive events in the subcategory Rest, while young women mention only very negative events.

*Young-Future* (M age W1 = 23.5 yrs)

– Young men are less positive about Finishing School in the future than young women.
– Young men are less positive about Beginning Work than young women are.

*Middle-Past* (M age W1 = 43.3 yrs)

– Middle-aged men are more negative about End Relations than middle-aged women.
– For middle-aged men Starting School was a more positive event than for middle-aged women.
– For middle-aged men Moving was a negative event in the past, while for middle-aged women it turned out to be a more positive event.
– Middle-aged men have experienced Birth Child as less positive than middle-aged women have.

*Middle-Future* (M age W1 = 43.3 yrs)

– There are no noticeable differences between men and women in affective rating of future events.

*Older-Past* (M age W1 = 67.4 yrs)

– Older men have more positive memories about Begin Relations than older women have.
– Changing Work and Work Rest were experienced not as positive by older men as by older women.
– Physical and Mental Health are rated less negative by older men than by older women.

*Older-Future* (M age W1 = 67.4 yrs)

– Death Partner is rated more negative by older women than by older men.

*In general:*

– Life events which refer to some beginning or personal development are evaluated as positive while events referring to problems or endings in life are evaluated as negative.

### 4.3.3 W1: Patterns of events

#### Categories per decade

In order to reveal the basic structure of the life-course in terms of important events, the distribution of events over categories per decade was studied. The number of events per decade was set at 100 percent both for the total group and for the past and future of young, middle-aged and older men and women. In this way the relative importance of categories per decade was determined. In order to compress the huge data set in a conveniently arranged table, the most frequently mentioned categories per decade were selected. This selection of main categories is based on the clinical rule of thumb that minor percentages (< 20 % of all events for at least two events per decade) are not reported. Table 4.4 shows the main categories (percents) per decade for the total group and by age group (young, middle, old), gender and event time. On the basis of the mean age per age group it was determined which decades are considered past and which are considered future. For instance, the mean age of the young age group is 23.5 years. In terms of decades the transition from past to future for this age group is closest to the transition from the second to the third decade, which is marked by a dotted line in Table 4.4. It should be noted that because of the age range within the subgroups, the recent past and near future for all subgroups are mixed up. For instance, the period from 21 to 30 years is for some respondents of the young age group (partly) future, for others partly past, dependent of their age on the time of measurement. From Table 4.4 can be read, for instance, that 33 percent of all events young men remember from the first decade of life belong to the category Growth.

*Total*

– A global picture of life emerges in which childhood and adolescence are dominated by School and Home, young adulthood by Relations, middle adulthood by Work, and late adulthood by Health and Death.

*Young-Past (0–20 yrs)* (M age W1 = 23.5 yrs)

– It is salient that young men recall more events from the category Relations in the period of 11 till 20 years than young women do in the same period.

*Young-Future (from 21 yrs)* (M age W1 = 23.5 yrs)
- Young men also mention more Relations related events in the period of 21 to 30 year of age than young women do.
- Young men expect Birth about a decade later (41–50 yrs) than young women (31–40 yrs).
- Young men mention more Death related events in the period from 41 to 60 years than young women do.

*Middle- Past (0–40 yrs)* (M age W1 = 43.3 yrs)
- Middle-aged men mention fewer memories concerning Relations in the period of 11 to 20 years of age than middle-aged women.
- Middle-aged men mention more Work related events in the period of 31 to 40 years than middle-aged women do.
- It is noticeable that Birth is mentioned by middle-aged men in their thirties but not by middle-aged women.

*Middle-Future (from 41 yrs)* (M age W1 = 43.3 yrs)
- Middle-aged men mention more events in the category Work in the period of 41 to 50 years of age than middle-aged women. Middle-aged women report more events concerning Health and Death in this period.

*Older-Past (0–70 yrs)* (M age W1 = 67.3 yrs)
- Older men do not mention Birth, while for older women this was a very important event in their twenties and thirties.
- From the age of thirty Work has been very important in the lives of older men, while Health played a prominent role in the lives of older women.

*Older-Future (from 71 yrs)* (M age W1 = 67.3 yrs)
- Older men more often mention events in the category Death in the period of 71 to 80 years than older women do.

*Another salient finding:*
- The older respondents are, the further they look into the future. Men do not look as far ahead in the future as women do. Women of all age groups mention events at a later age than men of these age groups do.

## Subcategories per decade

For a more detailed picture of the life-course the same procedure was repeated at the level of subcategories, i.e., the number of events per decade for the total group and for past and future of young, middle-aged and older men and women was set on 100 percent. The main subcategories per decade were selected, meeting two criteria of inclusion: (a) 10 percent or more of all events per decade, and (b) at least two reported events. The affect ratings of selected main subcategories per decade and subgroup were converted to a three point scale (negative, neutral, positive). Table 4.5 shows the main subcategories (percents) with mean affect per decade for the total group. In order to be able to compare categories and subcategories for the total group, the main categories per decade are also presented in this table. Compared to the structure of the life-course in terms of main categories per decade it is noticeable that:

*Total*
- In childhood all events concerning Home refer to Moving. Most events concerning School refer to Starting School at the age of six years. Besides Moving and Starting School Physical Health is also remembered as an important event from childhood.
- In adolescence most events concerning School refer to Starting School which can refer to go to Secondary School or to start studying at the age of eighteen.
- In young adulthood Relations are dominating of which most events concern Commitment. Birth Child and Finishing School are also important in this period of life.
- Although in the thirties Relations is the dominating category the most important subcategory in this period is Birth Child.

Table 4.4　W1: Main categories (percents; ≥20 percent of all events per decade and ≥2 events per category) per decade for the total group and by age group (young, middle, old), gender, past and future (dotted line).

| Decade | Young (23.5 yrs) | | Middle (43.3 yrs) | | Older (67.4 yrs) | | Total | Decade |
|---|---|---|---|---|---|---|---|---|
| | Men | Women | Men | Women | Men | Women | | |
| I: 0–10 | Growth (33) | Home (42) | School (50) Home (25) | School (40) Home (30) Growth (20) | Other (38) | Other (23) | School (21) Home (21) | I: 0–10 |
| II: 11–20 | Relations (21) School (21) Home (21) | School (31) Growth (23) | School (42) Growth (23) | School (26) Relations (23) | School (36) Other (29) | Other (26) Relations (22) | School (27) | II: 11–20 |
| III: 21–30 | Relations (33) School (27) Work (23.3) | School (26) | Relations (44) | Relations (54) | Relations (29) | Birth (31) Relations (27) | Relations (33) | III: 21–30 |
| IV: 31–40 | Growth (42) | Birth (43) School (29) | Work (35) Relations (24) Birth (24) | Relations (27) | Work (40) Health (20) Home (20) | Relations (28) Birth (20) | Relations (22) | IV: 31–40 |
| V: 41–50 | Birth (29) Death (29) | – | Work (37) Growth (26) | Health (31) Death (25) | Work (56) | Relations (33) Health (33) Work (22) | Work (30) | V: 41–50 |
| VI: 51–60 | Death (43) Health (29) | Health (40) Home (40) | Work (25) | Growth (40) Work (20) | Work (50) Death (33) | Work (33) Health (33) | Work (24) | VI: 51–60 |
| VII: 61–70 | – | Death (50) | Work (50) Health (25) | Health (40) Work (20) | Relations (33) Work (33) | Health (39) | Health (32) Work (25) | VII: 61–70 |
| VIII: 71–80 | – | – | – | Death (75) | Health (44) Death (44) | Health (67) | Health (43) Death (43) | VIII: 71–80 |
| IX: 81–90 | – | – | – | – | – | Health (67) | Health (50) | IX: 81–90 |
| X: 91–100 | – | – | – | – | – | – | Health (67) | X: 91–100 |

* Shaded area refers to the 'bump' period of life

- Besides Work related events as Changing Work in the forties and Stopping Work in the fifties, Death Parents is important in the period from 41 to 60 years of age.
- After the age of 60 Stopping Work, Physical Health and Death Partner are most important sub-categories.

**Table 4.5**  W1: Main categories (≥ 20% of all events per decade and ≥ 2 events per (sub)category) and main subcategories (≥ 10% of all events per decade and ≥ 2 events per (sub)category) with affect (+ = positive, 0 = neutral, − = negative) per decade for the total group.

| Decade | Category | % | Subcategory | % | Affect |
|--------|----------|---|-------------|---|--------|
| I: 0–10 | Home | 21 | Moving | 21 | 0 |
| | School | 21 | Starting School | 16 | + |
| | | | Physical Health | 11 | − |
| II: 11–20 | School | 27 | Starting School | 14 | + |
| III: 21–30 | Relations | 33 | Commitment | 20 | + |
| | | | Birth Child | 12 | + |
| | | | Finishing School | 11 | + |
| IV: 31–40 | Relations | 22 | Birth Child | 18 | + |
| V: 41–50 | Work | 30 | Changing Work | 18 | + |
| | | | Death Parents | 11 | − |
| VI: 51–60 | Work | 24 | Stopping Work | 16 | 0 |
| | | | Death Parents | 11 | − |
| VII: 61–70 | Work | 25 | Stopping Work | 23 | 0 |
| | Health | 32 | Physical Health | 21 | − |
| VIII : 71–80 | Health | 43 | Physical Health | 43 | − |
| | Death | 43 | Death Partner | 33 | − |
| IX : 81–90 | Health | 50 | * | * | * |
| X : 91–100 | Health | 67 | Physical Health | 67 | − |

\* = no subcategories in this decade which meet criteria of inclusion (10 percent or more of all events per decade, and at least two reported events).

*In general:*
- In the first half of life positive events are dominating, while in the second part of life negative events are dominating.

Table 4.6, Table 4.7 and Table 4.8 show the main subcategories (percents) per decade, the mean affect of these subcategories and a typical example of the subcategory for past and future (dotted line) of young, middle-aged and older men and women, respectively. It should be noted that in these tables mean age, time-perspective and age of the respondent are contaminated.

*Young-Past (0–20 yrs)* (M age W1 = 23.5 yrs)
- Moving in childhood (0–10 yrs) is remembered as a negative event by young men and as a positive event by young women.
- In adolescence (11–20 yrs) young men have had more Physical Health problems, while young women have experienced Growth Problems.
- Young men report from their adolescence (11–20 yrs) more relational events (Begin Relations) than young women do.

*Young-Future (21–60 yrs)* (M age W1 = 23.5 yrs)
- Young men have rather ambivalent feelings about Finishing School while young women are more positive.

**Table 4.6** W1: Main subcategories (percents) with affect (+ = positive, 0 = neutral, − = negative) and examples (catchwords) per decade for past and future (dotted line) of young men and women (age range 18–30 yrs, mean age = 23.5 yrs).

| | Young (M age = 23.5) | | | | | | | |
| | Men | | | | Women | | | |
| Decade | Subcategory | % | Affect | Example | Subcategory | % | Affect | Example |
|---|---|---|---|---|---|---|---|---|
| I: 0–10 | Relations Others | 17 | − | *Divorce parents* | Moving | 42 | + | *Moved a lot* |
| | Physical Health | 17 | − | *Hospitalization* | Physical Health | 17 | − | *Getting epilepsy* |
| | Growth Problems | 17 | − | *Feeling lonely* | Birth Family | 17 | 0 | *Birth of sister* |
| | Growth Rest | 17 | + | *Happy childhood* | | | | |
| | Moving | 17 | − | *Relocation* | | | | |
| II: 11–20 | Physical Health | 14 | − | *Accident* | School Rest | 13 | 0 | *Good school time* |
| | Moving | 14 | 0 | *Relocation* | Growth Problems | 13 | − | *Adolescence problems* |
| | Begin Relations | 12 | + | *Falling in love* | Starting School | 10 | + | *Starting college* |
| | Starting School | 12 | 0 | *Starting college* | | | | |
| III: 21–30 | Finishing School | 23 | 0 | *Graduating* | Finishing School | 23 | + | *Graduating* |
| | Beginning Work | 20 | + | *Find a job* | Commitment | 17 | + | *Living together* |
| | Commitment | 10 | 0 | *Living together* | Mental Health | 14 | − | *Depression* |
| | End Relations | 10 | − | *Splitting up* | Birth Child | 14 | + | *Having a baby* |
| IV: 31–40 | Commitment | 17 | + | *Marriage* | Birth Child | 43 | + | *Birth of children* |
| | Individual Growth | 17 | + | *Peace of mind* | Finishing School | 29 | + | *Graduating* |
| | Growth Problems | 17 | − | *Deep crisis* | | | | |
| | Birth Child | 17 | + | *Start a family* | | | | |
| V: 41–50 | Birth Child | 29 | + | *Birth of children* | * | * | * | * |
| | Death Parents | 29 | − | *Death of parent* | | | | |
| VI: 51–60 | Death Parents | 43 | − | *Death of parent* | Health Rest | 40 | − | Physical decline |
| | | | | | Home Others | 40 | − | Children leaving |
| VII: 61–70 | * | * | * | * | * | * | * | * |
| VIII: 71–80 | * | * | * | * | * | * | * | * |

* = no subcategories in this decade which meet criteria of inclusion (10 percent or more of all events per decade, and at least two reported events).

- Young men expect Birth Child later (31–50 yrs) than young women do (21–40 yrs).
- Young men expect Birth Child and Death Parents to happen in the period of 41 to 50 years, while young women do not have any idea of what will happen in this period.
- Young men also expect Death Parents in the period of 51 to 60, while young women are more focused on their own family (Home Others = children leaving home) and on events concerning Health in this period.

*Middle-Past (0–40 yrs)* (M age W1 = 43.3 yrs)

- Middle-aged men report fewer memories concerning Relations from adolescence (11–20 yrs) than middle-aged women.
- Middle-aged men report Birth Child at a younger age (21–40 yrs) than middle-aged women (31–40 yrs).
- In the period of 31 to 40 years Work issues are more prominent in the lives of middle-aged men than of middle-aged women (Problems Work, Changing Work).

**Table 4.7**  W1: Main subcategories (percents) with affect (+ = positive, 0 = neutral, − = negative) and examples (catchwords) per decade for past and future (dotted line) of middle-aged men and women (age range 31–55 yrs, mean age = 43.3 yrs) (Shaded area refers to the 'bump' period of life).

| | Middle (M age = 43.3) | | | | | | | |
| | Men | | | | Women | | | |
| Decade | Subcategory | % | Affect | Example | Subcategory | % | Affect | Example |
|---|---|---|---|---|---|---|---|---|
| I: 0–10 | Starting School | 50 | + | Elementary school | Moving | 30 | + | Relocation |
| | Moving | 25 | − | Relocation | Starting School | 20 | − | Primary school |
| | | | | | Problems School | 20 | − | Bad school time |
| II: 11–20 | Starting School | 35 | + | Secondary school | Begin Relations | 16 | + | Courting |
| | Beginning Work | 12 | + | Nursing | Individual Growth | 13 | + | Feeling accepted |
| III : 21–30 | Commitment | 19 | + | Marriage | Commitment | 27 | + | Marriage |
| | Begin Relations | 15 | + | Meeting wife | End Relations | 12 | − | Divorce |
| | Birth Child | 15 | + | Birth children | | | | |
| IV : 31–40 | Birth Child | 24 | 0 | Becoming father | End Relations | 14 | − | Splitting up |
| | Work Problems | 18 | − | Layoff | Birth Child | 14 | + | Birth daughter |
| | Commitment | 12 | + | Steady relation- | | | | |
| | Changing Work | 12 | _ | ship | | | | |
| | Death Parents | 12 | − | Starting own business | | | | |
| | | | | Death of father | | | | |
| V: 41–50 | Changing Work | 26 | + | Other job | Changing Work | 13 | + | Other job |
| | Individual Growth | 21 | + | Solving problems | Health Rest | 13 | − | Menopause |
| | Death Parents | 16 | − | Death mother | | | | |
| | End Relations | 11 | − | Divorce | | | | |
| | Physical Health | 11 | − | Physical complaints | | | | |
| VI: 51–60 | Stopping Work | 25 | 0 | Early retirement | Growth Others | 30 | 0 | Problems children |
| | | | | | Stopping Work | 20 | 0 | Early retirement |
| VII: 61–70 | Stopping Work | 50 | 0 | Retirement | Physical Health | 33 | − | Disabilities |
| | | | | | Stopping Work | 13 | + | Retirement |
| | | | | | Individual Growth | 13 | + | Reflect on life |
| VIII: 71–80 | * | * | * | * | Death Partner | 50 | − | Husband dies |

* = no subcategories in this decade which met criteria of inclusion (10 percent or more of all events per decade, and at least two reported events).

- Death Parents is mentioned by middle-aged men in the period of 31 to 40 years but not by middle-aged women.
- In contrast to middle-aged men middle-aged women mention End Relations in the period of 21 to 40 years.

*Middle-Future (41–80 yrs)* (M age W1 = 43.3 yrs)

- Middle-aged men mention End Relations in the period of 41 to 50 years which is a decade later than middle-aged women do.
- Middle-aged men are very focused on Stopping Work in the period of 51 till 70 years.

**Table 4.8** W1: Main subcategories (percents) with affect (+ = positive, 0 = neutral, − = negative) and examples (catchwords) per decade for past and future (dotted line) of older men and women (age range 56–84 yrs, mean age = 67.4 yrs)(Shaded area refers to the 'bump' period of life).

| | Older (M age = 67.4) | | | | | | | |
|---|---|---|---|---|---|---|---|---|
| | Men | | | | Women | | | |
| Decade | Subcategory | % | Affect | Example | Subcategory | % | Affect | Example |
| I: 0–10 | Other Rest | 25 | + | *Getting a special present* | War | 23 | − | *Outbreak of WW II* |
| | | | | | Relations Others | 15 | − | *Parents are fighting* |
| | | | | | Starting School | 15 | + | *Primary school* |
| | | | | | Birth Family | 15 | 0 | *Birth of sister* |
| II: 11–20 | War | 29 | − | *Japanese camp* | War | 22 | − | *WW II* |
| | Starting School | 14 | + | *Studying* | Beginning Work | 17 | + | *First job* |
| | Finishing School | 14 | + | *Leaving school* | | | | |
| | Death Parents | 14 | − | *Mother died* | | | | |
| III : 21–30 | Commitment | 25 | + | *Marriage* | Birth Child | 31 | + | *Having a baby* |
| | Physical Health | 17 | − | *Serious disease* | Commitment | 23 | + | *Marriage* |
| | Finishing School | 13 | + | *Diploma* | War | 12 | − | *End of WW II* |
| | War | 13 | 0 | *Liberation* | | | | |
| IV : 31–40 | Changing Work | 20 | + | *Promotion* | Birth Child | 20 | + | *Getting children* |
| | | | | | Moving | 12 | + | *Relocation* |
| V : 41–50 | Changing Work | 44 | + | *Becoming director* | Problems Relations | 22 | − | *Bad marriage* |
| | | | | | Health Others | 22 | − | *Illness parents* |
| VI : 51–60 | Changing Work | 33 | − | *Merger of companies* | Health Others | 22 | − | *Illness husband* |
| VII : 61–70 | Stopping Work | 33 | − | *Retirement* | Health Others | 22 | − | *Illness husband* |
| | | | | | Physical Health | 17 | − | *Very ill* |
| | | | | | Birth Grandchild | 17 | + | *Getting grandchild* |
| | | | | | Stopping Work | 11 | 0 | *Retirement* |
| VIII : 71–80 | Physical Health | 44 | − | *Requiring help* | Physical Health | 67 | 0 | *Getting ill* |
| | Death Partner | 33 | − | *Death of wife* | | | | |

- Middle-aged women also mention events in other domains.
- Middle-aged men do not look further ahead than Stopping Work in the seventh decade, while middle-aged women expect Death Partner between 71 to 80 years of age.

*Middle-Memory Bump (10–30 yrs)* (M age W1 = 43.3 yrs)

- The most important events in the bump period for middle-aged men are Starting School and Beginning Work in adolescence (11–20 years), and Relation-related events and Birth Child in young adulthood (21–30 years).
- Middle-aged women mainly recall Begin Relations and Individual Growth from adolescence, and Commitment and End Relations from young adulthood.
- Most events from the period of 11 to 30 years of age are positive events, referring to some beginning (Starting School, Begin Relations, Beginning Work, Commitment, Birth Child) or personal development (Individual Growth).

*Older-Past (0–70 yrs)* (M age W1 = 67.4 yrs)
- The Second World War (WWII) has had great impact in childhood and adolescence on men and women of this older age-group.
- Older men mention more events concerning School (Starting and Finishing School) in the age of 11 to 30 years than older women do.
- Older men report Death Parents in adolescence while older women do not mention this event in any period.
- From the age of thirty older men mainly recall Changing Work and Stopping Work, while older women were confronted with problems in different domains (Relations, Health Others and Physical Health).
- Stopping Work in the sixties is experienced mainly as a negative event by older men and as a neutral event by older women, i.e., by some women as positive, by others as negative.
- Older men do not mention Birth Grandchild but for older women this is a positive event.

*Older-Future (70–80 yrs)* (M age W1 = 67.4 yrs)
- It is remarkable that relatively often older men report Death Partner as an expected event before their own death.

*Older-Memory Bump (10–30 yrs)* (M age W1 = 67.4 yrs)
- Older adults hold more negative memories of the period of 11 to 30 years of age than middle-aged adults which is mainly due to the effect of the Second World War.
- Other negative memories of older men concern Death Parents in adolescence and Physical Health in the twenties. Positive events for older men in the period of 11 to 20 years of age were Starting and Finishing School and in the period of 21 to 30 years of age Finishing School and Commitment.
- Older women hold positive memories of Beginning Work in adolescence and Commitment and Birth Child in young adulthood.

*Other salient findings:*
- Young men more often report Begin Relations (e.g., falling in love) from the period of 11 to 20 years than young women do, but for the middle-aged group it is the other way around; middle-aged women more often report Begin Relations from this period than middle-aged men.
- Young women look forward to Commitment (e.g., marriage) but, in retrospect, this often has ended in a divorce for middle-aged women.
- Young women report Commitment and Birth about one decade ahead of young men in their future but middle-aged and older men and women report Commitment and Birth Child from the same decade in their past. However, End Relations is reported more at an older age by middle-aged men than by middle-aged women.
- Death Parents is mentioned more often by men than by women.
- Young women mention Home Others (e.g., children leaving home) in the future. Middle-aged and older women, however, do not mention this event in the past.

## 4.4 Discussion

In this chapter the content of life stories was analysed at the event level. First, the basic elements of the life story, the life events, were classified into nine categories and 40 subcategories. The effect of age, gender and time on the distribution of events over categories was determined. Then, the structure of the life-course in terms of most dominating events per decade including ratings of affect of such events was determined for the total group and for men and women of three age groups for past and future separately. In this way a linear, chronological structure of the life-course was obtained for the total group as well as for men and women of a young, middle and older age-group in terms of most important events per decade.

## Age-Period-Cohort

In a cross-sectional study with period (time of measurement) being constant, it is not always clear whether differences between age groups refer to an age or a cohort effect (Schaie, 1965). It seems to be logical that the finding that younger respondents are more focused on the domains School and Growth than older respondents, while older respondents are more focused on Health and Work is an effect of age rather than of cohort in this LIM-study. A clear cohort effect in this sample is the impact of the Second World War which is mentioned by the oldest LIM-group. Another example of a cohort effect is the fact that older men mention relatively many School related events in young adulthood in contrast to older women. These older men, who had not so much schooling, took extra training courses and classes to work their way up. But it is less clear whether, for instance, Moving is a cohort or an age effect. Moving is relatively often mentioned by young and middle-aged respondents in childhood but not by older respondents. It is likely that younger adults had to move more often in their youth, for instance, because of their parent's career or parent's divorce. An alternative explanation would be that the effect of Moving fades away as people grow older.

## Gender

As was shown in Chapter 2, men and women show the same pattern concerning the number and distribution of events over the lifespan. Conway, Wang, Hanyu and Haque (2005) found this pattern to be very robust as it was also found across cultures. The content of memories, however, seems to be sensitive to gender-differentiated socialization processes (Davis, 1999) and cultural influences related to the nature of the self (Conway et al, 2005). In this LIM-study it was found that, in general, men are more oriented towards Work while women are more oriented towards Health and Birth which is in accordance with results of other studies (Baum & Stewart, 1990; Brugman, 2000; deVries & Watt, 1996; Rönka, Oravala & Pulkkinen, 2003). The LIM-study shows that young women are focused on starting a family and do not mention events concerning Work in the future. Young men expect Birth Child about one decade later than young women do. Older men mainly remember Work-related events from their adult life while for older women Birth Child was very important. As Sterns and Huyck (2001) state, Work is at the centre of life for men, while women's development is more varied. The LIM-study shows that middle-aged and older women show a larger variety in types of events than middle-aged and older men do.

Although the life expectancy for women is higher than for men, at old age women have a longer period in which they suffer from illnesses than men have (Bee, 1995; Deeg, 2002). Therefore, it is not surprising that women mention more events in this domain. Besides, middle-aged and older women are also more likely than men to be active in taking care of frail elderly (Bee, 1995; Moen, 1996). Table 4.8 shows that for older women Health Others was an important issue during their forties, fifties and sixties. As women have a higher life expectancy than men, it is remarkable that older man mention more often Death Partner in the future. Besides, women are generally younger than their partner. But as men generally derive more social and emotional support from marriage than women do, the impact of the death of one's spouse may be higher for men (Moen, 1996).

## Time perspective

In the LIM-study respondents are first asked to report important events from their past and then to mention events they expect for their future. Respondents of all age groups mention more events in the past than in the future. Most respondents found it difficult to form a picture of their future life. When considering the type of events respondents mention in the past and in the future it is striking that for the future respondents foresee mainly normative events, while from the past they report normative as well as non-normative events. As defined by Baltes, Reese and Lipsitt (1980) normative age-graded events occur at about the same time to all individuals in a given (sub)culture (e.g., going to kindergarter at age four), while non-normative events do not occur in any normative age-graded or history-graded manner to most individuals (e.g., having an accident). In the LIM-study the middle-age group, for instance, reports normative events from the past, like Starting School, Begin Relations, Commitment, as well as non-normative events like Moving, Problems Work, Changing Work, End Relations and Problems School. In the future they expect normative events such as Death Parents, Stopping Work and Physical Health problems. Non-normative events are not included in the picture people have of their future. This was also found by Gergen (1988) who asked college students to create narrative expositions of their lives; young individuals had a prototypical image of their future of a consistent happily-ever-after age 25, with a regressive downturn at life's end. Newby-Clark and Ross (2003) found that students mainly expected desirable events for the future as graduation, gainful employment, marriage, children and exotic travel. As was mentioned in Chapter 3, Berntsen and Rubin (2002) made a conceptual distinction between life narrative and life script. The results of the present study show that when young, middle-aged and older people are asked to tell about their past and future life, their past life story consists of personal memories (life narrative) while their future life story is more general and prototypical (life script).

## Affect

Overall, it can be stated that events that implicate problems or losses (Problems Relation, Problems School, Problems Work, End Relation, Death) elicit negative emotions, while events concerning the start of a new stage in life (Starting School, Begin Relations, Commitment, Beginning Work, Changing Work, Birth Child, Birth Grandchild) or relating to Growth (Individual Growth) elicit positive emotions. The fact whether an event happens on-time or off-time is also of influence on the emotions it elicits. Neugarten (1970, 1977) claimed that it is the unanticipated (off-time), not the anticipated (on-time), that is likely to represent the traumatic event and to require greater adjustment. For instance, in the LIM-study some older men mention Death Parents in adolescence which, when it happens in this period of life, is an off-time event.

Some events like Stopping Work, Moving, Growth Others and Birth Family are rated neutral, meaning that these events can be positive as well as negative. Retirement, for instance, can mean the beginning of a period in which individuals experience maximum autonomy and which offers time and opportunities to realize one's own plans and goals. Retirement can also be experienced as a loss of position in society and of meaning and structure in life. Besides, individuals show less retirement satisfaction and adjustment when they stop working involuntary (Kim & Moen, 2001). Moving is mentioned as an important event in childhood and adolescence by young and middle-aged adults but by some respondents it is experienced as a positive event, by others as a negative event. According to Sandoval (2002), moving means a hazardous time for children but it also may offer possibilities to obtain resources to cope with other life events.

## Structure of the life-course

On the basis of results of the LIM-study a linear, chronological structure of the life-course was generated, i.e., ten periods of ten years, in which each period is characterized by one or more dominant life theme(s). For the total group it turned out that childhood and adolescence are characterized by School and Home, young adulthood by Relations, middle adulthood by Work, and older adulthood by Health and Death. Stage models of the life-course have always been very popular in life-course psychology. From the time of Aristotle, who discerned three stages of life (i.e., youth, the prime of life and old age) (Birren & Schroots, 2001), people have divided the life-course in separate periods with specific characteristics (Erikson, 1950; Lowenthal, 1975; Levinson, 1986; 1996; Kohli, 1986; Grob et al., 2001). However, in such general stage models of the life course it is not clear from whose perspective the life course is viewed; age, gender and time perspective are all mixed up. As Neugarten (1979) already stated, the view individuals have of previous life events, life periods, and the life story depends on the age at which they look back. Similarly, the expectations individuals hold for their future, depend on the age from which they look forward. Therefore, besides a general basic model of the life course (see Table 4.5), a modal life course for men and women of different age groups (see Table 4.6, Table 4.7 and

Table 4.8) was generated in this study. The results favour a more dynamic view of the life-course taking into account the changing view people have on their past and future over the lifespan.

In order to reveal the pattern of events over the life-course it was determined what type of events is dominating within each decade of life, resulting in the relative importance of events per decade. All decades were considered equal which is based on the concept of calendar or clock time. Calendar time is conceived as linear and as a quantity that can be added, subtracted, multiplied, and divided regardless of the age of the individual. This implicates, for instance, that the first ten years of human life are the same as the middle ten years of life and that, consequently, it would not make any difference if a person loses a parent at the age of eight years or at the age of forty-eight. The absolute distribution of events over the lifespan, however, shows that not all decades that are equal from a calendar time perspective are equally important in the subjective perception of respondents. The period of about 10 to 30 years, the bump period, for example, is perceived as far more outstanding than other periods of life and is characterized by a density of events. Older adults have disproportionally more memories from this period of life than from other periods of life. Memories from this bump period, mainly memories referring to School (2nd decade) and Relations (3rd decade), form the frame of reference from which middle-aged and older people view their past. It is hypothesized that events that happened in this period have more impact than when the same event would have happened at a later age. Fromholt et al. (2003), for instance, found that memories of the occupation in Denmark during the Second World War were reported more often if they had occurred during the bump years.

On the basis of the foregoing, it can be stated that a model of the life-course should take into account the age of the individual and his or her subjective perception of past and future. For instance, young adults report most memories from their recent past and expect more events in the near future than in the distant future. When older people look back on their past they do not mention so many memories from the period of 0–10 years of age. But from the period of 10 to 30 years of age they report relatively many memories, most of which are positive like Starting and Finishing School, Beginning Work, Commitment and Birth Child. After this period there is a kind of latency stage from which older people hold relatively few memories. Around the present age older respondents hold somewhat more memories and expectations than from the latency stage, but not as many as from the bump period (see Chapter 2). Events expected in the future are mostly negative and refer to Health and Death.

In concluding this chapter, it can be stated that:

– Per age group the distribution of autobiographical memories and expectations over the lifespan shows a robust pattern with recency/proximity effects and a bump period, whereas the content of autobiographical memories and expectations varies within this pattern and seems to be more sensitive to social and cultural influences.

– The patterns of events show an age-dependent content shift of past memories and future expectations over the lifespan, supporting a more dynamic view on the human life-course. Memories from the past are more personal and include normative as well as non-normative events, while expectations for the future are more generic and predominantly normative.

– A non-linear model, i.e., a model in which some periods in life are more prominent in memory – concerning the number of events recalled – than other periods in life would be more appropriate to describe the life-course as it takes into account the difference in subjective meaning perceived by individuals at different ages.

# Chapter 5
# Dynamics

## 5.1 Introduction

So far the analysis of LIM data resulted in a description of the modal life course in terms of most important events per decade for men and women of a young, middle and older age group. Autobiographical memory, however, is not static but has a dynamic character and is subject to continuous changes, as was shown, for instance, in Chapter 2 with respect to the ratio of past and future events and the distribution of events over the lifespan. Concerning the content of memories and expectations over time, some events may be forgotten or may have lost their significance while new events have to be integrated in the life story. As Bluck and Habermas (2000) state, the life story must be updated as life is being lived. Remote events may lose or gain significance over time (Linde, 1993) as they are reinterpreted (Karney & Coombes, 2000) or as their remembered emotional intensity changes over time (Levine, 1997).

The cross-sectional analysis of the first wave showed an age-dependent content shift of past memories and future expectations over the lifespan. However, differences between age groups are not the same as changes within age groups, since the time parameters Age and Cohort are confounded in cross-sectional research. It is not clear whether differences between age groups concerning past and future events can be explained by differences in age or are due to different cohorts. For instance, in this study Moving is relatively often remembered by young and middle-aged respondents from childhood but not by older respondents. It is possible that younger people had to move more often in their youth, but an alternative explanation would be that the effect of Moving fades away as people grow older.

In order to describe stability and change in autobiographical memories within an individual's life it is necessary to conduct longitudinal research. However, when conducting longitudinal research, the time parameters Age and Period are confounded. It is not clear whether changes in the content of memories and expectations can be explained by age or by time-of-measurement (Schaie & Hofer, 2001). For instance, when the young age group is very optimistic about finding a good job in the future at the first wave but more pessimistic two years later, this can be a consequence of economic changes or of a more realistic view when growing older. Time-of-measurement effects can only be identified if a minimum of two cohorts are followed over similar age ranges (Schaie & Hofer, 2001) which was not the case in this study. The effect of time-of-measurement, then, has to be taken for granted but can be considered negligible over a period of five years.

In the present study the LIM was administered three times over a period of five years. The questions to be answered concern the stability and change in the content of the LIM| Life story over this period. The content of the LIM|Life story will be limited to the basic elements of the life story, i.e., memories respondents report from their past and expectations they have for their future. *Stability*, then, is defined as recalling similar events, i.e., events which are classified into the same (sub)category, at different points in time by the same (group of) respondents. *Change* is defined as recalling different events from one point of measurement to the other, i.e., omitting or adding events in the second and third wave, by the same (group of) respondents. The results of the first wave make up the base line from which the stability and change in content of retrospective and prospective memory over a period of two and five years will be analyzed.

Most studies on stability and change have been conducted with regard to recalling the same events at two different sessions (Thorne, Cutting, & Skaw, 1998). For instance, Anderson, Cohen and Taylor (2000) had a young and an older age group recall two events. Two months later they were asked to recall the same two events. Anderson et al. (2000) were surprised about the low level of memory stability. Memory stability was greater in the older group. In the young age group 46 percent of the facts in the repeated memory task were the same as in the original memory task, while in the older group this percentage was 58 percent. Older memories were more stable than relatively recent ones. When recalling events respondents omitted information or added new information rather than contradict or falsify the original information. Rubin, Schrauf and Greenberg (2004) asked 30 undergraduates to recall the same 20 autobiographical memories at two sessions with an interval of two weeks and investigated the stability of subjects' ratings of various aspects of these memories. The dating of a memory appeared to be more stable than other properties of the memory such as visual imagery or whether the memory came in words. Findings of various other studies (Christiansen & Safer, 1996; Josselson, 2000; Thompson, Skowronski, Larsen, & Betz, 1996; Wagenaar, 1986; Wagenaar & Groeneweg, 1990) showed that central features of events that are highly emotional and surprising are rather stable over time (Thorne et al., 1998).

As far as known, there are no longitudinal studies in which respondents are asked to report spontaneously events they remember from their past and expect for their future. Birren and Hedlund (1987) had 25 respondents (age range 22–81) list the major branching points in their lives. At the follow-up, two years after the first measurement, participants got a copy of the original branching points but they were encouraged to make any changes or additions they wished. On basis of the average number of branching points at the first measurement and the number of omitted events at the second measurement it can be deduced that about 84 percent of the events that were considered major branching points at the first measurement were still considered to be important two years later. It should be noticed, however, that participants got a copy of their original list of major branching points in stead of being asked to recall branching points spontaneously. Thorne et al. (1998) asked 46 young adults to report memories concerning relationships with an interval of six months and found that only 12 percent of the memories which were told at the first interview were also told six months later. Although not a longitudinal study, Robinson and Taylor (1998) asked fourteen middle-aged women to review their lives. When they had finished this task, they were asked to review their lives once more but to focus now on the disruptions, detours, surprises, choices, and turning points, both good and bad that may have occurred. At the second telling 39 percent of topics referred to similar topics in the first tellings and 61 percent were new. Bourque and Back (1977) investigated to what extent individuals have a relatively constant picture of their lives (past as well as future). They asked 371 participants in the age between 45 to 70 years to draw their life graph two times within a 4-year interval. The general view individuals had of their lives turned out to be quite stable. It seemed that life events had some influence on the life perspective as measured by the life graph especially as they occurred at the wrong moment, i.e., off-time events. Death events had a strong impact on all respondents and generally had the power to generate a turning point or to change the life graph.

In spite of the lack of longitudinal data about the content of autobiographical memory, a few hypotheses can be generated concerning the stability and change of autobiographical memories on the basis of previous results of the LIM-study and results of other studies. The patterns for the distribution of events over the lifespan show two phenomena, the autobiographical memory bump and the recency/proximity effect (see Chapter 2). The bump in this study is fixed in the period of about 10 to 30 years of age with a peak in the period of 20 to 30 years of age; older respondents hold disproportionally more memories from this period of life than from other periods of life. As Rubin, Rahhal and Poon (1998) state "Things learned in early adulthood are remembered best" (p. 3). Therefore, it is expected that for older adults events recalled from the bump period are rather stable over time. The recency/proximity effect – people remember more events from their recent past than from their distant past and expect more events in the near future than in the distant future – is moving with age. The period which is the recent past at the first wave, has become a more distant past at the second and third wave. Some events will be forgotten according to the forgetting curve and new events will have happened in the mean time and will be recalled. Some of these events were expected in the near future at the first wave, while other events were not foreseen. As a consequence, a lot of change can be expected in the content of memories and expectations around the present age of the respondent.

Concerning the affect of events different studies have shown that highly emotional and surprising features of events are rather stable over time (see for an overview Thorne et al., 1998). It can be expected that memories and expectations which are rated 'very positive' or 'very negative' are more stable than events which are not accompanied by such strong emotions. Besides, the LIM-study showed that respondents remember more 'very negative' events than 'very positive' events. It was argued in Chapter 3 that it is adaptive for human beings to respond more strongly to bad than to good. Consequently, it can be expected that, in general, '(very) negative' events are more stable in the life story than '(very) positive' events. The LIM-study also showed that positive and negative events are not distributed equally over the lifespan. For instance, respondents remember more positive events from the bump period than from other periods of life. The question, then, is whether there is a difference in the stability of positive and negative events in different periods of life.

Concerning the content of events it can be expected on the basis of cross-sectional research that some type of events become more important as people grow older while other types of events lose their significance over time. For instance, it can be expected that for the youngest age group events within the category Work will become more important, while events within the category School will be mentioned less often as time passes by. Events which are mentioned by all age groups, for instance Commitment, are expected to be rather stable over time.

Besides determining the stability and change of memories and expectations over a period of five years, the stability or robustness of 'patterns of events' will be studied in the present chapter. In Chapter 4 the LIM-data of the first wave were analyzed resulting in different patterns of events for men and women of different age groups. Examples of such patterns are: older respondents mainly remember events from the bump period which indicate a beginning or a development and which are rated positively; men appear to be more focused on Work while women are more focused on Health and Birth; older adults mention fewer events in the category Growth than younger adults. The question now is: "Are these patterns also found when administering the LIM a second and a third time". In other words: "How stable or robust are these patterns?" A pattern or phenomenon is considered to be stable when it is found in all three waves of this LIM-study. When the pattern is also found in other studies, using different methods and on different samples, the pattern can be considered robust. In an earlier chapter, the 'bump phenomenon' and the 'principle of the constant life perspective' turned out to be very robust patterns as they were found in all three waves and also in other studies when using other methods and other samples (see Chapter 2). In order to determine which patterns concerning the content of life events are stable, the second and third wave will be content-analyzed in the same way as the first wave and the results of the three waves will be compared to each other. Because of the great amount of data results of the three cross-sectional analyses will be fully presented only in the enclosed CD.

In sum, the aim of the present chapter is twofold:
– First, the LIM-data of three waves will be analyzed independent from each other in order to identify which patterns of events are stable over three waves and which patterns change over time.
– Second, longitudinal data of 74 respondents who participated at all three waves will be analyzed in order to determine the intra-individual stability and change of memories and expectations over periods of two and five years.

The first wave will be taken as base-line and the number (percentage), affect and content of (un) stable events will be determined, taking into account the effect of gender, age and time (past, present and future). Besides, stability and change in two specific periods of life, i.e., the bump period and the period around the moving age will be studied in more detail. As the intra-individual variability of changes turned out to be rather large, it is rather difficult to describe group findings concerning change (Saldana, 2003); the focus in this chapter, therefore, will be on describing group findings concerning the stability of (patterns of) memories and expectations.

## 5.2   Method

First, the three waves will be treated as three cross-sectional studies (N = 98, 83 and 77 respectively) and each study will be analyzed separately and independently from the other studies with regard to the content of events in the same way as was done for the first wave in the previous chapter. Because of the enormous amount of data full results of the first, second and third wave will be presented only in the enclosed CD. In the Results section of this chapter a summary of the results will be presented.

Next, longitudinal data of 74 respondents who participated in all three waves will be analyzed concerning the content of life events in order to describe intra-individual stability and change in autobiographical memories and expectations over the lifespan. The first wave will be taken as point of departure and it will be determined (a) which percentage of events reported at the first wave is reported at the second and/or third wave, (b) which percentage of positive and negative events reported at the first wave is reported at the second and/or third wave, (c) what type of events, reported at the first wave, is also reported at the second and third wave, and (d) which changes take place in the content of events in the bump period and in the period around the recent past/near future.

### Analysis
Before analyzing categorical LIM-data, it is necessary to define and discuss the following issues and concepts:

– *Stability* of memories and expectations in the present study refers to mentioning similar events, i.e., events that are categorised in similar (sub)categories by about the same group of respondents (to this type of analysis will be referred to by the heading W1 | W2 | W3) or by the same respondents (to this type of analysis will be referred to by the heading W1 → W2 → W3) when telling the life story at three different points in time.

– *Change* in memories and expectations can refer to (1) omitting events when telling the life story a second and third time by about the same group of respondents (W1 | W2 | W3) or by the same respondents (W1 → W2 → W3), or (2) adding events at the second and/or third wave by the same group of respondents (W1 | W2 | W3) or by the same respondents (W1 → W2 → W3).

– *Past, Present and Future.* When determining the intra-individual stability of events for past and future separately, it has to be kept in mind that the individual past and future are changing constantly as time is passing by; for instance, the past at the third wave is five years longer than the past at the first wave, while the future is five years shorter. In order to compare the same periods over different waves, at each wave the past is defined as the period from the moment of birth till the age at the first wave while the future is defined as the period from the age at the third wave till the moment of expected death. The five years between the first and third wave will be treated as a special period and will be called 'Present'. This period is the near future at the first wave, partly near future and partly recent past at the second wave and recent past at the third wave. For instance, when a respondent is 24 years at the first wave, 26 years at the second wave and 29 years at the third wave, the past at each wave is the period of 0 till 24 years, the present is the period of 24 till 29 years and the future is the period of 29 years till death.

## 5.3   Results

### 5.3.1   W1 | W2 | W3: Content of events
#### Event distribution over categories
For each wave the percentage of events per category was determined for the total group and for the past and future of younger, middle-aged and older men and women (see CD : Table A5.1a and Table A5.2a for W1, Table A5.1b and Table 5.2b for W2, and Table A5.1c and Table 5.2c for W3). The distribution of events over categories for men and women, for young, middle-aged and older respondents and for

past and future are presented in Table A5.2a for the first wave, in Table A5.2b for the second wave and in Table A5.2c for the third wave (see CD).

A 2(Gender) x 3(Age Group) x 2(Event Time: Past and Future) x 9(Category) analysis of variance was conducted with repeated measures on the last two factors and with the logarithmic transformation [ln(number+1)] of the highly skewed event distribution per category as the dependent variable. Not surprisingly, the following effects were found in all three waves (in Chapter 4 results of only the first wave were reported):

– *Category.* There is a main effect of category. Overall, most events are mentioned in the categories Relations and School, respectively.

– *Category x Age group.* There is an interaction effect of Category and Age group; the older respondents are the fewer events they mention in the category School. The middle-age group mentions at each wave more events in the category Work than the young age group. Older adults mention fewer events in the category Growth than younger adults.

– *Category x Gender.* There is a trend that women report more events in the category Health.

– *Event time.* In all three waves more events per category are mentioned in the past than in the future.

– *Event time x Age group.* The older respondents are the more events per category they report in the past and the fewer events per category they report in the future.

– *Category x Event time.* In all three waves more events are mentioned in the past than in the future in the category Relations and more events are mentioned in the future than in the past in the categories Work and Death.

– *Category x Event time x Age group.* At each wave this interaction effect was found meaning, for instance, that the young age group mentions more events in the category Work in the future and the oldest age group in the past.

### Event distribution over subcategories
Next, per wave the percentage of events per subcategory was determined for the total group and for past and future of younger, middle-aged and older men and women (see CD: Table A5.3a, Table A5.3b and Table A5.3c for W1, W2 and W3, respectively). The following most noticeable differences between men and women of three age-groups were found in all three waves.

*Young* (M age W2 = 24.7 yrs)
–  Young men mention more Relations Others in the past than young women.
–  Young men expect more Problems Growth in the future than young women.
–  Young men less often mention Birth Child in the future than young women.

*Middle* (M age W2 = 45.4 yrs)
–  Middle-aged men more often mention Stopping Work in the future than middle-aged women.
–  Middle-aged men less often mention Physical Health in the future than middle-aged women.
–  Middle-aged men more often mention Death Parents in the future than middle-aged women.

*Older* (M age W2 = 68.7 yrs)
–  Older men more often mention Changing Work in the past than older women.
–  Older men less often mention Health Others in the past than older women.
–  Older men more often mention Death Parents in the past than older women.
–  Older men more often mention Death Partner in the future than older men.

In all three waves Physical Health, Commitment, Birth Child and Starting School belonged to the subcategories which were mentioned most frequently.

## 5.3.2 W1 | W2 | W3: Affect of events
The mean affect of events per subcategory was determined, both for the total group and for the past and future of young, middle-aged and older adults for three waves (see CD: Table A5.4a, Table A5.4b

and Table A5.4c for W1, W2 and W3, respectively) and for the past and future of young, middle-aged and older men and women, separately (see CD: Table A5.4d, Table A5.4e and Table A5.4f for W1, W2 and W3, respectively). Events were rated on a five point Likert scale, varying from very negative (–2), negative (–1) and neutral (0) to positive (+1) and very positive (+2) affect. The following most noticeable results were found in all three waves:

- Only Birth Grandchild has a mean rating of 1.0 or higher at all three waves.
- Events in the categories Health and Death are always rated (very) negative. Events that refer to Problems are also rated negative.
- Events which are rated neutral in all three waves are: Growth Others (e.g. children having problems), Moving, Birth Family (e.g. birth of sister) and Other Rest (e.g. financial problems).
- There are no differences between men and women concerning the affective rating of events that were found in each wave.
- The following patterns of differences between age groups were found:
- End Relations (e.g. divorce) is rated more negative by middle-aged adults than by older adults in the past.
- Individual Growth (e.g. personal development) is rated more positive by middle-aged adults than by young adults in the past.
- Growth Rest (e.g. happy childhood) is rated more positive by younger adults than by older adults.
- The younger respondents are the more negative they rate Death Parents.
- For the sake of completeness it has to be mentioned that Other Rest (e.g. getting a present) is rated more positive in the past by older adults than by younger adults. As this subcategory contains events which do not belong in any other subcategory no value can be attached to this result.
- Another interesting finding is that the youngest group looks forward to Birth Child in the future, while, in retrospect, the middle-aged group is less positive about this event.

## 5.3.3  W1 | W2 | W3: Patterns of events
### Categories per decade
Per wave the number of events per decade for young, middle-aged and older men and women was set on 100 percent. The main categories per decade were selected, meeting two criteria of inclusion: (a) 20 percent or more of all events per decade, and (b) at least two reported events (see CD: Table A5.5a for W1, Table A5.5b for W2 and Table A5.5c for W3). Table 5.1 shows the categories which appeared to be relatively important in a certain decade at all three waves for the total group and for men and women of three age groups. From table 5.1 can be read, for instance, that at all three waves 20 percent or more of all events mentioned in the period of 41 to 50 years by young men belong to the category Death. Table 5.1 shows the following patterns:

*Total*
- In general, childhood and adolescence are characterized by School, young adulthood by Relations, middle adulthood by Work, and older adulthood by Health and Death.

*Young* (M age W2 = 24.7 yrs)
- Young men expect events concerning Growth in the period of 31 to 40 years of age, while young women are focused on Birth in this period.
- Young men expect Death related events in the period from 41 to 50 years unlike young women.

*Middle* (M age W2 = 45.4 yrs)
- Middle-aged men mention Birth (of children) in their thirties but middle-aged women don't.
- Middle-aged men more often mention events in the category Work in the period of 41 to 50 years of age than middle-aged women.
- Middle-aged men expect Work-related events in the period of 61 to 70 years of age, while middle-aged women expect Health-related events in this period.

**Table 5.1** W1 | W2 | W3: Main categories per decade over three waves – at each wave each category contained 20 percent or more of all events mentioned in the particular decade and included 2 or more events – by the total group and by young (M age W2 = 24.7), middle-aged (M age W2 = 45.4) and older (M age W2 = 68.7) men and women.

| Decade | Young | | Middle | | Older | | Total | Decade |
|---|---|---|---|---|---|---|---|---|
| | Men | Women | Men | Women | Men | Women | | |
| I: 0–10 | – | – | – | School / Home | – | Other | School | I: 0–10 |
| II: 11–20 | School | School | School | School | School | Relations | School | II: 11–20 |
| III: 21–30 | – | – | Relations | Relations | Relations | Relations / Birth | Relations | III: 21–30 |
| IV: 31–40 | Growth | Birth | Birth | – | Work | Birth | – | IV: 31–40 |
| V: 41–50 | Death | – | Work | – | Work | – | Work | V: 41–50 |
| VI: 51–60 | – | – | Work | Work | Work | Health | Work | VI: 51–60 |
| VII: 61–70 | – | – | Work | Health | Work | – | Health | VII: 61–70 |
| VIII: 71–80 | – | – | – | – | Death | – | Health / Death | VIII: 71–80 |

Shaded area refers to the 'bump' period of life.

*Older* (M age W2 = 68.7 yrs)
– From adolescence older men hold more memories concerning School while older women have more memories concerning Relations.
– Older men do not mention Birth, while for older women Birth (of children) was a very important event in the period of 20 to 40 years of age.
– From the age of thirty the lives of older men have been dominated by Work which is not the case for older women. For older women, Health is important in the period of 50 to 60 years of age.

## Subcategories per decade

Per wave the number of events per decade for young, middle-aged and older men and women was set on 100 percent. The main subcategories per decade were selected, meeting two criteria of inclusion: (a) 10 percent or more of all events per decade, and (b) at least two reported events. The mean affect ratings of selected main subcategories per decade and subgroup were converted to a three point scale (negative, neutral, positive). Results per wave are presented in the enclosed CD (Table A5.6a, Table A5.6b and Table A5.6.c for W1, W3 and W3, respectively). In order to show stability and change in patterns over time, the most important subcategories per decade per wave with mean affective rating for respectively young men and women, middle-aged men and women and older men and women are presented below in Table 5.2a, Table 5.2b and Table 5.2c, respectively. Memories and expectations which are mentioned at all three waves by the same subgroup in the same decade are printed in italics. On the basis of the mean age per subgroup per wave it was determined which decades are considered past and which are considered future. For instance, the mean age of young men at the third wave is 28.0 years. In terms of decades the transition from past to future for this age group is closest to the transition from the third to the fourth decade, which is marked by a dotted line in Table 5.2a. It should be noted that because of the age range within the subgroups, the recent past and near future for all subgroups are confounded. For instance, the period from 21 to 30 years is for some respondents of the young age group (partly) future and for others partly past, dependent of the age on the time of measurement. Below, per subgroup the mean age at the second wave is mentioned. From Table 5.2a can be read, for instance, that 22 percent of all events young men mention from the first decade of life at the third wave belongs to the subcategory Moving.

*Young men-Past* (M age W2 = 24.9 yrs) (Table 5.2a)
– Relations Others, Moving and Starting School are recalled at each wave from childhood and adolescence.
– Physical Health is reported only at the first wave, as well from childhood as from adolescence.
– Starting School is mentioned in adolescence at each wave. Furthermore, young men remember different events from adolescence at each wave.

*Young men-Future* (M age W2 = 24.9 yrs) (Table 5.2a)
– Finishing School is expected at the first and second wave in the period of 21 to 30 years of age. At the third wave, when the period of 21 to 30 years of age has become past, this event is not reported anymore.
– Beginning Work is at each wave an important event which is expected to happen or has happened at the third decade.
– Commitment, Birth Child and Death Parents are also reported at all three waves.
– Stopping Work is expected from the second wave.
– Birth Child is mentioned at each wave in the fourth decade.
– In the period of 41 to 50 years of age Death Parents is expected at each wave.

*Young women-Past* (M age W2 =24.6 yrs) (Table 5.2a)
– Young women recall at each wave different events from childhood and adolescence.

*Young women-Future* (M age W2 =24.6 yrs) (Table 5.2a)
– Finishing School and Commitment are mentioned at the first and second wave in the future and at the third wave in the past.

**Table 5.2a** W1 | W2 | W3: Main subcategories (percents) with affect (+ = positive, 0 = neutral, – = negative) per decade for young men and women (mean age at W2 = 24.7 yrs) for three waves (italics refer to similar subcategories per decade at all three waves; dotted line refers to transition past – future)

| | Young | | | | | |
| --- | --- | --- | --- | --- | --- | --- |
| | **Men** | | | **Women** | | |
| Decade | Wave 1 (Mean age = 23.3) | Wave 2 (Mean age = 24.9) | Wave 3 (Mean age = 28.0) | Wave 1 (Mean age = 23.6) | Wave 2 (Mean age = 24.6) | Wave 3 (Mean age = 28.2) |
| I: 0–10 | *Relations Others (17)* –<br>*Physical Health (17)* –<br>*Growth Problems (17)* –<br>*Growth Rest (17)* +<br>*Moving (17)* – | *Relations Others (25)* –<br>Starting School (17) –<br>School Rest (17) –<br>*Moving (17)* +<br>– | *Relations Others (22)* –<br>*Moving (22)* +<br>Other Rest (14) –<br>– | Moving (42) +<br>Physical Health (17) –<br>Birth Family (17) 0 | Starting School (38) + | Physical Health (25) – |
| II: 11–20 | Physical Health (14) –<br>Moving (14) 0<br>Begin Relations (12) +<br>*Starting School (12)* 0 | Problems Growth (14) –<br>*Starting School (12)* 0 | *Starting School (17)* –<br>Moving (13) –<br>Leaving Home (13)<br>Problems Growth (10) – | School Rest (13) 0<br>Problems Growth (13) –<br>Starting School (10) + | Starting School (15) 0<br>Finishing School (11) –<br>Travel (15) + | Finishing School (13) +<br>Problems Growth (13) –<br>Travel (13) + |
| III: 21–30 | *Finishing School (23)* 0<br>*Beginning Work (20)* +<br>Commitment (10) 0<br>End Relations (10) – | Finishing School (16) 0<br>*Beginning Work (13)* + | End Relations (10) +<br>*Beginning Work (10)* + | *Finishing School (23)* +<br>*Commitment (17)* +<br>Mental Health (14) –<br>Birth Child (14) + | *Commitment (17)* +<br>*Finishing School (14)* +<br>Beginning Work (11) –<br>+ | Begin Relations (10) +<br>*Finishing School (14)* +<br>*Commitment (14)* + |
| IV: 31–40 | Commitment (17) +<br>Ind. Growth (17) +<br>Problems Growth (17) –<br>*Birth Child (17)* + | Commitment (21) +<br>*Birth Child (21)* + | *Birth Child (22)* +<br>Problems Growth (17) +<br>Death Parents (17) –<br>Beginning Work (11) 0<br>Ind. Growth (11) + | *Birth Child (43)* +<br>Finishing School (29) + | *Birth Child (29)* + | *Birth Child (50)* +<br>Death Parents (11) – |
| V: 41–50 | Birth Child (29) +<br>*Death Parents (29)* – | *Death Parents (60)* +<br>– | *Death Parents (50)* – | – | – | Death Parents (60) – |
| VI: 51–60 | Death Parents (43) – | Death Parents (75) – | Pr. Growth (50) – | Health Rest (40) –<br>Home Others (40) – | –<br>– | Death Parents (40) – |
| VII: 61–70 | – | Stopping Work (40) | *Stopping Work (44)* + | – | – | – |
| VIII: 71–80 | – | – | – | – | – | – |

**Table 5.2b** W1 | W2 | W3: Main subcategories (percents) with affect (+ = positive, 0 = neutral, − = negative) per decade for middle-aged men and women (mean age at W2 = 45.4 yrs) for three waves (shaded area refers to the 'bump' period of life; *italics* refer to similar subcategories per decade at all three waves; dotted line refers to transition past - future)

| | Men | | | Women | | |
|---|---|---|---|---|---|---|
| Decade | Wave 1 (Mean age = 41.7) | Wave 2 (Mean age = 43.6) | Wave 3 (Mean age = 47.3) | Wave 1 (Mean age = 44.9) | Wave 2 (Mean age = 47.2) | Wave 3 (Mean age = 49.8) |
| *I: 0–10* | Starting School (50) +<br>Moving (25) − | Growth Rest (25) +<br>Moving (25) − | Problems School (33) −<br>Growth Rest (33) + | *Moving (30)* +<br>Starting School (20) −<br>Problems School (20) − | *Moving (44)* + | *Moving (30)* 0<br>Relation Others (22) − |
| *II: 11–20* | *Starting School (35)* +<br>Beginning Work (12) + | *Starting School (27)* +<br>Problems Growth (18) −<br>Ind. Growth (14) + | *Starting School (19)* 0<br>Problems School (13) −<br>Problems Growth (13) +<br>Beginning Work (13) + | Begin Relations (16) +<br>Ind. Growth (13) + | Leaving Home (17) 0<br>Starting School (17) +<br>Finishing School (10) + | Starting School (22) +<br>School Rest (11) −<br>Moving (11) −<br>Relations End (11) − |
| *III: 21–30* | Commitment (19) +<br>*Begin Relations (15)* +<br>Birth Child (15) + | *Begin Relations (17)* + | Commitment (18) +<br>Birth Child (18) +<br>*Begin Relations (12)* +<br>End Relations (12) − | *Commitment (27)* +<br>End Relations (12) − | *Commitment (22)* +<br>Birth Child (19) +<br>Starting School (11) + | Birth Child (27) +<br>*Commitment (20)* + |
| *IV: 31–40* | *Birth Child (24)* 0<br>Problems Work (18) −<br>Commitment (12) +<br>Changing Work (12) −<br>Death Parents (12) − | *Birth Child (24)* +<br>Problems Work (14) − | *Birth Child (29)* +<br>Problems Work (13) −<br>Death Parents (13) − | *End Relations (14)* −<br>Birth Child (14) + | Growth Rest (18) −<br>End Relations (12) +<br>Death Parents (12) | Starting School (10) 0<br>Finishing School (10) +<br>Growth Rest (10) +<br>*End Relations (10)* −<br>Physical Health (10) +<br>Birth Child (10) −<br>Stop Working (10) − |
| *V: 41–50* | Changing Work (26) +<br>Individual Growth (21) +<br>Death Parents (16) −<br>End Relations (11) −<br>Physical Health (11) − | Growth Rest (22) +<br>Problems Work (17) −<br>Changing Work (11) +<br>Birth Child (11) + | Problems Work (25) +<br>Mental Health (13) − | Changing Work (13) +<br>Health Rest (13) − | Finishing School (14) +<br>Changing Work (14) − | Pr. Relations (13) −<br>Physical Health (13) 0<br>Mental Health (13) −<br>Individual Growth (13) + |
| *VI: 51–60* | *Stopping Work (25)* 0 | *Stopping Work (47)* 0<br>Death Parents (20) −<br>Physical Health (13) − | *Stopping Work (29)* 0<br>Death Parents (21) − | Growth Others (30) +<br>Stopping Work (20) 0 | Stopping Work (30) +<br>Death Rest (20) − | Birth Grandchild (18) +<br>Physical Health (14) − |
| *VII: 61–70* | *Stopping Work (50)* 0 | *Stopping Work (40)* 0 | *Stopping Work (50)* + | *Physical Health (33)* −<br>Stopping Work (13) +<br>Ind. Growth (13) + | *Physical Health (17)* −<br>Ind. Growth (17) +<br>Birth Grandchild (17) +<br>Death Rest (17) − | Stopping Work (33) 0<br>Health Rest (25) −<br>*Physical Health (17)* − |
| *VIII: 71–80* | − | − | − | Death Partner (50) − | *Physical Health (50)* − | − |

**Middle**

- Birth Child is expected at each wave in the future. However, at the first wave this event is expected in the period of 21 to 40 years of age and at the second and third wave in the period of 31 to 40 years of age.
- It is significant that young women expect Death Parents at the third wave in the future but that they do not mention this event at the first and second wave in contrast to young men who mention this event at each wave.

*Middle-aged men-Past* (M age W2 =43.6 yrs) (Table 5.2b)
- From childhood middle-aged men recall at each wave different events.
- From adolescence Starting School is remembered at each wave. For the rest, middle-aged men remember at each wave different events from this period.
- From young adulthood they remember events concerning Begin Relations (e.g. falling in love).
- Birth Child and Problems Work are mentioned in the period of 31 to 40 years of age at each wave.

*Middle-aged men-Future* (M age W2 =43.6 yrs) (Table 5.2b)
- At the first and second wave middle-aged men expect Changing Work in the future. At the third wave this event is not mentioned anymore.
- In the period of 41 to 50 different events are expected / remembered at each wave.
- After the age of 50 Stopping Work is an important issue at all three waves.

*Middle-aged women-Past* (M age W2 = 47.2 yrs) (Table 5.2b)
- From childhood middle-aged women remember at all three waves Moving, which was a positive event for them.
- From adolescence they report different memories at each wave.
- From young adulthood they mention consistently Commitment.
- End Relations is mentioned consistently in the period of 31 to 40 years of age. At the third wave middle-aged women report very different memories from the period of 31 to 40 years of age.

*Middle-aged women-Future* (M age W2 = 47.2 yrs) (Table 5.2b)
- From the period of 41 to 50 years of age middle-aged women also expect/remember different events. At the first and second wave they mention Changing Work but at the third wave this event is not mentioned anymore.
- In contrast to middle-aged men Problems Work are not reported by middle-aged women.
- Events concerning Physical Health are expected in the period of 61 to 70 years of age at all three waves.

*Older men-Past* (M age W2 = 69.2 yrs) (Table 5.2c)
- From childhood and adolescence Death Parents is recalled at each wave.
- War and Starting School are reported from adolescence at the first and third wave.
- From young adulthood older men recall consistently Commitment.
- It is noticeable that older men do not recall Birth Child at the first wave but they do at the second and third wave.
- From middle adulthood older men recall Changing Work at each wave and from the age of 60 they mention Stopping Work. This event is rated negative at the first wave and positive at the second and third wave.

*Older men-Future* (M age W2 = 69.2 yrs) (Table 5.2c)
- In the future older men fear at all three waves Death Partner.

*Older women-Past* (M age W2 = 68.5 yrs) (Table 5.2c)
- Older women hold strong memories concerning the War from childhood and adolescence.
- Relations Others (e.g., divorce parents) and Starting School are remembered from childhood at two waves.
- From young adulthood older women recall Commitment (marriage) and Birth Child at each wave.
- From the fourth decade they remember Birth Child and Moving at each wave.

**Table 5.2c** W1 | W2 | W3: Main subcategories (percents) with affect (+ = positive, 0 = neutral, – = negative) per decade of older men and women (mean age at W2 = 68.7 yrs) for three waves (W = Wave; shaded area refers to the 'bump' period of life; italics refer to similar subcategories per decade at all three waves; dotted line refers to transition past - future)

| | Older | | | | | |
|---|---|---|---|---|---|---|
| | **Men** | | | **Women** | | |
| **Decade** | Wave 1 (Mean age = 69.0) | Wave 2 (Mean age = 69.2) | Wave 3 (Mean age = 72.3) | Wave 1 (Mean age = 66.2) | Wave 2 (Mean age = 68.5) | Wave 3 (Mean age = 69.1) |
| I: 0–10 | Other Rest (25) + | Death Parents (40) – | School Rest (29) 0; Death Parents (29) – | Relations Others (15) –; Starting School (15) +; Birth Family (15) 0 | *War (27)* –; Relations Others (18) –; Physical Health (18) +; 0 | Starting School (25) +; *War (25)* – |
| II: 11–20 | *War (29)* –; Starting School (14) +; Finishing School (14) +; Death Parents (14) – | – | Starting School (22) +; *War (22)* + | *War (22)* –; Beginning Work (17) + | *War (23)* –; Begin Relations (14) +; Commitment (14) + | *War (18)* – |
| III: 21–30 | *Commitment (25)* +; *Physical Health (17)* –; *Finishing School (13)* +; *War (13)* 0 | *Commitment (31)* +; *Birth Child (23)* –; *Beginning Work (15)* +; 0 | *Commitment (33)* +; *Finishing School (13)* +; *Birth Child (13)* + | *Birth Child (31)* +; *Commitment (23)* +; *War (12)* – | *Birth Child (32)* +; *Commitment (26)* +; – | *Birth Child (53)* +; *Commitment (13)* + |
| IV: 31–40 | *Changing Work (20)* + | *Changing Work (33)* + | Commitment (40) +; *Changing Work (40)* + | Birth Child (20) +; Moving (12) + | Birth Child (21) +; Moving (14) +; Health Others (14) – | Birth Child (23) +; Relations End (15) 0; Mental Health (15) –; Moving (15) + |
| V: 41–50 | Changing Work (44) + | Changing Work (67) + | – | Problems Relation (22) –; Health Others (22) – | Health Others (33) – | Health Others (20) – |
| VI: 51–60 | Changing Work (33) – | Changing Work (43) – | – | Health Others (22) – | Health Others (24) –; Problems Work (18) –; Death Partner (12) – | |
| VII: 61–70 | *Stopping Work (33)* – | *Stopping Work (25)* –; *Death Family (25)* | *Stopping Work (25)* +; *Death Parents (25)* – | *Health Others (22)* –; *Physical Health (17)* –; *Birth Grandchild (17)* +; *Stopping Work (11)* 0 | *Health Others (23)* –; *Birth Grandchild (15)* +; 0 | Other Rest (25) +; *Health Others (19)* –; Relations Rest (13) +; Death Family (13) – |
| VIII: 71–80 | Physical Health (44) –; *Death Partner (33)* – | *Death Partner (50)* – | *Death Partner (50)* – | Physical Health (67) 0 | – | Physical Health (18) –; Health Rest (18) –; Other Rest (18) + |
| IX: 81–90 | – | | – | – | Physical Health (50) – | – |

- In middle and older adulthood Health Others is remembered consistently. Older women mention consistently more different events in this period of life than older men do. Older men mention consistently only events concerning Work.

*Older women-Future* (M age W2 = 68.5 yrs) (Table 5.2c)
- Problems with Physical Health are feared at each wave in the future by older women.

*Overall, it is notable that:*
- Men mention more often Relations Others (e.g., divorce parents), Death Parents and Death Partner in their life story than women do.
- From the second part of the bump period many positive events are recalled such as: Begin Relations, Commitment, Birth Child, Finishing School and Beginning Work.
- For men of all age groups Work is more important than for women.
- Women of the middle and older age group expect consistently events within the subcategory Physical Health in the future contrary to men of these age groups.
- Women report more different types of events over their lifespan compared to men, especially as they get older.

*Patterns which turned out to be not stable over a period of five years are:*
- The pattern that young women are about one decade ahead of young men concerning Commitment and Birth Child is not found at the second and third wave.
- The pattern that women look further ahead into the future than men do is not found in the second and third wave. Evidently, the difference in development between men and women diminishes when growing older.

## 5.3.4 W1 → W2 → W3: Number of stable events

In order to determine the intra-individual stability and change in the content of autobiographical memories over a period of two and five years, longitudinal data of 74 respondents who took part in all three waves were analyzed. The content of life events at the first wave was taken as baseline.

### Percentage of stable events

First, the number of events for the Total life and for Past (birth – age at first wave), Present (age at first wave – age at third wave) and Future (age at third wave – death), separately, was determined per respondent for the first wave. Second, it was determined how many of these events were also mentioned at the second wave, at the third wave and at both the second and third wave by the same respondent in the same period (Total life, Past, Present and Future). The number of events at the first wave was set at 100 percent and the number of stable events was expressed as a percentage of the number of events at the first wave in order to control for differences in event number. The results are shown in Table 5.3. From Table 5.3 can be read, for instance, that overall 51 percent of the subcategories that are recalled at the first wave are also recalled at the second wave and that 35 percent of the subcategories that are recalled at the first wave are recalled at both the second and third wave.

*Total life: Category*

In order to determine the effect of gender, age group and wave on the percentage of similar categories over the total life a 2(Gender) x 3(Age Group) x 3(Wave) analysis of variance was conducted with repeated measures on the last factor and with the percentage of similar categories over the total life as dependent variable. There was only a main effect of wave for categories, $F(2, 67) = 128.813$, $p < .001$. Paired sample t-tests showed that there was a statistically significant difference in the mean percentage of similar categories between the first and second wave and between the first and third wave ($p < .001$), but not between the second and third wave. Next, a one-way analysis of variance was conducted to determine the effect of age and gender on the mean percentage of similar categories for the total life which were reported in all three waves. No effect of age and gender was found.

**Table 5.3**  W1→W2→W3: Percentage of categories and subcategories mentioned at the first wave that are also mentioned at the second wave (W1→W2), at the third wave (W1→W3) and at both the second and third waves (W1→W2→W3) for the Total life and for Past (birth – age W1), Present (age W1 – age W3) and Future (age W3 – death).

|          | W1 | | W1→W2 | | W1→W3 | | W1→W2→W3 | |
|----------|----------|-------------|----------|-------------|----------|-------------|----------|-------------|
|          | Category | Subcategory | Category | Subcategory | Category | Subcategory | Category | Subcategory |
| Total    | 100      | 100         | 65       | 51          | 64       | 48          | 52       | 35          |
| Past     | 100      | 100         | 62       | 51          | 56       | 46          | 44       | 35          |
| Present  | 100      | 100         | 50       | 43          | 39       | 24          | 26       | 20          |
| Future   | 100      | 100         | 40       | 34          | 49       | 36          | 29       | 20          |

*Total life: Subcategory*

The above mentioned analysis was repeated with the percentage of similar subcategories over the total lifespan as dependent variable. There was, again, a main effect of wave, $F (2, 67) = 308.629$, $p < .001$. Paired sample t-tests showed that the mean percentage of similar subcategories was significantly different between the first and second wave, and between the first and third wave ($p < .001$), but not between the second and third wave. There was no effect of age or gender on the mean percentage of stable subcategories which were mentioned in all three waves for the total life.

*Past: Category*

There was an effect of wave – $F (2, 67) = 114.654$, $p < .001$ – on the percentage of similar categories in the past. Paired sample t-tests showed that the difference in the percentage of similar categories was significant between the first and second wave, between the second and third wave ($p < .001$) and between the first and third wave ($p < .01$). There was no effect of age and gender on the percentage of similar categories mentioned in all three waves in the past.

*Past: Subcategory*

For subcategories there was also an effect of wave, $F (2, 67) = 165.519$, $p < .001$. Paired sample t-tests showed that the decrease in similar subcategories was significant between the first and second wave, between the first and third wave ($p < .001$) and between the second and third wave ($p < .05$). There was no effect of age and gender on the mean percentage of subcategories that were mentioned in all three waves in the past.

*Present*

Because many respondents do not mention events in the present in all three waves it is not possible to conduct statistical tests. Table 5.3 shows that the stability of categories and subcategories is lower in the present than in the past. Table 5.3 also gives the impression that the percentage of stable categories and subcategories decreases between the second and third wave.

*Future: Category*

For similar categories in the future there was an effect of wave, $F (2, 52) = 59.732$, $p < .001$. Paired sample t-tests showed that the difference in similar subcategories was statistically significant between the first and second wave and between the first and third wave ($p < .001$) but not between the second and third wave. Table 5.3 shows that the percentage similar categories is even a bit higher, although not statistically significant, after five years than after two years. There was no effect of age and gender on the mean percentage of categories that were mentioned in all three waves in the future.

*Future: Subcategory*

For similar subcategories in the future there was an effect of wave, $F (2, 52) = 94.455$, $p < .001$. Paired sample t-tests showed that the decrease in similar subcategories was significant between the first and second wave and between the first and third wave ($p < .001$) but not between the second and third wave. Table 5.3 shows that the percentage of stable subcategories is also somewhat higher after five years than after two years. There was no effect of age and gender for subcategories that were mentioned in all three waves in the future.

*Past and Future*

Over three waves a greater percentage of categories and subcategories turned out to be stable in the past than in the future (p < .01).

*Past and Present*

Paired t-tests showed that over three waves a greater percentage of events (categories and subcategories) is stable in the past than in the present (p < .05).

*Present and Future*

Over three waves there was no statistically significant difference between the stability of events (categories and subcategories) in the present and future.

*In sum, concerning the percentage of stable events it can be stated that:*
- Overall, over a period of five years about half of the categories and about one third of the subcategories is rather fixed in the life story.
- The decrease of stable memories and expectations is significant between the first and second wave but in most cases not between the second and third wave.
- The past is more stable than the present and the future.

## Distribution of stable events over the lifespan

In order to determine the distribution of stable events over the lifespan, first, the number of similar events (categories and subcategories) across three waves per decade was determined for men and women of three age groups. Second, the number of similar events over the whole lifespan was set at 100 percent per subgroup and the number of similar events per decade was transformed into a percentage of the total number of similar events. Figure 5.1 shows the distribution of similar categories and similar subcategories, i.e., categories and subcategories which are mentioned in all three waves for respectively young, middle-aged and older men and women over the lifespan. The mean age per age group at the second wave is indicated by a vertical line.

*Young-Category* (M age W2 = 24.7 yrs)
- For the youngest group there is a strong recency effect for similar categories and also a proximity effect.
- The proximity effect is somewhat stronger for young women than for young men.
- Besides, there are no events within the same category that are expected by young adults at all three waves in the same decade after the age of 30.

*Young-Subcategory* (M age W2 = 24.7 yrs)
- Young men recall many similar events from the period of 11 to 20 years of age in all three waves.
- For young women there is a strong recency/proximity effect; events mentioned in the period of 11 to 30 years are very stable.
- Young men report more stable memories from childhood than young women do.

*Middle-Category* (M age W2 = 45.4 yrs)
- For the middle-aged group there is roughly a bump and a recency effect for categories. – It is noticeable that middle-aged men do not recall similar events from childhood at all three waves in contrast to middle-aged women
- Middle-aged men recall more stable memories from the period of 31 to 40 years of age than middle-aged women do.

*Middle-Subcategory* (M age W2 = 45.4 yrs)
- For middle-aged women a bump can be discerned concerning stable memories, which is situated in the third decade.
- Middle-aged men hold most stable memories from the period of 31 to 40 years of age; bump and recency effect are confounded in this period.
- There is a very small bump around the age of 65 years for middle-aged women.

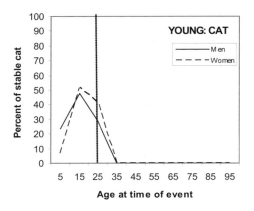

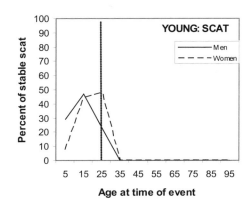

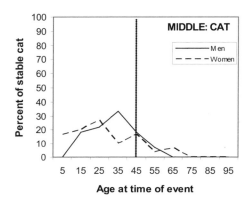

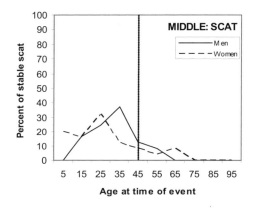

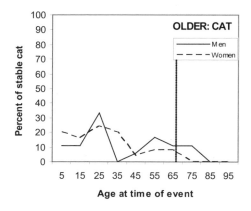

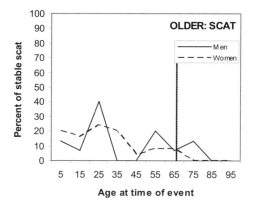

**Figure 5.1** W1→W2→W3: Distribution of stable categories (CAT) (left panel) and stable subcategories (SCAT) (right panel) for young (top panel; M age W2 = 24.7), middle-aged (middle panel; M age W2 = 45.4) and older men and women (bottum panel; M age W2 = 67.4) over the lifespan (vertical line indicates transition from past events to future events for the W2).

- Middle-aged women have more stable memories from childhood than middle-aged men.

*Older-Category* (M age W2 = 67.4 yrs)
- For the oldest group there is a clear bump.
- The bump lasts longer for older women than for older men (older men: peak from 21 to 30 years of age, older women: till 40 years of age).
- There is a small recency effect for older women and a recency and proximity effect for older men.
- The percentage of similar categories at childhood is higher than would be expected on the basis of the distribution of categories over the lifespan in general, especially for older women.

*Older-Subcategory* (M age W2 = 67.4 yrs)
- For older men there is a bump concerning stable memories in the period of 21 to 30 years of age and for older women in the period of 10 to 40 years.
- There is a recency effect for older women while older men recall relative many similar memories from the period of 50 to 60 years of age and expect most similar events in the period of 70 to 80 years of age.

*Overall comparison*
- Comparing the pattern of the distribution of events in general (see Chapter 2) to the pattern of the distribution of stable events over the lifespan it is noticeable that the percentage of stable events in childhood is higher than would be expected on the basis of the distribution of events in general.

## Stability per decade

The total number of events at each decade at the first wave was put at 100 percent for men and women of three age groups. For all six subgroups it was determined which percentage of these events was recalled at both the second and third wave. Figure 5.2 shows the percentage of stable categories and of stable subcategories per decade for respectively young, middle-aged and older men and women. The mean age per age group at the second wave is indicated by a vertical line.

*Young-Categories* (M age W2 = 24.7 yrs)
- For young men stability is highest in childhood and decreases then.
- For young women stability is highest in the period of 11 to 30 years of age.

*Young-Subcategories* (M age W2 = 24.7 yrs)
- Young men hold more stable memories from childhood than young women.
- Young women hold many stable memories/expectations from the period of 20 to 30 years of age.
- Expectations after the age of 30 are very unstable and are different at each wave for young adults.

*Middle-Categories* (M age W2 = 45.4 yrs)
- Middle-aged women have more stable memories from childhood than middle-aged men who have more stable memories from the period of 31 to 40 years of age.

*Middle-Subcategories* (M age W2 = 45.4 yrs)
- Middle-aged women relatively hold the most stable memories from childhood while middle-aged men do not have stable memories from this period.
- Middle-aged men have most stable memories from the period of 31 to 40 years of age and expect similar events at all three waves in the period of 51 to 60 years of age.

*Older-Categories* (M age W2 = 67.4 yrs)
- Older women have very stable memories from childhood.
- Older men as well as older women hold relatively stable memories from the period of 20 to 30 years of age.
- The period of 50 to 60 is rather stable for older women. For older men the period of 50 to 80 is rather stable.

*Older-Subcategories* (M age W2 = 67.4 yrs)
- Older women have very stable memories from childhood.
- From the period of 41 to 50 both older men and women hold least stable memories.
- From the period of 21 to 30 (bump) both men and women hold rather stable memories.

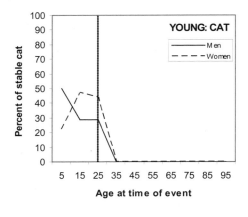

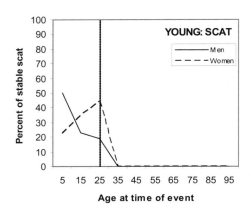

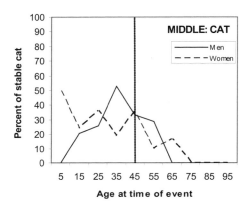

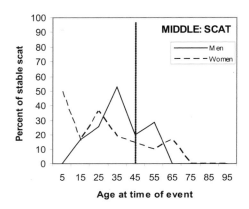

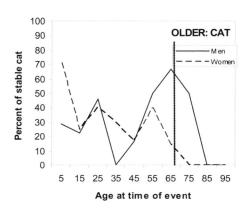

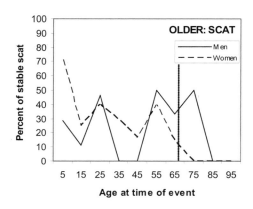

**Figure 5.2** W1→W2→W3: Percent of stable categories (CAT) (left panel) and stable subcategories (SCAT) (right panel) per decade for young (top panel; M age W2 = 24.7), middle-aged (middle panel; M age W2 = 45.4) and older men and women (bottum panel; M age W2 = 67.4) (vertical line indicates transition from past events to future events for W2).

- After the age of fifty memories/expectations are rather stable for both men and women.

*In sum, concerning the distribution of stable events it can be stated that:*
- The distribution of stable events over the lifespan for three age groups follows roughly about the same patterns as the distribution of events over the lifespan in general.
- Young men hold more stable memories from childhood than young women, while for the middle and older age group it is the other way around.
- Young women report similar events at each wave from the present.
- Young adults have a very unstable view of the future.
- Middle-aged men report relatively many similar events from the period of 30 to 40 years of age.
- Older adults hold rather stable memories from the period of 20 to 30 years of age.
- Older men have relatively rather stable memories from the recent past and stable expectations for the near future.

### 5.3.5 W1 → W2 → W3: Affect of stable events

#### Positive and negative stable events

In Chapter 3 it was found that at the first wave respondents, in general, mentioned as many positive events as negative events over their whole lifespan and over past and future separately. Is there a difference in the stability of positive and negative events? In order to answer this question, first, the number of positive and of negative events for the Total life and for Past (birth – age W1), Present (age W1 – age W3) and Future (age W3 – death), separately, was determined per respondent for the first wave and was set at 100 percent. Second, it was determined what percentage of these events was also mentioned at the second wave, at the third wave and at both the second and third wave by the same respondent in the same period. The results are shown in Table 5.4 for the total group and for men and women separately. From Table 5.4 can be read, for instance, that of all positive events men report from their past, 40 percent is also reported at the second wave, 28 percent is mentioned at the third wave and 17 percent is mentioned at all three waves.

In order to determine the effect of wave, gender and age on the percentage of stable positive and stable negative events a 2(Gender) x 3(Age Group) x 3(Wave: W1, W1 → W2, W1 → W3) x 2(Affect: positive and negative) analysis of variance was conducted for the total life and for the past with repeated measures on the last two variables and with the percentage of stable positive and stable negative events as the dependent variable.

*Total life*

– *Affect.* For the total life there is a main effect of affect, $F (1, 65) = 6.450$, $p < .05$; the percentage of stable negative events is higher than the percentage of stable positive events.

– *Affect x Gender.* There is an interaction effect of affect and gender, $F (1, 65) = 7.842$, $p < .01$; negative events turn out to be more stable for men than for women while positive events are more stable for women than for men. Paired t-tests showed that for men negative events are more stable

**Table 5.4**  W1→W2→W3: Percentage of positive (+) and negative (–) events that are recalled at the second wave (W1→W2), at the third wave (W1→W3) and at all three waves (W1→W2→W3) by the total group and by men and women separately for the Total life and for Past (birth – age W1), Present (age W1 – age W3) and Future (age W3 – death).

| | W1→W2 | | | | | | W1→W3 | | | | | | W1→W2→W3 | | | | | |
|---|---|---|---|---|---|---|---|---|---|---|---|---|---|---|---|---|---|---|
| | Total | | Men | | Women | | Total | | Men | | Women | | Total | | Men | | Women | |
| | + | – | + | – | + | – | + | – | + | – | + | – | + | – | + | – | + | – |
| Total life | 44 | 55 | 36 | 60 | 52 | 50 | 41 | 52 | 33 | 60 | 48 | 45 | 28 | 37 | 19 | 43 | 37 | 32 |
| Past | 45 | 59 | 40 | 59 | 49 | 60 | 36 | 56 | 28 | 62 | 44 | 50 | 26 | 46 | 17 | 51 | 34 | 42 |
| Present | 40 | 45 | 24 | 57 | 53 | 25 | 25 | 27 | 18 | 29 | 31 | 25 | 22 | 18 | 18 | 29 | 25 | 0 |
| Future | 43 | 26 | 30 | 29 | 58 | 23 | 45 | 30 | 40 | 38 | 51 | 23 | 31 | 8 | 19 | 11 | 43 | 5 |

than positive events while for women positive and negative events are about equally stable (p < .05).

 – *Wave.* There was an effect of wave, F (2, 64) = 293.130, p < .001. Paired t-tests showed that the percentage of stable positive and stable negative events was different between the first and second wave, the first and third wave but not between the second and third wave.

 – *Affect x Wave.* There was an interaction effect of affect and wave, F (2, 64) = 3.240, p < .05. The decrease in stability over three waves is higher for positive than for negative events.

 – *Affect x Wave x Gender.* There was an interaction effect of affect, wave and gender, F (2, 64) = 3.861, p < .05. For stable positive events the decrease over waves is higher for men than for women, while for stable negative events the decrease is higher for women, i.e., negative events are more stable for men while positive events are more stable for women.

In order to determine the effect of gender and age group on the percentage of stable positive and stable negative events over three waves a 2(Gender) x 3(Age Group) x 2(Affect: positive and negative) analysis of variance was conducted with repeated measures on the last variable and with the percentage of stable positive and stable negative events as the dependent variable.

- There was an effect of gender on the percentage of positive and negative events that was mentioned at all three waves, F (2, 64) = 4.508, p < .05.
- Over three waves the stability of negative events is higher for men than for women, while the stability of positive events is higher for women than for men.
- Paired t-tests showed that for men negative events are more stable than positive events while for women positive and negative events are about equally stable.

*In sum, for the total life it was found that:*
- Negative events are more stable in the life story of men than of women while positive events are more stable in the life story of women than of men.
- Negative events are more stable than positive events in the life story of men while negative and positive events are about equally stable in the life story of women.
- The percentage of stable positive and negative events remains about the same between the second and third wave.
- There is no effect of age on the stability of positive or negative events.

*Past*

 – *Affect.* For the past there is a main effect of affect, F (1, 59) = 8.201, p < .01; the percentage of stable negative events in the past is higher than the percentage of stable positive events.

 – *Wave.* There was an effect of wave, F (2, 58) = 176.274, p < .001. Paired t-tests showed that the percentage of similar positive and negative events was different between the first and second wave and between the first and third wave. The percentage of stable positive events was also different between the second and third wave meaning that there is a significant decrease of stable positive events between the second and third wave while the percentage of stable negative events remains the same.

 – *Affect x Wave.* There was an interaction effect of affect and wave, F (2, 58) = 4.107, p < .05. The decrease in stable past events is higher for positive than for negative events.

- There was no statistically significant effect of age or gender on the percentage of stable positive and negative events mentioned in the past at all three waves.

*In sum, for the past it was found that:*
- Negative events are more stable than positive events.
- There is no statistical significant effect of age or gender on the stability of negative and positive events.
- Between the second and third wave the percentage of stable positive events decreases significantly in contrast to the percentage of negative events.

*Present*

Because of small numbers it was not possible to conduct statistical analyses to determine the effect of gender, age and wave on the percentage of stable positive and stable negative events in the present. Descriptive statistics (see Table 5.4) suggest that:

– Negative events are more stable in the present for men, while positive events are more stable for women.

*Future*

For the future it also was not meaningful to conduct statistical analyses because of small numbers. Results presented in Table 5.4 suggest that:

– Positive events are more stable in the future life story of women than of men.
– For men positive and negative events are about equally stable in the future, while for women positive events are more stable in the future than negative events.

*In sum, the data suggest that:*

*In the present*:

– Negative events are more stable for men, while positive events are more stable for women.

*In the future:*

– Positive events are more stable for women than for men.
– For men, positive and negative events are about equally stable.
– For women positive events are more stable than negative events.

## Stability of affect per decade

The total number of positive and of negative events at each decade at the first wave was put at 100 percent for men and women of three age groups. For all six subgroups it was determined which percentage of these events was recalled at both the second and the third wave. In Figure 5.3 the percentage of positive and negative events which are recalled at both the second and third wave are presented per decade for young men and women, middle-aged men and women and older men and women. From Figure 5.3 can be read, for example, that about 60 percent of all negative events which are remembered from childhood by young men at the first wave are also recalled at the second and third wave. The mean age at the second wave per age group is indicated by a vertical line.

*Young* (M age W2 = 24.7 yrs)

– *Young men* recall more negative than positive memories from childhood and these negative memories turn out to be far more stable than positive memories. From adolescence young men recall about the same number of positive and negative events. Negative events however, are more stable. There are only few stable positive memories in the life story of young men and these memories are reported from the period of 11 to 30 years of age.

– *Young women* recall as many positive as negative events from childhood at the first wave but negative events turn out to be far more stable than positive events from this period. From adolescence young women also recall as many positive as negative events and these events are about equally stable. For the period of 21 to 30 years of age young women report far more positive than negative events and these positive events turn out to be rather stable.

*Middle* (M age W2 = 45.4 yrs)

– *Middle-aged men* recall at the first wave far more positive than negative events from the period of 11 to 30 years of age but negative events turn out to be far more stable. For the period of 51 to 60 positive events are more stable than negative events.

– *Middle-aged women* hold relatively many stable positive and negative memories from childhood. Middle-aged women recall about the same number of positive and negative events from the period of 11 to 30 years of age; for adolescence positive and negative memories are equally stable, while for the period of 21 to 30 years of age negative memories are more stable than positive memories. Positive events for the period of 51 to 70 years of age are more stable than negative events for this period.

*Older* (M age W2 = 67.4 yrs)

– *Older men* hold about as many positive as negative memories from childhood and adolescence at the first wave but negative events are far more stable. From the period of 21 to 30 years of age older men have far more positive than negative memories and these positive memories are rather stable. From the period of 51 to 60 years of age they recall more negative than positive events. Positive events

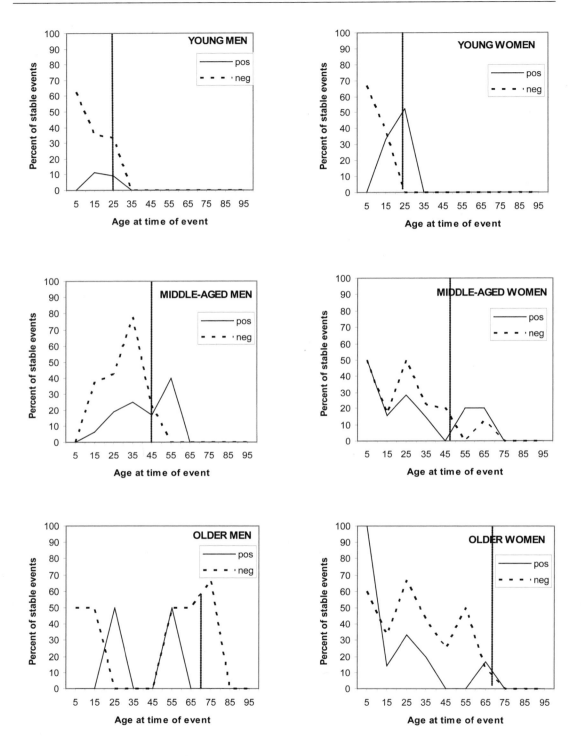

**Figure 5.3** W1→W2→W3: Percent of stable positive and stable negative events per decade for young (top panel; M age W2 = 24.7), middle-aged (middle panel: M age W2 = 45.4) and older (bottum panel; M age W2 = 67.4) men (left panel) and women (right panel) (vertical line indicates the transition from past events to future events for W2).

from this period are more stable than positive events from other periods of life (except period of 21 to 30 years of age). From the period of 51 till 80 negative events are also rather fixed in the life story.

   – *Older women* remember more negative than positive events from childhood but positive events are more fixed in the life story than negative events from this period. From the period of 21 to 40 years of age older women have more positive than negative memories but negative events are more stable.

   *It sum, it can be stated that:*
- Negative memories from childhood are very stable for the young and old age group and for middle-aged women; for middle-aged and older women positive memories from childhood are also very stable.
- All subgroups have positive stable memories/expectations from part of the bump period (21 to 30 years of age) but negative memories/expectations from this period are relatively more stable, except for young women and older men.

## 5.3.6 W1 → W2 → W3: Content of stable events
### Stable events in past-present-future
In order to determine which type of events is stable and is reported each time respondents tell their life story, it was determined which percentage of each (sub)category mentioned at the first wave was also mentioned at both the second and third wave (= stability) in Past (birth – age W1), Present (age W1 – age W3), Future (age W3 – death) and over the total life course by the same young, middle-aged and older men and women. In the enclosed CD the stability of (sub)categories over three waves for the total group and for men and women of three age groups is presented. In these tables the distribution of events over (sub)categories (= frequency) at the first wave is also presented (see Table A5.7a for the total group and the young age group, A5.7b for the middle-aged group and Table 5.7c for the older age group). In Table 5.5 an overview is given of the most stable categories and subcategories for the total group over the whole life course with frequency and stability. A (sub)category is considered to be stable when 50 percent or more of the events within the (sub)category which are mentioned at the first wave are also mentioned at both the second and third wave. This criterion is empirically based; it turned out that using this criterion it made some sense to construct the core life story of different subgroups. From Table 5.5 can be read, for instance, that 2.1 percent of all events mentioned at the first wave belong to the subcategory End Relations and 54 percent of these events are also recalled at the second and the third wave. Relations turned out to be the most stable category, while the most stable subcategories were Relations Others and Travel. Events within the categories Growth and Home turned out to be least stable while events in the subcategories Rest and Other were never mentioned at all three waves.

**Table 5.5**  W1→W2→W3: Overview of stable and unstable categories and subcategories for the total group over the total lifespan (past and future) with Frequency (f: percentage of events mentioned within (sub)category at W1) and Stability (Stab.: percent of events within (sub)category which are recalled at both W2 and W3).

| Category | | | | | | Subcategory | | | | | |
| --- | --- | --- | --- | --- | --- | --- | --- | --- | --- | --- | --- |
| Stable | | | Unstable | | | Stable | | | Unstable | | |
| Cat | f | Stab. | Cat | f | Stab. | Scat | f | Stab. | Scat | f | Stab. |
| Relations | 17.4 | 64 | Growth | 11.1 | 43 | Relations Others | 2.5 | 69 | Relations Rest | 0.2 | 0 |
| School | 15.6 | 55 | Home | 8.8 | 43 | Travel | 1.1 | 67 | School Others | 0.4 | 0 |
| Death | 9.4 | 55 | | | | Problems Work | 1.7 | 56 | Work Others | 0.8 | 0 |
| Other | 4.2 | 55 | | | | Death Family | 1.7 | 56 | Health Rest | 1.7 | 0 |
| | | | | | | End Relations | 2.1 | 54 | Growth Others | 0.8 | 0 |
| | | | | | | Birth Family | 0.4 | 50 | Home Rest | 0.2 | 0 |
| | | | | | | War | 1.5 | 50 | | | |
| | | | | | | Other Rest | 1.5 | 50 | | | |

**Table 5.6** W1→W2→W3: Stable subcategories (≥ 50% of subcategories mentioned at W2 and W3; Stab = Stability) with frequency ($f$) in Past (birth-age W1), Present (age W1- age W3) and Future (age W3-death) for young men and women (M age W2 = 24.7 yrs), middle-aged men and women (M age W2 = 45.4 yrs) and older man and women (M age W2 = 67.4 yrs).

| | Young | | | | | | Middle | | | | | | Older | | | | | |
| | Men | | | Women | | | Men | | | Women | | | Men | | | Women | | |
| | Subcategory | $f$ | Stab | Subcategory | $f$ | Stab | Subcategory | $f$ | Stab | Subcategory | $f$ | Stab | Subcategory | $f$ | Stab | Subcategory | $f$ | Stab |
|---|---|---|---|---|---|---|---|---|---|---|---|---|---|---|---|---|---|---|
| Past | Relations Oth. | 8.2 | 100 | Travel | 4.3 | 100 | Death Parents | 5.6 | 100 | End Relations | 3.8 | 100 | Death Partner | 4.2 | 100 | Pr. Relations | 2.9 | 100 |
| | Moving | 16.3 | 50 | Other Rest | 4.3 | 100 | Begin Relations | 5.6 | 75 | Moving | 8.8 | 86 | Commitment | 8.3 | 75 | Moving | 2.9 | 100 |
| | Pr. Growth | 8.2 | 50 | | | | Problems Work | 5.6 | 75 | Ph. Health | 3.8 | 67 | Death Parents | 8.3 | 50 | Death Family | 5.9 | 75 |
| | End Relations | 4.1 | 50 | | | | End Relations | 4.2 | 67 | Starting School | 5.0 | 50 | Begin. Work | 4.2 | 50 | Health Others | 8.8 | 67 |
| | | | | | | | School Rest | 2.8 | 50 | Leaving Home | 2.5 | 50 | Stopping Work | 4.2 | 50 | Begin Relations | 4.4 | 67 |
| | | | | | | | | | | Death Family | 2.5 | 50 | War | 4.2 | 50 | Starting School | 4.4 | 67 |
| | | | | | | | | | | Travel | 2.5 | 50 | Other Rest | 4.2 | 50 | Ph. Health | 4.4 | 67 |
| | | | | | | | | | | | | | | | | War | 7.4 | 60 |
| Present | – | | | Birth Child | 16.7 | 50 | Birth Child | 20.0 | 50 | | | | – | | | – | | |
| Future | Finish. School | 11.5 | 67 | Finish. School | 7.1 | 50 | Stopping Work | 21.1 | 75 | Stopping Work | 13.8 | 50 | – | | | Ph. Health | 33.3 | 100 |
| | Death Parents | 15.4 | 50 | Birth Child | 21.4 | 50 | | | | Birth Gr. Child | 6.9 | 50 | | | | | | |

In Table 5.6 stable subcategories – subcategories of which 50 percent or more of the events that are recalled at the first wave are also recalled at both the second and third wave – and their frequency are presented for the Past, Present and Future of young, middle-aged and older men and women. Subcategories are only presented if they contain at least two events at the first wave. From Table 5.6 can be read, for instance, that 8.2 percent of all events young men mention at the first wave in their past belong to the subcategory Relations Others and 100 percent of these events are reported at both the second and third wave.

*Young-Past* (M age W2 = 24.7 yrs)
- For young men Relations Others (e.g., divorce parents) is very fixed in their life story. 16.3 percent of the events mentioned in the past by young men belongs to the subcategory Moving and half of these events are mentioned in all three waves.
- For young women all events within the subcategories Travel and Other Rest (e.g., being raped) are mentioned in all three waves although both subcategories contain only 4.3 percent of all events mentioned in the past by young women.

*Young-Present* (M age W2 = 24.7 yrs)
- For young men there are no stable events in the present.
- For young women half of the events within the subcategory Birth Child is mentioned in all three waves in the present.

*Young-Future* (M age W2 = 24.7 yrs)
- Finishing School (e.g., graduating) and Death Parents are stable events (stab. = 67 and 50 %, respectively) in the future of young men and are mentioned rather often in the future (f = 11.5 and 15.4% respectively).
- For young women Finishing School is also a stable event in the future (50%) although it is not mentioned very often (f = 7.1%). Birth Child is expected more often (f = 21.4%) and half of the events within this subcategory is mentioned in all three waves.

*Middle-Past* (M age W2 = 45.4 yrs)
- For middle-aged men stable events in the past are Death Parents (100%), Begin Relations (75%; e.g., meeting wife), Problems Work (75%), End Relations (67%; e.g., divorce) and School Rest (50%; e.g., boarding school).
- For middle-aged women End Relations is a very stable event in the past (100%). Moving and Physical Health also turn out to be stable events (86 and 67% , respectively).

*Middle-Present* (M age W2 = 45.4 yrs)
- For middle-aged men Birth Child is a stable event in the present (50%).
- For middle-aged women there are no stable events in the present.

*Middle-Future* (M age W2 = 45.4 yrs)
- For middle-aged men Stopping Work is mentioned frequently (f = 21.1%) in the future and 75 percent of events in this subcategory are mentoned in all three waves.
- For middle-aged women Stopping Work is also a rather stable event in the future (50%) as is Birth Grandchild (50%) which is mentioned less often (f = 13.8 versus 6.9%, respectively).

*Older-Past* (M age W2 = 67.4 yrs)
- For older men Death Partner (100%) and Commitment (75%) are very stable events in the past. Death Parents, Beginning Work, Stopping Work, War and Other Rest (e.g., finances) are also rather stable events (50%) in the past of older men.
- For older women Problems Relations and Moving are not recalled frequently (f = 2.9%) but are very stable (100%). Death Family (75%), Health Others, Begin Relations, Starting School, Physical Health (67%) and War (60%) are also stable events.

*Older-Present* (M age W2 = 67.4 yrs)
- There are no stable events in the present for older men and women.

*Older-Future* (M age W2 = 67.4 yrs)
- For older men there are no stable events in the future.
- For older women Physical Health is a very stable event in the future (100%).

*In sum, concerning the content of stable events it can be stated that:*
- Events within the category Relations are most stable in the life story followed by School, Death and Other, while events concerning Growth and Home are least stable.
- Events within the subcategories Relations Others, Travel, Problems Work, Death Family, End Relations, Birth Family, War and Rest which are generally accompanied by a negative affect – except for Travel and Birth Family – are most stable.

## Content stable events per decade

In order to determine stable events per decade, first, the number of events per decade at the first wave was set at 100 percent for younger, middle-aged and older men and women. In this way the relative importance of subcategories per decade was obtained. Next, it was determined per decade which percentage of each subcategory was also reported at both the second and third wave by the same respondents. Subcategories of which at least 20 percent were also mentioned at the second and third wave and which contained at least two events at the first wave are presented in Table 5.7 for young, middle-aged and older men and women. The frequency of the subcategory per decade at the first wave is also presented. From table 5.7 can be read, for instance, that 20 percent of all events young men reported at the first wave in the first decade belong to the subcategory Relations Others and all these events are also reported at the second and third wave (= 100%).

*Young* (M age W2 = 24.7 yrs)
- Young men mainly hold negative stable memories from childhood. Relations Others and Moving are fixed in their memory.
- Young women do not hold stable memories from childhood.
- From adolescence young men also mainly hold stable negative memories. They do not report frequently Relations Others (f = 6%) but when they do, it is a very stable event.
- Young women mainly hold stable positive memories from adolescence. Travel (e.g., world tour) is very fixed in the life story.
- From the period of 21 to 30 years of age young men do not hold positive stable memories or expectations.
- In contrast, young women are very positive about this period (21 to 30 yrs.). Commitment is a very stable event in this period (83%).
- From the age of 30 young men and women do not have stable expectations for specific decades in the future.

*Middle* (M age W2 = 45.4 yrs)
- From childhood middle-aged men do not have stable memories while Moving is remembered often (f = 30%) and consistently (100%) from this period by middle-aged women as a positive event.
- For middle-aged men Problems Growth is a rather stable negative event in adolescence (50%) although it is not mentioned very often (f = 8%).
- From young adulthood both middle-aged men and women hold rather stable memories concerning Begin Relations or Commitment which are positive events.
- From the period of 31 to 40 years of age Death Parents is remembered consistently (100%) by middle-aged men, while middle-aged women remember consistently End Relations (100%). Problems Work is also a very stable event for middle-aged men (67%). It is salient that Birth Child is a more stable event for middle-aged men (50%) than for middle-aged women (0%).
- Middle-aged men mention End Relations a decade later than middle-aged women. Middle-aged women do not mention the same events in the period of 41 to 50 years of age.
- Middle-aged men do not report the same events after the age of 50 at each wave. Middle-aged women mention at each wave Stopping Work in the period of 51 to 60 years of age (50%).

*Older* (M age W2 = 67.4 yrs)
- Older women at each wave report memories concerning the War from childhood (50%), while older men do not report the same events from this period.

**Table 5.7** W1→W2→W3: Stable subcategories over three waves (≥ 20% of subcategories mentioned at W1 is also mentioned at W2 and W3; St = stability) with frequency ($f$) per decade at first wave and mean affect at first wave (Af = Affect; + = positive, 0 = neutral, − = negative) for young, middle-aged and older men and women.

| Decade | Young (W2: 24.7 yrs) — Men | f | St | Af | Young — Women | f | St | Af | Middle (W2: 45.4 yrs) — Men | f | St | Af | Middle — Women | f | St | Af | Older (W2: 67.4 yrs) — Men | f | St | Af | Older — Women | f | St | Af |
|---|---|---|---|---|---|---|---|---|---|---|---|---|---|---|---|---|---|---|---|---|---|---|---|---|
| I: 0–10 | Relations Oth. | 20 | 100 | − | − | | | | − | | | | Moving | 30 | 100 | + | − | | | | War | 29 | 50 | − |
| | Moving | 20 | 100 | − | | | | | | | | | Prob School | 20 | 50 | − | | | | | | | | |
| | Ph. Health | 20 | 50 | − | | | | | | | | | | | | | | | | | | | | |
| II: 11–20 | Relations Oth. | 6 | 100 | − | Travel | 6 | 100 | + | Prob Growth | 8 | 50 | − | Finish. School | 12 | 33 | + | | | | | Begin Relations | 13 | 50 | 0 |
| | Prob Growth | 9 | 67 | − | Fin. School | 9 | 33 | + | Begin. Work | 13 | 33 | + | | | | | | | | | | | | |
| | Moving | 17 | 33 | 0 | Prob Growth | 9 | 33 | − | | | | | | | | | | | | | | | | |
| | | | | | St. School | 13 | 25 | + | | | | | | | | | | | | | | | | |
| | | | | | School Rest | 16 | 20 | 0 | | | | | | | | | | | | | | | | |
| III: 21–30 | End Relations | 10 | 50 | − | Commitment | 22 | 83 | + | Beg. Relations | 13 | 33 | + | Commitment | 32 | 43 | + | Commitment | 31 | 75 | + | Birth Child | 40 | 50 | + |
| | Finish. School | 33 | 29 | 0 | Fin. School | 30 | 50 | + | Commitment | 22 | 20 | + | | | | | Finish. School | 23 | 33 | + | Commitment | 33 | 20 | + |
| | | | | | Begin. Work | 7 | 50 | + | | | | | | | | | | | | | | | | |
| | | | | | Birth Child | 19 | 40 | + | | | | | | | | | | | | | | | | |
| IV: 31–40 | − | | | | − | | | | Death Parents | 12 | 100 | − | End Relations | 13 | 100 | − | − | | | | Mental Health | 12 | 50 | − |
| | | | | | | | | | Prob Work | 18 | 67 | − | Moving | 13 | 50 | + | | | | | Birth Child | 18 | 33 | + |
| | | | | | | | | | Birth Child | 24 | 50 | 0 | | | | | | | | | | | | |
| | | | | | | | | | Commitment | 12 | 50 | + | | | | | | | | | | | | |
| V: 41–50 | − | | | | − | | | | End Relations | 13 | 50 | − | − | | | | − | | | | Health Others | 33 | 50 | − |
| | | | | | | | | | Chang. Work | 33 | 20 | + | | | | | | | | | | | | |
| VI: 51–60 | − | | | | − | | | | − | | | | Stop. Work | 20 | 50 | 0 | Chang. Work | 33 | 50 | 0 | Health Others | 40 | 50 | − |
| VII: 61–70 | − | | | | − | | | | − | | | | Ph. Health | 42 | 20 | − | Ph. Health | 33 | 50 | − | Health Others | 29 | 25 | − |
| VIII: 71–80 | − | | | | − | | | | − | | | | − | | | | Death Partner | 33 | 50 | − | − | | | |

Shaded area refers to the 'bump' period of life

 - From adolescence older women hold rather stable memories concerning Begin Relations (50%), while older men do not mention similar events at each wave in this period.
 - Both older men and women hold positive memories from young adulthood; for older men Commitment is a stable event (75%), while older women recall consistently Birth Child (50%).
 - Older men do not mention the same events in the period of 31 to 40 years of age while older women mention Mental Health (50%) and Birth Child (33%) in this period at each wave.
 - Older men do not have stable memories from the period of 41 to 50 years of age. From the period of 50 to 60 years of age older men remember consistently (50%) Changing Work; this is perceived as a negative event. Older women remember consistently Health Others at each decade after the age of 40.
 - Older men expect rather consistently Physical Health (50%) and Death Partner (50%) in the period of 71 to 80 years of age while older women do not mention similar events at each wave in this decade.

*In sum, concerning the content of stable events per decade it can be stated that:*
 - Stable events reported in the life story of young men are mainly negative events like Relations Others and Moving, while stable events in the life story of young women are mainly positive events like Travel and Commitment.
 - Death Parents and Problems Work are stable events in the life story of middle-aged men while Moving and End Relations are very stable events in the life story of middle-aged women.
 - Older men and women have stable positive memories from the period of 21 to 30 years of life (bump period) which include Finishing School, Commitment and Birth Child.

### 5.3.7 W1 → W2 → W3: Bump and Present
#### Stability and change in the 'bump'
Because the period of 10 to 30 years of age is a special period in life from which older people hold disproportionally more memories than from other periods of life, this period will be analyzed in more

Table 5.8a W1→W2→W3: Subcategories mentioned by eight men of the older age group (Respondent 1 to 8) at the first, second and third wave in the period of 11 to 20 years of age and 21 to 30 years of age.

| Older men (M age W2 = 69.2) | | | | | |
|---|---|---|---|---|---|
| Resp. | I: 11–20 yr | II: 11–20 yr | III: 11–20 yr | I: 21–30 yr | II: 21–30 yr | III: 21–30 yr |
| 1 | Death Parents | – | – | Begin. Work Commitment | Begin. Work Commitment Birth Child | Begin. Work Commitment Birth Child |
| 2 | Leaving Home | Starting School | Starting School | – | Commitment | Commitment |
| 3 | – | – | – | Finish. School Commitment Birth Child | Commitment Birth Child | Finish. School Commitment Birth Child |
| 4 | Starting School | – | – | War Commitment | Commitment Birth Child | Commitment Death Family |
| 5 | Ind. Growth Probl. School Finish. School | School Rest Finish. School | Probl. School | Ind. Growth Finish. School Finish. School | Starting School Ind. Growth Begin Relations Finish. School | Death Rest Prob. Relations Finish. School |
| 6 | – | War Work Rest | Begin. Work War | Commitment | – | Begin Relations Commitment |
| 7 | Probl. Growth | Probl. Growth | War Probl. Growth Leaving Home | Begin Relations | – | – |
| 8 | Starting School Finish. School | Leaving Home | Starting School Finish. School | Moving | Begin. Work | War |

detail for the oldest group. In order to answer the question whether there is some pattern concerning omitting or adding memories in the bump period, events mentioned in the period of 11 to 20 years of age and 21 to 30 years of age of each respondent of the older age group at each wave were listed per respondent. In Table 5.8a results for older men are presented and in Table 5.8b for older women.

*Bump period: 11–20 yrs*
- As was shown before (see Figure 5.2) the period of 11 to 20 years is not a very stable period for the oldest group. The percentage of stable subcategories over three waves was 11 percent for older men and 25 percent for older women.
- Table 5.8a shows that only Problems Growth is mentioned at all three waves by one male respondent.
- Table 5.8b shows that Relations Others, Leaving Home, Begin Relations and Commitment are stable events in the life stories of older women in this period. Most events, however, are not mentioned consistently at each wave in the period of 11 to 20 years of age.
- Table 5.8 conveys the impression that older respondents recall rather arbitrarily different events from adolescence, the period of 11 to 20 years of age, at each wave.

*Bump period: 21–30 yrs*
- Memories from young adulthood, the period of 21 to 30 years of age, are more stable. For older

**Table 5.8b** W1→W2→W3: Subcategories mentioned by ten women of the older age group (Respondent 1 to 10) at the first, second and third wave in the period of 11 to 20 years of age and 21 to 30 years of age.

| | | | | | | |
|---|---|---|---|---|---|---|
| **Older women (M age W2 = 66.0)** | | | | | | |
| Resp. | I: 11–20 yr | II: 11–20 yr | III: 11–20 yr | I: 21–30 yr | II: 21–30 yr | III: 21–30 yr |
| 1 | War<br>Probl. Growth | Starting School | Finish. School | Ph. Health | Commitment | Begin Relations<br>Ph. Health |
| 2 | Ind. Growth | Health Others<br>Commitment | – | Commitment | Birth Child | Birth Child |
| 3 | Relations Others<br>Leaving Home | Relations Others<br>Leaving Home | Relations Others<br>Leaving Home | – | – | Probl. Relations |
| 4 | – | Begin Relations | Moving | Commitment<br>Birth Child | Relations Others<br>Birth Child | Birth Child |
| 5 | Probl. Growth<br>Starting School<br>Pr. School | Starting School | Ind. Growth | – | – | – |
| 6 | Death Parents<br>Starting School<br>War | Death Parents | Begin. Work<br>War | Commitment<br>Birth Child | Commitment<br>Birth Child | Commitment<br>Birth Child |
| 7 | Begin. Work<br>Begin Relations | War<br>Begin Relations<br>Relations Rest | War<br>Begin Relations<br>Relations Rest | Commitment<br>Moving<br>Work Others | Moving | Commitment<br>Moving |
| 8 | Commitment | War<br>Changing Work<br>Commitment | Commitment | – | – | – |
| 9 | Begin Relations | Commitment | – | Birth Child (4x)<br>Death Family | Death Family<br>Birth Child | Birth Child (4x)<br>Death Family |
| 10 | War | Begin Work<br>War | – | Commitment | Commitment | Birth Child |

men 46 percent of events from this period are stable and for older women 40 percent. This is mainly due to events such as Commitment and Birth Child which are mentioned rather often at all three waves.

*In sum:*
- Older people recall more events from the bump period of life than from other periods of life.
- From the period of 11 to 20 years of age older men and women recall many different events and events are not stable over three waves. The period of 21 to 30 years of age turned out to be most stable; events older adults recall consistently from this period are particularly Commitment and Birth Child.

## Stability and change in the recent past – distant past

As was shown in Chapter 2, people recall more events from the recent past than from the distant past which is called the 'recency effect'. What happens to the memories which are mentioned in the recent past as time passes by? In the present study, the recent past was defined as the period which covers the recent five years. The events which were reported from this period at the first wave were listed. Five years later at the third wave, events which were reported from that same period which is at that time five till ten years ago were listed again. In this way it became clear which events were still included in the life story and which events had been omitted from or had been added to the life story. In Table 5.9 (see enclosed CD) the number of events per (sub)category which were mentioned in the recent past at the first wave and at the third wave – when this period is 5 till 10 years ago and has shifted into a more distant past – are presented for men and women of three age groups. In case the difference between the first and third wave is more than 2 events, results will be mentioned below.

*Young* (M age W1 = 22.7 yrs)
- Overall, the young age group, men and women, reported at the first wave 52 events from the recent past (Mean: 2.00 events per respondent). Five years later they reported 43 events from the same period which is then the more distant past (Mean: 1.65 events per respondent).
- When the recent past has shifted into a more distant past, young men mention fewer events concerning Relations (Begin Relations and Problems Relations) and Health (Physical Health), while young women mention fewer events concerning Starting School and Home (Moving and Leaving Home).
- But there are also events which were not reported in the recent past at the first wave but which are reported as the recent past has turned into a more distant past like School (Starting School) by young men and Finishing School and Other (Travel) by young women.

*Middle* (M age W1 = 43.5 yrs)
- Overall, the middle age group reported at the first wave 26 events from the recent past (Mean: 0.87 events per respondent). Five years later they reported 32 events from the same period (Mean: 1.07 events per respondent).
- When the recent past has shifted into a more distant past, middle-aged women report fewer events concerning Death.
- Events that were not reported as often in the recent past at the first wave as in the more distant past at the third wave are for middle-aged men events concerning Health, and for middle-aged women Relations and School (Starting School).

*Older* (M age W1 = 65.5 yrs)
- Overall, the older age group reported at the first wave 8 events from the recent past (Mean: 0.44 events per respondent). Five years later they reported 13 events from the same period (Mean: 0.72 events per respondent).

*In sum:*
- The young age group mentions fewer events after five years in the period which shifts from the recent past into the distant past.
- Young men omit events concerning (Begin) Relations and Health.

- Young women omit events concerning Starting School and Home.
- Contrary to expectations, the middle and older group mention more events in the period which shifts from the recent past to the more distant past after five years.

### Stability and change in the near future – recent past

People expect more events in the near future than in the distant future, a phenomenon which was called the proximity effect. The question is what happens when time passes by and the near future shifts into the recent past. Which events that were expected in the near future have actually occurred and are recalled from the recent past? Which events that were not anticipated in the future have occurred and are recalled from the recent past? And which events that were expected are not mentioned anymore? The near future was defined as the period which covers the next five years. First, it was determined which events were expected in the near future at the first wave. Second, it was determined which events were mentioned in the same period at the third wave when this period has turned into the recent past. In Table 5.10 (see enclosed CD) the number of events per (sub)category is shown for men and women of the young, middle and older age group for the near future at the first wave and the recent past at the third wave. In case the difference between the first and third wave is more than 2 events, results will be mentioned below.

*Young* (M age W1 = 22.7 yrs)
- Overall, young adults expected 22 events in the near future at the first wave (Mean: 0.85 events per respondent). Five years later when the near future has become recent past 58 events are recalled from the same period (= 2.23 events per respondent).
- Events which were not expected in the near future by young men but have occurred and are mentioned when the near future has shifted into the recent past are Relations (End Relations; Relations Rest, e.g., friendship), Health (Health Others, e.g., illness sister) and Growth (Growth Rest, e.g., difficult period).
- Events which were not expected in the near future by young women but are mentioned when the near future has shifted into the recent past are Relations (Begin Relations, e.g., falling in love, End Relations), School (Problems School, e.g., difficulties study; School Rest, e.g. getting a high grade), Health (Mental Health, e.g. depression; Health Others), Home and Death Family.
- Finishing School is expected often in the near future by young men and women but is mentioned less often when the near future has turned into the recent past.
- Birth Child is expected by young women at the first wave and this event is mentioned also five years later.

*Middle* (M age W1 = 43.5 yrs)
- Overall, 14 events are expected in the near future at the first wave by the middle age group (Mean: 0.47 events per respondent). Five years later when the near future has become recent past 41 events are reported from the same period (Mean: 1.37 events per respondent).
- Middle-aged men: Events that were not expected in the near future at the first wave but are mentioned in the recent past at the third wave are Problems Work (e.g., problems with superior), Health (Health Others, e.g., mother having cancer) and Growth (e.g., midlife crisis).
- Middle-aged women: Events that were not expected in the near future at the first wave but are mentioned in the recent past at the third wave are Work, Health (Physical Health), Growth and Birth (Birth Grandchild).
- Changing Work and Birth Child are expected by middle-aged men at the first wave and are mentioned five years later.

*Older* (M age W1 = 65.5 yrs)
- Overall, in the near future 11 events are expected at the first wave by the old age group (Mean: 0.61 events per respondent). Five years later when the near future has become recent past 19 events are mentioned in the same period (Mean: 1.06 events per respondent).
- Older men: Events that were not anticipated in the near future but have occurred and are mentioned in the recent past are Health (e.g., surgery).

- Older women: Events that were not anticipated in the near future but have occurred and are mentioned in the recent past are Relations (e.g., falling in love), Growth (e.g., problems children) and Death (Partner).
- Health Other is expected in the near future by older women and is also mentioned from the recent past five years later.

*In sum:*

- Many more events actually happen than respondents expect to happen in the near future and most of these events are negative events. The younger respondents are, the stronger this pattern.

## 5.4  Discussion

In this chapter the dynamics of autobiographical memory are studied with regard to the content of memories and expectations over a period of two and five years. This was done for men and women of three age groups. Dynamics refers to stability and change (in patterns) of events over time. First, methodological limitations which are met when studying changes in categorical data over time are discussed. Second, results concerning the stability of (patterns in) memories and expectations over a period of five years are discussed. Finally, the focus is on changes in the content of (patterns in) memories and expectations over a period of five years.

### Methodological remarks

– *Group versus individual.* In the present chapter stability was defined as recalling the same event by the same group of respondents and by the same respondent. At the group level, the frequency with which an event is mentioned at each wave determines whether an event and, consequently, specific patterns of events are considered to be stable. At the individual level, however, frequency and stability are independent of each other. Events, which are mentioned very rarely and do not turn up in the modal life story of a group of respondents can be very stable factors in the individual life story. This difference in the meaning of 'stability' has to be kept in mind when evaluating and discussing the results of this chapter.

– *Turning points and events.* Respondents are required to draw their life-line and are asked to label each peak and each dip by chronological age and to tell what happened at a certain moment or during an indicated period. The event a respondent mentions at a peak or dip is classified into one of the 9 categories and 40 subcategories. Often, however, respondents mention more events at one peak or dip (Schroots, Kunst & Assink, 2006). For instance, at the first wave a respondent tells that at the age of 18 he moved to Amsterdam and started to study psychology there. This event is classified into the subcategory 'Moving'. At the second wave this respondent tells that at the age of 18 he started to study psychology which is classified as 'Starting School'. At the third wave the same respondent tells that at the age of 18 he finished high school and went to live in Amsterdam to study psychology. This event is classified as 'Finishing School'. At each wave the respondent refers to another aspect of the turning point which occurred at the age of 18 and the result is that this event is considered to be unstable. This also means that changes in the life story, which are defined as omitting or adding events, do not necessarily imply that events are not mentioned anymore or that the event was not mentioned at a previous wave. It only means that these events are not coded as the most important event at a peak or dip. Life stories have to be analyzed in more detail to deal with this artifact of the coding instruction.

– *Small numbers.* A problem in this chapter is the relative small number of respondents compared to the number of (sub)categories resulting in statistical problems when testing differences between subgroups. As was discussed before, the purpose of this explorative study is to describe trends/patterns in stability and change of autobiographical memory over the lifespan. Hypotheses which can be generated from this study can be tested then on a larger sample of participants, or on other specific groups of respondents.

– *Time.* Stability of events was determined over the total lifespan, over past, present and future and per decade. Events were considered to be stable when a certain percentage of events in a specific period of time was recalled at each wave. This means that an event can appear to be stable, for instance, in the future but does not turn up as a stable event in a specific decade in the future. For instance, many young men refer consistently to Death Parents in the future but at each wave they situate this event in another decade. It also happens that at each wave respondents place the same event at another age. For instance, at the first wave the respondent says he was 30 years old when his first child was born and at the second wave that he was 31 years old. In the first case the event is situated in the third decade and in the second case in the fourth decade. All these factors have the effect of lowering the number (percentage) of stable events that emerge in this study. It seems that in this study a more conservative estimation of the stability of turning points over a period of five years is given.

In sum, despite the above constraints the longitudinal content analysis of LIM-events led to some interesting results which are discussed in more detail below.

## Stable patterns

Description of the modal life course of different groups of respondents revealed some typical patterns of events at the first wave. In spite of error, effect of testing, attrition and the passage of time (Drenth & Sijtsma, 2006) a number of patterns show up in all three waves and can be considered as stable patterns in this study.

– *Men are focused on Work; women are focused on Relations and Health.* A pattern which turns out to be very robust, i.e., which is also found in other samples, in other studies and using other methods, is that in general men are more focused on Work than women are (Baum & Stewart, 1990; Brugman, 2000; deVries & Watt, 1996; Rönka, Oravala & Pulkkinen, 2003). In the LIM-study young men mention Beginning Work, middle-aged men mention Problems Work and Stopping Work, and older men mention Changing Work and Stopping Work. Women, in general, are more focused on Relations and Health; young women are looking forward to start a family, middle-aged women mention at each wave Commitment, End Relations and in the future Physical Health, and older women recall consistently events concerning Commitment, Birth and Health Others. Another notable difference between young men and young women is that the core life story of young women covers only a small part of the lifespan. Young women are very focused on Finishing School, Commitment and Birth Child and they are very positive about these events. In relation to these events, other events shrink into insignificance. The core life story of young men covers a greater part of the lifespan and involves more events and different types. It is remarkable that for older men and women it is the other way around; older women have a more differentiated life story than older men have.

– *Women are more self-reliant than men.* Another strong pattern that turns up in each wave is that men seem to be more dependent on parents and partner than women are. Young men more often mention Divorce Parents and Death Parents in their life story than young women do. Older men in all three waves mention the expectation of the death of their wife before their own death, while older women do not mention this event. It is possible that in our sample more young men than young women happen to have experienced the divorce of parents in their youth. But this does not explain the fact that young men consistently mention the death of parents in their future. When we consider the fact that older men are afraid to loose their partner we can recall what was stated in the previous chapter that men get more social and emotional support from marriage than women do (Moen, 1996). Women mostly maintain family relationships and invest in care-giving and kin-keeping activities (Putney & Bengtson, 2001). So men generally are more inconvenienced by the loss of their wife than women by the loss of their husband. In general, men seem to be more vulnerable to events which concern the loss of parents or partner than women are.

– *Young adults are more focused on Growth than older adults.* Overall, younger adults report more events in the category Growth than older respondents. This could be a cohort effect. Maybe younger adults are more used to speak in terms of personal growth while in the period older adults grew up there was less thought for personal growth and growth problems. Another explanation is that younger adults are in the phase of their life in which they develop themselves and are also facing more growth problems than older people do. Over time these events fade away as events in the category Growth turned out to be rather unstable. The older people get, the less growth they show.

– *The 'rosy view' is a robust phenomenon.* At all three waves young women look forward to Commitment (e.g. marriage) but for middle-aged women this has often ended in a divorce. Probably, this is due to the phenomenon of the 'rosy view', i.e., people's expectations of an event are more positive than their experience during the event itself, and their subsequent recollection of that event is more positive than the actual experience (Mitchell, Thompson, Peterson & Cronk, 1997). Another example of this 'rosy view' in the LIM-study is that middle-aged men are less positive about Work – Problems Work are often mentioned by this group – than younger and older men. Young men are looking forward to Beginning Work and older men have mainly positive feelings about their career (Changing Work). Older men recall Stopping Work as a negative event at the first wave but as a positive event at the second and third wave when more time has passed since the event. There are also other signs in this study which indicate that (very) negative events are rated less negatively with the passage of time. For instance, End Relations is rated more negatively by middle-aged women than by older women; Death Parents is rated less negatively by older respondents than by younger respondents. It can be concluded that the anticipation and afterglow of events which are usually considered as positive, is often perceived as more positive than the event itself. Negative events tend to become less negative as time passes. After all, time is the great healer.

– *Older respondents mainly recall positive events from the period between 20 to 30 years old.* The pattern that older respondents mainly recall positive memories from the 'bump' period also turns out to be stable. This applies especially for the period of 20 to 30 years of age. As the positive events most frequently mentioned in this period are Begin Relations, Commitment and Birth Child, this period could be called the Commitment period.

### Stable events

The question to be answered is 'which elements of the life story are being repeatedly reported over a period of five years?' Since we do not know of longitudinal studies concerning the development of autobiographical memory over the lifespan, results of this LIM-study cannot be compared to results of other studies. LIM-results make it clear that the life story has a stable core, which consists of at least about one third of all events mentioned when telling the life story at a certain point in time. Beside these stable events respondents omit events and add other events each time they tell their life story. Factors which were found to have an effect on the stability of memories and expectations are:

– *Time interval: Decrease in stability is significant after two years and then seems to stabilize.* In general it can be concluded that 65 percent of the categories is stable over a period of two years and 64 percent over a period of five years. For subcategories these percentages are respectively 51 and 48 percent. These data show that stability does not decrease in a linear way over time. The decrease in stability is significant between the first and second wave but not between the second and third wave. About one third of events (subcategories) is fixed in memory and it can be concluded that these events make up the core of a person's life story. The question is how long it takes before there is a significant decrease in the stability of memories and expectations. Glickman, Hubbard, Liveright and Valciukas (1990) asked 1669 respondents in the age of 45 to 84 years to fill in the Life Events Questionnaire. Respondents were asked how often and when each of 35 events had occurred in the previous year. Because of the great number of respondents it was assumed that in both intervals of six months the frequency of reported events should be equal. However, the authors found that from the period 7 to 12 months ago 21 percent fewer events were reported than in the period up to six months ago. So after six months there is already a significant decrease in stability of memorized events. More research is needed, with measurement points at different intervals, to find out exactly how much stability decreases over time.

– *Time perspective: The past is more stable than the future.* Memories from the past turned out to be more stable than expectations for the future, which does not come as a surprise as past events belong to the world of actual reality whereas expectations for the future belong to the world of possibilities (Whitehead, 1929). However, there is disagreement among scientists as to the nature of the conceptions of past and future. According to Frankl (1978), "The present is the borderline between the unreality of the future and the eternal reality of the past" (p. 111). This view is completely in contrast with the constructivistic view hold by Mead (1964) who suggested that the past is as hypothetical as the future. According to McAdams (1996) life stories are based on empirical facts but are not simply objective accounts of 'what really happened' in the past. Life stories are psychosocial constructions that go beyond facts. The results of the present study show that both past and future are reconstructed over time but that the future is reconstructed to a greater degree than the past.

Bernsten and Rubin (2002) made a distinction between life narrative and life script. The life narrative is concrete and consists of personal memories, while the life script is generic and consists of cultural expectations. Apparently, the life narrative is more stable than the life script as the life narrative refers to the past and the life script to the future.

Markus and Nurius (1986) introduced the concept of 'possible selves' which refer to the future of an individual. 'Possible selves' represent individuals' different scenarios for their future, ideas of what they might become, what they would like to become, and what they are afraid of becoming. Hooker (1999) views goals people have in different domains of their lives in terms of possible selves. Goals can change as people grow older, or are replaced by other goals. Subsequently, the 'possible self' can change from one measurement point to another. Besides, events that have happened in the mean time will also have an influence on how the future is perceived. The LIM-study shows that more events, especially negative events, happen than people do expect and anticipate. These unexpected events change the future perspective and can even direct the future into a completely other direction.

*– Period in life: Memories of childhood and of the Commitment period are relatively stable.* When correcting for the differences in number of recalled or expected events per decade memories from childhood turned out to be most stable for young men, middle-aged women and older women. Although respondents do not report many events from childhood, events they recall have made a very deep impression. Mostly, these memories refer to negative events such as divorce of parents, war and moving. Studies about first memories in life also show that these memories mostly concern negative events often accompanied with feelings of fear (Blonsky, 1929 in: Draaisma, 2001). Peterson, Grant and Boland (2005) investigated the earliest memories of children between the ages of 6 and 19. They found that memories of older children were more likely to involve negative affect. Josselson (2000) had 24 respondents, at age 21, 33 and 43 years, recall their two earliest memories from childhood. She found that one third of all respondents recalled at all three interviews at least one similar event and that earlier memories become more stable as people grow older. This finding indicates, according to the author, that when personality consolidates, the core themes in life become more persistent. In the LIM-study stability of childhood memories is higher for young men than for young women. An explanation could be that young women are very focused on the present and near future and less on the past. As a consequence, at each wave they might recall different events from childhood. Young men, however, seem to be more focused on childhood and recall more similar events from this period. For the middle-aged group it is the other way around; probably, for middle-aged women memories of childhood are activated by having children of their own and they recall more similar events over time. Middle-aged men, however, live very much in the present and are focused on their work. They are not occupied with childhood memories and mention different events at each wave from this period. Older men have more stable memories of childhood than middle-aged men; when getting older people generally reflect on their whole life. For older women applies that memories from childhood are very stable; especially events concerning World War II have made a profound impression on these women.

As older respondents report relatively many events from the period of 10 to 30 years of age, it was expected that they also have stable memories from the bump period of life. However, only the third decade of life turned out to be a comparatively stable period in life. About forty percent of memories from this period is recalled at each wave. Contrary to expectations stability turned out to be rather low in the period of 11 to 20 years. Older respondents hold many memories from this period but at each wave other memories are recalled. A possible explanation is that adolescence is a period of turmoil and of chaos. Many important events occur and are encoded in memory. It can be hypothesized that a network of associated events is formed from which at each wave other events are recalled. Between 21 and 30 years of age the 'knots' in the network become clearer and at each wave these 'knots' are recalled resulting in more stable memories from this period of life. It is the period from which respondents mainly recall events concerning Relations and Birth Child. In fact, the bump could be divided into two different periods; a period of Turmoil in adolescence and a period of Commitment in young adulthood.

   *– Age of respondent: Life story of older people is more stable than of younger people.* Although stability was not significantly different for different age groups, there were indications that the life story is somewhat more stable for older respondents than for younger respondents. For instance, stability of subcategories over three waves for the past was 32 percent for young adults, 34 percent for middle-aged adults and 40 percent for older adults. For the future these percentages were 13 percent, 24 percent and 20 percent, respectively. Besides, more changes take place in the Present for young adults than for older adults; for young adults the change in ratio of actual events and events expected in the near future was higher than for older adults. It also turned out that more systematic changes take place in the modal life story of young adults than of older adults and that patterns concerning the modal life story are less stable for younger adults than for older adults.

   *– Affect of event: Negative events are more stable than positive events.* For the past it was found that negative events are more fixed in the life story than positive events. In Chapter 4 it was discussed that it is adaptive for human beings to respond more strongly to negative, bad events than to positive, good events. Consequently, it will be more adaptive to keep remembering negative events better than positive events in order to be better prepared for future negative events (Baumeister et al., 2001). Following this line of thought it is not surprising that negative events are more fixed in autobiographical memory and are recalled more consistently than positive events. Another explanation for the greater stability of negative events is that negative events have a more intense and longer lasting impact than positive events (Baumeister et al., 2001) as was discussed in Chapter 3. After a very positive event there is a short peak in happiness but then people become accustomed to the new situation and are not happier than they were before the event. After a traumatic event, however, people need much more time and it costs much more effort to adjust to the new situation which will result in more intensive encoding and, consequently, in a greater stability of negative events than of positive events.

   For the present and future, however, there is a difference between men and women in the stability of positive and negative events; negative events are more stable for men than for women, while positive events are more stable for women than for men. A possible explanation could be that from an evolutionary perspective men are supposed to protect their family and should be more prepared for threats and danger. In a study concerning processing visual information William and Mattingley (2006) found that subjects gave priority to pictures of angry men to pictures of neutral faces. Men, however, were faster in identifying angry faces while women were faster in identifying emotions such as happiness, sorrow and surprise. It seems that men are more focused on signals of danger, more prepared for negative events to happen.

   *– Type of event: Events concerning Relations are very stable.* Some types of events are more stable and are mentioned at each version of the life story, while other types of events are more variable and are mentioned only once or twice. Overall, most events which are stable in the life story over a period of five years refer to the categories Relations, School and Death. These types of events are printed in memory and are (part of) the core of a life story. Some non-normative events, which do not happen very often, are also very stable. These are events which are categorized in the category 'Other', such as War, Travel and Other Rest (e.g., being adopted, being raped). Events which refer more to a process in stead of to a concrete event like Growth (Individual Growth) and events which refer to other persons like Home Others, Growth Others and Work Others turned out to be rather unstable in the life story.

These events are mentioned when they are relevant, close to the time they happen, but fade away after some time. It is also important in which period of life an event has taken place. It seems that Moving is more stable in the life story and has more impact when it occurs in childhood than when it occurs in another period of life.

### Changes in patterns of events

Cross-sectional analysis of the first wave resulted in a description of the modal life story for men and women of three age-groups. It can be expected that as time passes by the modal life story of the youngest group will start to look like the modal life story of the middle-aged group and the model life story of the middle-aged group like that of the oldest group. Comparison of the modal life stories of three waves showed such a change only for young men.

*Generally*
- There are more systematic changes in the life story of younger adults than of older adults.

*Young*
- Young men mention Finishing School (graduating) at the first and second wave in the period between 21 to 30 years of age but not at the third wave, which is in accordance with the modal life story of middle-aged men. It seems that when men finish school, this event looses its importance. Also, young men do not mention Stopping Work in the future at the first wave but they do so at the second and third wave, which is also in accordance with the life story of middle-aged men.
- A change in the modal life story of young women is the postponement of Birth Child as they grow older. At the first wave they place this event in both the third and fourth decade, at the second and third wave this event is expected only in the fourth decade. Most of these women were students at the first wave. Postponing Birth is a well-known phenomenon for women who have an academic education (Beets, Dourleijn, Liefbroer & Henkens, 2000). Another change in the life story of young women is that they do not mention Death Parents at the first and second wave in their future but they do at the third wave. It is not clear why young women mention this event at that moment. Maybe illness of parents or becoming a parent themselves has activated the expectation of this event.

*Middle*
- The life stories of middle-aged men and women show only a systematic change concerning Changing Work in the future. At the first and second wave this event is expected in the future but at the third wave this event is not mentioned anymore. It is possible that this event has taken place in the mean time or that this event is overruled by other more important events.

*Older*
- In the modal life stories of older men and women almost no patterns of change can be discerned. It is interesting that older men do not recall Birth Child at the first wave but they do at the second and third wave. This might be because of the social desirability effect. After having told their life story the first time they could have realized that they had 'forgotten' this event and that it is socially undesirable not to recall the births of children.

Although the changes are very small, the results suggest that more systematic changes take place within the young age group than within the older age group. This is in accordance with the dynamics of the event distribution over the lifespan. For older respondents life has crystallized out; there is a fixed bump followed by a period from which few events are remembered, and a rather flat recency/proximity effect. For younger respondents a bump is developing and the recency/proximity effect is rather steep as many changes take place in this period. Besides, as young people grow older the future self is extending and new events expected in the distant future are included in the life story. For instance, young men mention Stopping Work in their life story as soon as they have started their working life. For older adults future time perspective decreases and, consequently, no new events will be included in the future life story.

## Changes: adding and omitting events

About one third of all events recalled at the first wave turned out to be very stable over a period of five years and one third turned out to be rather stable and was also recalled at either the second or third wave. New or other events are recalled and added to the life story at the second and/or third wave. Although a detailed analysis of the total life story is necessary to ascertain exactly which changes actually occur in the life story, some explanations for omitting events from the life story and adding other events can be suggested on the basis of theories of memory and on the basis of different versions of the life story.

*Over time memories fade away*

According to Schachter (2001) 'transience' is one of the seven sins of memory. "Transience refers to a weakening or loss of memory over time" (p. 4). As time is passing by, memories fade away resulting in the classical 'forgetting curve' or the 'recency effect'; respondents recall more events from their recent past than from their distant past. Over a period of five years this effect only turns up for the youngest age group. Middle-aged and older respondents recall more events from the period more than five years ago than from the recent past. For the middle-age group the bump and recency effect are contaminated. For the older age group the recency/proximity effect is more flat and seems to cover a longer period than for the young age group. However, there is no clear definition of the recency effect. It can be seen that a period of five years has a different meaning for people of different ages. For the youngest group five years take up about one quarter of their lifespan while for older groups five years represent a smaller percentage of their lifespan. Saldana (2003, p. 5) quotes Hawking: "In the theory of relativity there is no unique absolute time, but instead each individual has his own personal measure of time that depends on where he is and how he is moving" (1988, p. 33). When examining the power curve of the recency effect, it is clear that for young people this curve is much steeper than for older people. It is hypothesized that the peak for young respondents is a combination of bump and recency (and proximity) effect. The bump is fixed while the recency/proximity effect is moving. But the recency effect seems to be steeper for young respondents than for older respondents since more memories fade away in five years for young respondents than for older respondents. Memories which are remembered from the past five years at the first wave by young adults but have faded away at the third wave five years later are: Relations (Begin Relations and Problems Relations), Health (Physical Health), Starting School and Home (Moving and Leaving Home). Evidently, these events are not important enough to be included in the core of the life story. They have lost their importance and other more actual events have taken their place in memory. However, these memories can regain significance again after some time when they are activated by other events (Linde, 1993).

*Over time memories are reorganized*

Besides omitting events, transience can also result in another organisation of events. "Transience involves a gradual switch from reproductive and specific recollections to reconstructive and more general descriptions" (Schachter, 2001, p.16). In some cases, different events which are mentioned at the first wave are combined as one event at a following wave. For instance, a respondent of the young age group recalled at the first wave three different events from the time he was 17 years old. First he got an accident (Physical Health), then he was abandoned by his girl friend (End Relations) and next, his grandfather died (Death Family). At the next wave two years later this respondent drew one big dip at the age of 17 and told that this had been a very difficult period in his life (Growth Rest). The three separate events were joined together in one turning point.

*Traumatic events can result in dramatic changes of the life story*

Stressful, traumatic events have the power to elicit dramatic changes in the life story (Bourque & Back, 1977; Kenyon, Clark & deVries, 2001). When people experience a traumatic event other events may loose their significance and life is viewed from another perspective. Although LIM|Life stories are not analysed with this in mind, different versions of the life story provides indications of such changes. For instance, a young man recalled at the first and second wave several events which happened in his childhood and in adolescence. Between the second and third wave some major events took place in his life. His relationship ended, he lost his job, and, quite unexpectedly, he became a parent. At the third wave this respondent did not mention any event from childhood and adolescence but started his life story by telling about all these new events.

*New, unexpected events are integrated in the life story*

As time is passing by new events will happen which have to be integrated in the life story. More events actually happen than people expect to happen. Most of these events are negative events like the death of a beloved person, problems at work, relation problems and health problems. People do not expect negative events to happen and are often too optimistic about their near future. For instance, a 20-year respondent expects at the first wave one event to happen in the near future namely finishing his studies when he is 25 years old. Five years later when he is 25 years old two unforeseen, negative events have taken place in the period of 20 to 25 years of age; his parents have divorced and the relationship with his girl friend has broken up. The respondent has not finished his studies yet and expects to do so when he will be 27 years old. This result shows some similarity with results obtained by Zauberman and Lynch (2005) who found that people are under the illusion that they have more time in the future than they have in the present. They accept, for instance, invitations or make commitments weeks or months before the deadline, but later they regret their promise because they have less time to spare at that moment than they expected. Also in this respect, more events actually happen than were expected, i.e., people have more things to do at any moment in time than they expected. In the LIM-study this effect turned out to be stronger with younger respondents than with older respondents. Young respondents expect more events in the next five years than older respondents do. After five years more events have actually occurred in young people's lives than in older people's lives. These results suggest that the proximity effect is also related to age although there is not yet a clear definiton of the (length of the) proximity effect. Both recency and proximity effect seem to cover a shorter period for younger people than for older people; more changes take place around the present age for younger people than for older people.

*It takes some time to recognize events as turning points*

Especially for the middle and older age group it seems tot take some time before events are recognized as turning points. These groups mention at the third wave more events from the period more than five years ago than from the recent past. For instance, a woman who is 44 years at the third wave recalls that she started her study when she was 34 years old. At the first wave when she was 39 years old she did not mention this event. She was focused on the future when she expected to finish her study. The same was the case at the second wave. At the third wave she had finished her studies and only now mentions that she started to study. Retrospectively, this event is considered a turning point in her life. Birren and Hedlund (1987, p. 406) maintain that "… branching points become branching points by reviewing one's life rather than while they are actually occurring". When events actually take place, a person can not foresee in which way the event will change his life. As Kierkegaard observed, "Life has to be lived forward but can only be understood backward".

*Remote events can be activated by present events*

Remote events may lose significance over time but may also gain significance over time (Linde, 1993). In some periods of life people can be confronted with events that activate the recall of remote events or the expectation of similar events in the future. For instance, in the first wave young women expect Home Others (= children leaving home) while in the second and third wave this event is not mentioned. Probably, these young women went to live on their own at the first wave which has activated the expectation of children leaving home in the future. Another example is that as soon as young men start to work they mention Stopping Work in the future.

*The test-retest effect can result in a more social desirable life story*

Respondents know at the second and third wave what sort of response is expected of them and as a result will anticipate more during the LIM-interview. They report more events at the second and third wave. It is possible that they tell a more social desirable story by including events they did not mention at the first wave because later they think it was a mistake to leave them out. For instance, Birth

Child is not recalled by older men at the first wave but is recalled at the second and third wave. On the other hand events which are mentioned at the first wave are sometimes omitted at the following waves because they are embarrassing or too painful. For instance, a middle-aged woman told at the first wave she had had an extramarital relationship. At the next waves she did not mention this event anymore.

In concluding this chapter it can be stated that:

– The life story is reconstructed constantly to a considerable extent and according to specific patterns.
– Over a period of five years about one third of memories and expectations is fixed in memory while another third is mentioned irregularly and one third is not mentioned anymore.
– The view people have on events that happened in the past is more stable than on those in the future.
– Memories from childhood and the top of the bump period (20–30 yrs) especially, are relatively stable among older people.
– Life stories of younger adults are subject to more changes than life stories of older respondents.
– People, in general, have normative expectations for the future; they expect fewer events to happen in the near future than actually happen. Most of these unexpected events are negative non-normative events.
– For the past it was found that negative events are more fixed in memory than positive events, while negative events expected in the future are more stable for men than for women, and positive events are more stable for women than for men.

# Chapter 6
# General Discussion

## 6.1 Methodological issues

In the present study autobiographical memory (AM) was studied with respect to the stability and change in number, affect and content of important life events. Respondents of three age groups reported events which they recalled from their past and expected for their future over periods of two and five years by means of the Life-line Interview Method (LIM). Due to an explorative approach the study has yielded rich information about the dynamics of AM and the subjective life course. In connection with this approach some general methodological issues need to be discussed.

### Type of study
Since AM is a relatively new area of research and since no comprehensive theoretical framework covering the diversity of AM research is available as yet (Conway & Pleydell-Pearce, 2000), it is not feasible to study AM by testing specific hypotheses. In hypothesis testing the null hypothesis is either rejected or accepted. The disadvantage of this type of research is that the researcher does not utilise the data to its full maximum. Van Zuuren (2002) points out that in addition to the more deductive empirical-analytical research also other types of research exist such as the more inductive theoretical-interpretative, descriptive and explorative forms. On the basis of the collected data, hypotheses are generated which may contribute to the development of a theory. In the present study such an *explorative* approach was followed; no specific expectations or hypotheses were formulated on beforehand. The study yielded many results which would not have been found when only a strict hypothesis testing procedure had been followed. These results, then, can be tested in future research on larger samples and as such can contribute to the development of a theory about AM.

According to Van Zuuren (2002) a more qualitative type of research is more suitable for the generation of hypotheses and theory building in new areas of research. Through qualitative research the researcher may gain insight in the domain of research on the basis of a proper and elaborate description of the respondents' experiences. Interpretation and categorization of these subjective experiences and the explanation of relationships may further contribute to the development of theories. Faltermaier (1997) argues that qualitative methods are in particular suitable to the analysis of the life course and other kinds of biographical processes. As theories in this field become more and more complex, it is unsatisfactory to apply only models and to use only variables that can be tested statistically, even when using rather large samples. Also, in the study of the life course one has to deal with the passage of time and the process character of different phenomena which are difficult to put in statistical models, even operationalized in the form of a longitudinal design (Faltermaier, 1997). Drenth and Heller (2004) state that using a combination of different methods, qualitative as well as quantitative, often gives better results than using only a single method.

The present study can be seen as a combination of *qualitative and quantitative* research. The Life-line Interview Method yields a rich variety of qualitative data of which only the life events were analyzed in the present study. As far as possible these data were analyzed quantitatively and statistical relationships between different variables were determined. The life story, however, can give more insight in the feelings and experiences of respondents and in the dynamic processes underlying changes of autobiographical memory over the lifespan. For instance, inspection of the life story showed that over time events are sometimes reorganized by combining different events into one event. This way quantitative and qualitative analysis of the LIM-data can complement each other and the combination can be very productive.

The point of departure in this study was the construction of individual life stories by administering the LIM. These individual life stories were deconstructed at the event level. Next, modal life stories were reconstructed at the aggregate level for men and women of a young, middle and older age group. These modal life stories were analyzed as the result of which general patterns became visible. In this way an *idiothetic* approach was followed in the present study (Hooker, 2002); an idiothetic approach combines the idiographic approach to describe individual trajects with the nomothetic approach to generalize such trajects about individuals. It was Allport (1937), one of the founding fathers of personality psychology, who pleaded for an idiographic approach to personality, which, in contrast to the nomothetic approach, would discern the specific and individual patternings of particular lives (McAdams, 2000). On the basis of Kluckhohn and Murray's (1953, p. 53) classic dictum *'Every man is in certain respects (a) like all other men, (b) like some other men, (c) like no other man'* Runyan (1983) posed that the purpose of personality psychology is three-fold, namely to discover: (1) what is true for all human beings, (2) what is true for groups of human beings, and (3) what is true for individual human beings. For instance, the bump is found in different samples from different cultures (e.g. Conway & Haque, 1999) and can be considered to be a universal phenomenon. The finding in the LIM-study that young respondents expect to finish their studies in the third decade of life is true for a specific group (students). An example of what is true for individual human beings is the memory of an older respondent that he received a puppet theatre at his fifth birthday. For many patterns it is not clear whether the patterns are specific for this group of respondents or whether they can be generalized to other populations. For instance, Moving turned out to be an important event in the past for young men but not for young women. Further research can show whether the revealed patterns are also true for other groups of respondents.

## Managing autobiographical data

When studying (auto)biographical material many methodological problems have to be faced (Schroots & Birren, 2002). These problems concern, first of all, the question how to bring *order into the large quantity of unstructured qualitative data.* Thanks to the self-structuring quality of the LIM the respondent himself structures the data into a chronologically ordered life story of which the unit of analysis consists of the age at which the event took place, a short description of the event and an explanation of the event. These units of analysis can than be categorized into meaningful categories. In this study a systematic category list was constructed, consisting of 40 subcategories divided over 9 categories, in which all events could be classified.

A second problem with autobiographical data concerns the *analysis of categorical data.* In this study the percentage of events per (sub)category was established. Where possible the effect of agegroup, gender and time perspective on the frequency of events per (sub)category was determined. In case this was not possible, rules were generated in order to determine whether differences between subgroups could be established.

The third problem concerns the *representation of the large quantity of categorical data* in a clear and convenient way. In this study the most frequently mentioned (sub)categories or the most stable (sub)categories per decade were selected, resulting in an orderly description of the modal life course for different subgroups. A disadvantage of this method is some loss of information, but this is outweighed by the transparency of the presented information and the patterns found.

As was mentioned in Chapter 1 researchers vary with respect to their methods to study AM and life stories. Therefore, it is difficult to compare results of different studies with each other (Schroots & Assink, 2004). In this LIM-study a method is presented to gather, classify, analyze and present autobiographical data in an efficient, systematic way. This method is described in detail and can be replicated in other studies. In this way we trust to have contributed to the development of an efficient, well-organized and univocal method to deal with autobiographical material.

## 6.2  Autobiographical memory effects

Until now it was not clear to what extent (patterns of) memories and expectations change with time, which variables have an effect on stability and change, and whether there are specific patterns underlying the dynamics of AM. An important contribution of this study to the knowledge about AM, then, is the fact that it is a longitudinal study. Over a period of five years the LIM was administered three times to the same men and women of three age groups. This resulted in information about stability at the group level and about stability of life events at an individual level. Since studies on AM are nearly exclusively focused on retrospective AM another important contribution of this study is the inclusion of prospective AM. As this study has a longitudinal nature, it was possible to examine the development of both retro- and prospective memory over the lifespan. Three specific effects of AM were found – bump, recency and proximity effect – which will be discussed in more detail below.

### Bump effect

All studies about AM show that the period of about 10 to 30 years of age is, quantitatively as well as qualitatively, a very special period in the life of (older) respondents. The reported number of memories from this period is larger than expected and most events which are mentioned in the period of 20 to 30 years of age are positive events and are relatively stable in the life story. At the first wave 28 percent of all past events that were mentioned by older respondents, were situated in the period of 20 to 30 years of age. At the second and third wave these percentages were 22 and 23, respectively. These percentages were higher than the percentages of reported events from the most recent decade. At the first wave 10 percent of all past events mentioned by older respondents were situated in the ten years preceding the present age of the respondents, at the second wave 19 percent and at the third wave 15 percent. Therefore, it can be concluded that the bump effect is stronger than the recency effect.

Although the bump effect can only be clearly distinguished for older adults, Schroots and van Dijkum (2004) have shown that for young adults the bump is 'hidden' under the recency effect and that for middle-aged respondents the bump emerges and is partly confounded with the recency effect. Over the lifespan bump and recency effect increasingly separate from each other. The older people are, the longer the period between bump and recency effect, a period of low recall of events.

The precise location of the bump varies in different studies and depends on the method used to gather autobiographical information as well as on the type of event the respondent is asked to recall. For instance, when Rubin and Schulkind (1997) gave respondents a cue-word and asked to describe for each word a personal event, they found a peak in the second decade. When they asked respondents to describe the five most important events of their life they found a peak in the third decade. Janssen, Chessa and Murre (2005) asked almost 2000 respondents between the age of 11 and 70 years through the internet to recall and date autobiographical memories using the cue-word method, and observed a bump with peaks at ages 15–18 for men and 13–14 for women. Holmes and Conway (1999) found a bump for public events between 10 and 19 years of age. Sehulster (1996) reported an average age of 27.6 years at which participants had watched their favourite movie. Holbrook and Schindler (1989) found that participants gave the highest preference ratings to music hits that had come out when they were 24 years old (see also: Rubin, Rahhal & Poon, 1998). In the present LIM-study and in the studies of deVries and Watt (1996) and Holmes and Conway (1999) a peak for autobiographical memories is found between 20 and 30 years of age. In this LIM-study for the older age group a peak was found between the ages of 20 to 30 years in case the number of events per decade was determined and when results of three waves were combined. An interesting question is why the word-cue method results in an earlier bump than a method in which respondents are asked to recall important life events. As was hypothesized in the previous chapter, in adolescence a network of associated events is formed, but people are only aware of the "knots" in this network at a later age. The word-cue method probably elicits more different, isolated memories whereas methods which ask the respondent to generate important life events themselves appeal more to the "knots" in the network which are formed (encoded) at a later age (see also Schroots & van Dijkum, 2004). Follow-up studies on larger samples and using different methods can result in a more precise location of the bump for important life events in a lifespan perspective (Schroots, 2008a,b).

Individuals experience the bump period as the time of their life (Sehulster, 1996). The bump is the mental frame of reference for the rest of life. Preferences for different kinds of music, literature and film date from this period. It is possible, for instance, to predict on the basis of age what type of music an individual will like. Things people have learned and experiences they have had in this period are remembered best later (Rubin, Rahhal & Poon, 1998). The bump period is the best period to encode information and knowledge into memory. It is easier to learn things by heart in this period of life than later in life. The difference in frame of reference can give rise to problems between different generations, for instance in work situations (Schroots, 2003a) or in family life (e.g. generation conflict in the sixties). The phenomenon of the bump is also responsible for a feeling of nostalgia, the feeling that "it is not like in the good old days in our time of life"!

The LIM-study showed that respondents mention relatively few events from childhood but at the same time that these events are rather stable. From the bump period relatively many events are reported and these events are also rather stable, at least with respect to the period of 20 to 30 years of age. The question is, then, how childhood and bump are related to each other and to the rest of the life course. Is a problematic childhood followed by a difficult bump period, in which negative events overrule positive events? And what effect does the fact that an individual has experienced traumatic events during the bump have on the rest of the life course? A more detailed content analysis of the LIM-data can help to provide answers to these questions.

## Recency effect

In the present study a period of five years was taken for the length of the recency effect. It was expected that memories from the recent past fade away when the recent past (0–5 yrs) turns into the more distant past (5–10 yrs), but this could only be confirmed for the young age group. As there is no clear definiton of the recency effect it is difficult to determine the length of the recency effect. It seems, however, that the recency effect covers a longer period for older adults than for younger adults. It should also be noted that a period of five years is relatively a longer period for younger respondents than for older respondents. For the young age group five years cover about 20 percent of their life lived, while for older respondents five years cover only about seven percent of their life lived.

When distinguishing between positive and negative events it turned out that there is a strong recency effect for negative events. For positive events there is not always a recency effect and when there is such an effect it is only modest. Traumatic events, such as the Second World War, have the power to disturb the normal pattern and show a small negative bump. Traumatic events such as a war (Conway & Haque, 1999) or immigration (Schrauf & Rubin, 2001) can also extend the bump period. The question was raised whether very positive events can also disturb the normal pattern. The effect of very negative events can be studied on a group level since some negative events affect a whole group of people (e.g., war, economic depression, natural disasters) while very positive events, mostly, do not occur at the group level and their influence can therefore be studied only at the individual level. Besides, it is more difficult to adjust to negative events than to positive events. For instance, almost all older respondents mention the Second World War, a very negative event, in their life story. Only a few respondents mention the liberation, a very positive event, although all older respondents have experienced this event. It seems likely that very positive events do not affect a group of people as strongly as very negative events do, and, consequently, it is likely that very positive events do not have the power to change the normal pattern of distribution of positive events.

Apart from the length of the recency period it can be concluded that many events that are important at a certain moment in life fade away as time is passing by. Most of these events are negative events since events mentioned with respect to the recent past are mostly negative events. This implies that when people have experienced a negative event they need time to come into terms with this. Research shows that most individuals who have experienced a traumatic event are able to continue their life after some time without professional assistance. Other studies have even found that individual psychological debriefing soon after a traumatic event is not useful in reducing symptoms of Post Traumatic Stress Disorder (PTSD) and in some cases can even worsen psychological problems (Sijbrandij, Olff, Reitsma, Carlier, & Gersons, 2006). Only a small part of individuals who have experienced traumatic events develop a PTSD. In that case memories of the traumatic event do not fade away but keep dominating the individual's life. Apart from this, it can be concluded that time is the great healer.

## Proximity effect

Analogous to the recency effect a proximity effect was found for the future; respondents expect more events in the near future than in a more distant future. Respondents are also positive about the near future; for instance, young adults expect to finish their studies in the near future and do not expect problems concerning their studies. Respondents do not look very far ahead and have a prototypical image of their future, a so-called life script (Rubin & Berntsen, 2003). Besides, the perceptions respondents have of their future is rather instable, especially for the young age group. At each wave other events are mentioned in the future or similar events are mentioned but at another age. The fact that individuals do not look far ahead into the future has different consequences. For instance, it is difficult to motivate (young) adults to make arrangements for their pension plan, to change an unhealthy lifestyle, to save money instead of making debts, to finish school instead of leaving school without a certificate; mostly, it is only after a longer time that people are confronted with the consequences of their careless behaviour. "Let tomorrow take care of itself", they seem to think. Policymakers have to take this short-term thinking into account when setting out a policy, for instance with respect to health care and life course arrangements. Since most people are not inclined to change an unhealthy lifestyle, a policy of behavioral control is expected to be more effective than an appeal to people's own responsibility. Life course arrangements are not attractive for (younger) adults because they have to invest in something that can provide benefits only somewhere in the remote future.

The LIM-study shows that actually more events happen than have been expected before. In most cases these events are negative. For instance, only one respondent of the young age group expects the end of a relationship in the near future but five years later it turns out that five respondents of the young age group had to face this event. On the basis of these results it can be recommended to build in extra time when planning for the future. Often, unanticipated, unusual events occur. Musgrove (1985) stated that projects last at least twice as long as has been planned, depending on the number of steps that have to be taken within the project. The present study shows that the same happens at the individual level. People have an ideal, abstract picture of their future in mind, while in practice all kinds of unexpected events take place, causing delays or even a complete change of the course of life.

A more detailed analysis of the life story is necessary to answer the question to what extent expectations for the (near) future come true and to what extent expectations change when time is passing by. In the present analysis different explanations can be given in case respondents expect a specific event in the near future and this event is not mentioned when the future has become the recent past. It is possible that the event has taken place and is not mentioned anymore. It is also possible that the event has not taken place and is postponed or omitted because it is not important anymore. For instance, when a young adult expects to finish his studies in the near future and he does not mention this event in the recent past after five years he could have left university without graduation, he could have finished his studies without mentioning this event or his study progress could have been delayed and he still intends to finish his studies in the (near) future.

## 6.3 Autobiographical memory over the lifespan

Exploration of autobiographical memory from a lifespan perspective also generates knowledge of the human life course as experienced by individuals. As was mentioned in previous chapters, many different theories divide the life course in successive stages from birth till death (cf. Erikson, 1950; Levinson, 1986; Lowenthal, Thurner & Chiriboga, 1975). A few comments on these models can be given. First of all, the study of AM shows that not all stages in life are equal with respect to the number of events that are recalled or expected for that specific stage. As Kelly and McGrath (1988, p. 55) claim, people "do not experience time as a smooth linear flow of undifferentiated moments. Rather, they experience time as epochal and phasic in its flow. Different points in time and different periods of time seem to be qualitatively different from one another". Second, in the traditional stage models it is not clear from which perspective the life course is described. The stages are all described in an objective way but the LIM-study shows that the question how respondents experience a certain period in life depends on age, gender and time perspective. For instance, young women have very high expectations for the period of 30 to 40 years of age which is the (near) future for them, while middle-aged women who look back on this period are less positive about the same period of life. In the present study the life course is described from the perspective of men and women of three age groups. Their time perspective is changing as they grow older and, consequently, their perception of life, of past and future, changes.

### Age

This LIM-study shows that age plays an important role in how an individual evaluates his life, on which domains of life he is focused, how he views his past, what he expects from the future, how far he looks ahead and so on. An ageless life course, i.e., a life course in which age does not play a role, then, is unthinkable. The concept 'ageless life course' was introduced by Smolenaars (2005) who states that age should not be decisive for activities one performs; learning, working, caring and leisure activities are combined and alternated in different periods in life. But when planning the life course one has to take into account the biological peak of all kinds of physical and physiological functions, the period of fertility, the risks of illness and dying, the future time perspective and the life expectancy. For instance, loosing a parent will have more impact when it occurs at a younger age than when it occurs at middle-age when this event is anticipated (see also Neugarten, 1977). It is more likely for a middle-aged adult to take care of old, fragile parents than for a young adult. Age gives structure to the life course and is the most important singular predictor of all kinds of psychological phenomena in different areas of life (Schroots & Birren, 1990).

### Gender

In this study clear differences were found between the subjective life course of men and women. This is not surprising for the oldest age group because most men of this generation worked outside the house, while most women stayed home and took care of the children. However, a difference between the life course of men and women was also found for the youngest age group. Young women are focused on the near future in which they want to finish their studies and look forward to having a steady relationship and children. They have very high expectations of these events while young men seem to be more sober and mention more different events. Middle-aged men are focused more on Work than middle-aged women. Even though men and women get the same opportunities and have the same possibilities these days concerning education, work, making a career, taking care of children, working part-time, and even though women are encouraged to work more hours, in practice this policy does not always corresponds with the subjective experiences and expectations of men and women.

Men are also more vulnerable to loss of parents and partner. They mention these events more often than women do. Willitts, Benzeval and Stansfeld (2004) found that single women exposed a good mental health relative to other women, but the same was not true for single men relative to men who live in partnership. Concerning the future women are more optimistic than men are; positive events turned out to be more stable in the life stories of women, and negative events in the life stories of men. Women, with the exception of young women, have a more varied life story than men; they are more active at different domains of life, while men are focused mainly on their work. In short, it seems that women are the stronger sex.

Overall, it can be concluded that the present study has contributed to the development of a theory about life-course dynamics which should take into account the constantly changing perspective on past and future over the course of life and the difference in quantitative (number of events) and qualitative (affect) meaning of different periods in life. Besides, it can be concluded that the 'age-less non-sexist life course' is an ideological construct which does not match with the subjective feelings and experiences of people concerning their life course.

## Clinical application

Besides a method to gather autobiographical information for research purposes, the LIM offers various possibilities for application in the clinical practice. An important diagnostic characteristic of the LIM is that within about 45 minutes a clear, chronologically ordered overview of the total life course is obtained with all ups and downs which can be used, first of all, as the starting point for counseling in different areas. The LIM is a general instrument which yields information about different domains in life. As such it can be used, for instance, in pastoral work or when working with guided autobiography, life review and reminiscence (Birren & Deutchman, 1991; Schroots & Van Dongen, 1995). The LIM can also be applied in specific domains of life, for instance in educational or vocational counselling, in order to help a client to make proper educational and career decisions. In the field of health care the LIM can be used to determine how respondents experience transitions in the course of chronic diseases, which factors affect a more or less successful transition and what kind of assistance patients could be given at different transitions in different stages of their illness (De Lange & Van Staa, 2004).

Second, as different disorders affect AM in different ways, the LIM can be helpful as an instrument, for instance, for diagnosing depression and dementia. In the present study the LIM was administered to relatively healthy respondents. Results of this study can serve as a benchmark with which LIM-scores of other groups of respondents can be compared. For instance, Fromholt et al. (2003) found that older adults with Alzheimer's dementia mentioned fewer events than healthy adults (8 versus 18 events), but that the distribution of events over the lifespan showed the same pattern for both groups. Fromholt, Larsen and Larsen (1995) found that older respondents suffering from a major depression reported proportionally more negative events dating from the last five years than non-depressed older adults. Depressed individuals also show a tendency to be overgeneral, i.e., less specific, when recalling autobiographical memories (van Vreeswijk & de Wilde, 2004) and have problems imagining the future (Williams, Ellis, Tyers & Healy, 1996). Overgeneral autobiographical memory is also found to be characteristic for individuals who have been traumatized. Wessel, Merckelbach and Dekkers (2002) found that patients with various psychiatric diagnoses, who had all been exposed to war atrocities during their childhood, produced significantly less specific memories than did controls. DeVries, Suedfeld, Krell, Blando, and Southard (2005) found differences in the content of life stories of Holocaust survivors and of other groups; Holocaust survivors all started their life story at the beginning of the War in contrast to other groups, and life stories of Holocaust survivors were less varied than life stories of other groups.

Third, since the confrontation with one's own life, i.e., reflection on the past and anticipation of the future, can have a therapeutic effect the LIM can be used as the basis for therapeutic interventions such as cognitive therapy, client-centred therapy and narrative therapy. To this end a protocol was developed existing of seven sessions (Schroots, 2004). At the first and last session the LIM is administered for evaluation purposes according to the guidelines of the LIM-manual. At the sessions in-between and depending on the problems of the client different periods in life can be explored more intensively and different domains of life can be given specific attention.

## 6.4  Future studies

### LIM data set

The present study is part of the research program *Life-course Dynamics* (Schroots, 2003b). Meanwhile the fourth wave has been administered resulting in a longitudinal study extending over a period of ten years. Besides, respondents also completed several questionnaires at each wave including a personality questionnaire, a locus-of-control questionnaire, a coping questionnaire and a subjective well-being questionnaire.

First of all, the fourth wave can be analyzed in the same way as the first three waves. It would be particularly interesting to examine how the young age group has developed over a period of ten years, as changes in the life story turned out to be most prominent for this group. In a longitudinal study over a period of three years McAdams et al. (2006) found that young adults showed a clear development in their life stories: the emotional tone of the life story became more positive, life stories showed a greater level of emotional nuance and self differentiation, and a greater understanding of the own personal development.

Second, in addition to a series of temporally ordered life events administration of the LIM also yields both a life-line and a life story which can be analyzed separately and in relation to each other. Some aspects of the life-line, for instance its factor structure and time orientation, have been analyzed for the first wave (Schroots & Assink, 1998). The results showed that young adults are focused mainly on the future and the present, middle-aged adults on the past and the present and older adults on the past. A factor analysis of twelve characteristic measures of the life-line yielded five factors: one for each phase in life (adolescence, young adulthood, late adulthood and older age) and one for the emotional tone of the life story. The life story can also be analyzed at different levels. For instance, Schroots, Kunst and Assink (2006) simply counted the number of words respondents needed to tell their life story and found that respondents used more words to describe an event from the past than an event in the future and that negative events were described more extensively than positive events. As the LIM-study is a longitudinal study it is also possible to examine changes of different aspects of the life story over the lifespan. For instance, McAdams et al. (2006) studied the continuity of emotional tone, theme and structure of life stories over a period of three months and three years. They found a substantial continuity of the complexity and the emotional tone of the narrative and a moderate continuity of the themes power and growth.

Third, the relationship between different aspects of the life story and other variables can be explored. According to McAdams (1996; 2001) the narrative or life story is part of personality. Personality can be described on three, relatively independent non-overlapping levels. The first level is the level of personality traits which are rather stable over the lifespan (McCrae & Costa, 1990). The second level is called 'personal concerns' and relates to different constructs that are contextualized in time, place and role (for instance: personal strivings, defense mechanisms, goals, coping strategies). The third level concerns the level of the identity of an individual which is expressesed in the life story. This LIM-study has added to the body of knowledge at the third level. An interesting question is whether a connection exists between different levels of personality and whether specific patterns can be discerned. Since in the LIM-study also questionnaires concerning the first (personality traits) and second (coping, locus of control) level of personality were administered, it is possible to describe relations between the three levels of personality. McAdams et al. (2004) examined the relationship between the first and third level. They studied the relationship between the Big Five and some aspects of the life story (emotional tone, theme and structure). Openness was positively related to the construction of a more complex life narrative, Agreeableness was positively related to themes of communion and Neuroticism was positively related to an emotional negative tone in the life story. No relation was found between aspects of the life story and the traits Conscientiousness and Extraversion. Results of the subjective well-being questionnaire can also be related to different aspects of the life story. For instance, the relation between reported positive and negative life events and subjective well-being can be analyzed. Suh, Diener and Fujita (1996) found that only recent events, which had occurred in the preceding three months, had an effect on subjective well-being and on positive or negative affect. Their sample included students in the age of 20–21 years. The LIM-study shows a tendency that the recency effect covers a longer period for older respondents than for younger respondents. On the basis of this finding it can be hypothesized that the period in which events have an effect on subjective well-being is longer for older than for younger adults. Because most questionnaires have been administered at each wave the stability of variables measured by these questionnaires can be determined and can be related to (changes in) the life story.

## Prospective memory

Studies on AM have primarily focused on retrospective autobiographical memory. Prospective autobiographical memory, then, is a relatively unknown area and offers many possibilities for further research. The present study, for instance, shows that many respondents find it hard to identify events in the future. At the first wave ten percent of the respondents of the oldest group did not mention any event in the future. The question, then, is to what extent individuals occupy themselves with the future and how this is related to other variables. The LIM-study showed that respondents are more focused on the near future than on the more distant future. Fingerman and Perlmutter (1995) found that adults of all ages think most frequently about the next few months but that young adults also think frequently about more distant periods in contrast to older adults. Young and older individuals think more about the distant future when they have a feeling to control events expected in the near future.

Respondents in the LIM-study sometimes wanted to draw two future life-lines; a line in case everything worked out in a positive way and a line in case everything worked out in a negative way. This may relate to the concept of 'possible selves' introduced by Markus and Nurius (1986). Possible selves are ideas of what one might become in the future. This can refer to one's 'hoped for self', one's 'expected self' or one's 'feared self'. In the LIM-study we asked respondents to draw a future line which expresses their expectations, not their hopes or fears regarding the future. It would be interesting to find out to what extent this expected future corresponds with the future one hopes for and the future one fears, and to determine the impact of these possible futures on present behaviour.

When people talk about their future they reveal more or less explicitly their goals for the future. The life story could be analyzed with respect to the kind of goals respondents set for their future and how these goals change as people grow older. In their socio-emotional selectivity theory Carstensen, Isaacowitz and Charles (1999) pose that the perception of time plays a decisive role in choosing and pursuing social goals. When time is perceived as unlimited individuals give priority to knowledge based goals. When time is perceived as limited, emotional goals are given priority. It seems that the study of the future has the future!

# Chapter 7
# Summary and Conclusion

## 7.1 Summary

The main aim of this longitudinal, explorative study is to describe the dynamics of autobiographical memory (AM) over the lifespan. The study covers a period of five years in which the Life-line Interview Method was administered three times to 98 men and women about equally divided over a young (18–30 yrs), middle (31–55 yrs) and older age group (56–84 yrs). Autobiographical memories and expectations were analyzed from the perspective of number, affect and content of events. The effect of age, gender and time perspective on stability and change was determined.

In *Chapter 1* a short overview is given of the history and position of research on AM. In the present study 'autobiographical memory' is broadly defined as 'a type of episodic memory for both retrospective (memories) and prospective information (expectations) related to the self'. In studies on AM many different methods are used to collect autobiographical data. An overview of these methods is given in Chapter 1. In the present study autobiographical information was collected by means of the *Life-line Interview Method* (LIM), a semi-structured interview which combines a quantitative and a qualitative approach. The background and use of this method are described in detail. Administration of the LIM results in a life-line, a series of chronologically ordered life events and a life story. In this study analysis of the data was limited to the analysis of life events. A special LIM-category list was developed in order to classify reported events. Finally, a description is given of the design of the study, the respondents who participated in the study, the administration of the LIM and the statistical analysis of the LIM-data.

In *Chapter 2* the *number and distribution of events* respondents report over their lifespan is examined. In the LIM-study the average numbers of events respondents identify over the total lifespan for the first, second and third wave is 7.03, 7.52 and 8.25, respectively. A salient finding is that the sum of past and future autobiographical events turned out to be constant across the lifespan; this was called the *Principle of the Constant Life Perspective*. Life stories of all age groups are characterized by a greater number of past than of future events but the older the group, the greater the number of past events; in contrast, the younger the group, the greater the number of future events. Over three waves respondents mention significantly more events over their total lifespan, which is probably a test-retest effect. As respondents grow older the ratio of past and total number of events increases, i.e., respondents mention more events in the past and fewer in the future. The data indicate that the change in ratio of past and total number of events decreases as people grow older.

The distribution of past events shows a strong *recency effect* for the young age group, i.e., respondents recall more events from the recent past than from the distant past. For future events a *proximity effect* was found, i.e., respondents expect more events in the near future than in the distant future. This recency/proximity effect is moving with increasing age. For the older age group a recency/proximity effect is found and a *memory bump,* i.e., older respondents report a larger number of memories than expected on basis of the classical forgetting curve of Ebbinghaus for the period of late adolescence and early adulthood. The distribution of events for the middle age group shows an emerging bump and recency/proximity effects. Various explanations for the bump phenomenon are presented and discussed. In addition to the lifespan distribution of events it was found that the average age at which respondents situate the first event is about 12 years without an effect of age or gender. The mean age at which respondents expect the last event in life, which is mostly situated in the future, and at which respondents expect to die appears to depend on age; the older respondents are, the later in life they situate the last event and the moment of expected death.

In *Chapter 3* the *affective rating of events* was determined and the ratio of (very) positive and (very) negative affect was examined as well as the distribution of (very) positive and (very) negative affect over the lifespan. Overall, *respondents report as many positive as negative events for the total life and for the past and the future separately*, i.e., the overall affective rating of the total life and of the past and future was found to be neutral. A tendency was found that young women are more positive about their whole life than young men, while middle-aged men are more positive than middle-aged women and older men and women are about equally positive (or negative). It was also found that *the older respondents are, the more positive they are about the past and the more negative about the future*. Concerning the percentage of intense affect it was found that more events are accompanied by an intense affect in the past than in the future. A greater percentage of past events is rated as 'very negative' than as 'very positive', while the percentages of 'very positive' and 'very negative' events for the future do not differ significantly from each other.

The distribution of positive and negative events over the lifespan shows a *bump for positive events for the middle-aged and older age groups*. For the older age group there is also a narrow bump for negative events which starts at the beginning of the Second World War. Besides, for all age groups there are recency effects for negative events and proximity effects for positive events which move with increasing age. The distribution of 'very positive' and 'very negative' events shows about the same pattern for the young and middle age group as the distribution of positive and negative events. For the older age group 'very positive' and 'very negative' events are distributed irregular over the lifespan without a specific pattern. The first important event respondents recall from the past is predominantly accompanied by a negative affect; for the last event a tendency was found that older adults are most negative about this event. The *best period in life*, i.e., the decade for which the ratio of positive events to the total number of events is highest, is the period between about *20 to 40 years* of age. The *worst period in life*, i.e., the decade for which the ratio of the number of negative events to the total number of events is highest, is the period of *70 to 80 years* of age followed by childhood.

In **Chapter 4** the first wave is analyzed concerning the *content of memories and expectations and the main affect of these specific events*. To this end LIM-events were classified into forty subcategories divided over *nine categories: Relations, School, Work, Health, Growth, Home, Birth, Death and Other*. Per decade the distribution of events over (sub)categories was determined and the most frequently mentioned (sub)categories per decade were selected resulting in a description of the modal life course for the total group and for men and women of three age groups. For the total group it turned out that *childhood and adolescence are characterized by School and Home, young adulthood by Relations, middle adulthood by Work, and older adulthood by Health and Death*. The content of autobiographical memories and expectations turned out to be dependent of age and gender. For instance, young men expect Birth Child later than young women, Death Parents was mentioned more often by middle-aged men than by middle-aged women, and older men expected more often Death Partner in the future than older women. *The past is characterized by more personal memories, while the future is more prototypical.* As people grow older the view they have on their past and future changes, which favors a more dynamic view on the human life-course.

In **Chapter 5** *stability and change of (patterns of) life events* over a period of two and five years are analyzed. First, the second and third wave were content-analyzed in the same way as the first wave and the results of the three waves were compared to each other. Examples of patterns that appeared to be stable are: *older respondents recall mainly events from the bump period which indicate a beginning or a development and which are rated positively; men appear to be more focused on Work while women are more focused on Health and Birth; men are more dependent on parents and partner than women; older adults report fewer events in the category Growth than younger adults*.

Second, the intra-individual stability of events over three waves was determined. Stability was defined as recalling similar events, i.e., events that are classified into the same (sub)categories, by the same respondents at different points in time. *Over a period of five years about one third of memories and expectations is mentioned at each wave. The view people have of the past is more stable than that of the future.* Especially young adults have a very unstable view of the future. The periods in life from which respondents report most similar events over three waves are childhood and the period of 20 to

30 years of age. For the past negative events are more fixed in memory than positive events. For the future it was found that negative events are more stable for men while positive events are more stable for women. Events within the category Relations are most stable in the life story followed by School, Death and Other, while events concerning Growth are least stable. Events within the subcategories Relations Others, Travel, Problems Work, Death Family, End Relations, Birth Family, War and Rest, which are generally accompanied by a negative affect – except for Travel and Birth Family –, are most stable. *In general, people have normative expectations for the future. They also expect fewer events to happen in the near future than actually happen. Most of these unexpected events are negative non-normative events.* The younger respondents are, the stronger this pattern. The present study focuses on the stability of events. On the basis of theories of memory and on the basis of inspection of different versions of the life story possible explanations for changes in the life story are provided. It is concluded that the life story is constantly being reconstructed.

In **Chapter 6** different aspects of the methodological approach followed in this study – *explorative, quantitative and qualitative, more inductive than deductive, and idiothetic* – are discussed. It is argued that due to the chosen approach the study has yielded rich information about AM and the subjective life course. An important contribution of the present study to the body of knowledge about AM is the fact that it is a longitudinal study and that both *retrospective and prospective AM* are included. Practical implications of findings of this study for the individual life and for setting out a policy in different areas are mentioned. Next, various possibilities for *clinical application* of the LIM are discussed; the LIM can be used as the starting point for counseling, as a diagnostic instrument and as a therapeutic tool. Finally, *future research* is outlined, based on the full LIM-data set, including a fourth wave, a life-line, a life story and several questionnaires.


## 7.2   Conclusion

The LIM-study has yielded a large quantity of information about AM and about the subjective life course of individuals. In the following, conclusions with regard to the main findings of the study will be presented in terms of *Principles* (P), i.e., robust results for which a strong effect was found and which are also found in other studies, *Hypotheses* (H), i.e., significant results which were only found in this particular LIM-study, and *Trends* (T), i.e., results for which a trend was found. Hypotheses and trends need to be tested in follow-up studies on larger samples. Generally, it is concluded that the contours of the dynamics of autobiographical memory over the lifespan have been marked.

### Events of life
*P:* The Principle of the Constant Life Perspective, i.e., the sum of past and future autobiographical events is constant across the lifespan.
*P:* Respondents of all age groups mention more events in the past than in the future. The ratio of past and future events changes over time, i.e., as people grow older the proportion of past events increases whereas the proportion of future events decreases.
*T:* The change in the ratio of past and future events is most prominent for the young age group.
*P:* The distribution of events over the lifespan shows strong recency and proximity effects for the young age group, an emerging bump and a recency and proximity effect for the middle age group, and a clear bump and a recency/proximity effect for the older age group. The recency/proximity effect is moving with calendar age of the respondent by definition, while the bump has a fixed peak between 20 to 30 years of age, the period of Commitment.
*T:* The recency effect seems to cover a longer period for older respondents than for younger respondents; the frequency of events in the recent past, however, is much lower for older respondents than for younger respondents.

*P:* The average age at which the first and last event are situated, is dependent on the method used. The average age of the first event is independent of respondent's age, while the average age of the last mentioned event depends on age: the older respondents are, the later they situate the last event.

*H:* The older respondents are the later they situate the moment of expected death.

## Stability of events

*H:* The life story has a stable core which contains about one third of all events respondents mention over their total lifespan over a period of five years.

*T:* The life story of older adults is more stable than the life story of younger adults.

*H:* The past is more stable than the future and especially young adults have a very unstable view of the future.

*H:* Childhood and the period of 20 to 30 years of age are the most stable periods in life; at each wave respondents mention more similar events in these periods than in any other period of life. From adolescence older respondents did not recall the same events at different measurement points.

*H:* More events in the near future actually happen than respondents expect to happen. The younger respondents are, the stronger this pattern.

## Affect in life

*H:* Overall, life is perceived as affective neutral.

*P:* As people grow older the past is valuated more positive and the future more negative.

*T:* Young women are more positive about their whole life than young men, while middle-aged men are more positive than middle-aged women and older men and women are about equally positive (or negative).

*H:* The first mentioned event is mostly a negative event.

*T:* The affect of the last mentioned event is depending on age: the last event older adults report is more often negative than the last event younger adults report.

*P:* The distribution of negative events shows a forgetting curve for all subgroups and for older adults also a small bump which correspondents with the beginning of the Second World War.

*P:* The distribution of positive events shows a bump for middle-aged and older age groups.

*H:* The distribution of positive events shows a proximity effect.

*H:* Respondents have more intense feelings about the past than for the future.

*H:* Respondents mention more extreme negative than extreme positive events in the past.

*T:* Women report more very positive events from the past than men do.

*T:* Overall, respondents expect the same numbers of very positive and very negative events in the future but the older individuals are the fewer 'very positive' events are exptected for the future.

*H:* The distribution of intense affect over the lifespan follows about the same pattern as the distribution of positive and negative events over the lifespan for the young and middle-age group.

*T:* For the older age group intense affects are distributed irregularly over the lifespan.

*P:* Traumatic events have the power to disturb the normal pattern (of distribution) of events over the lifespan and can cause a negative bump or an extension of the bump period.

*T:* Young adults, who look forward to, and older adults, who look back at certain events, for instance Commitment and Work-related events, are more positive about these events than middle-aged adults who actually experience these events (rosy view phenomenon).

*T:* The period between 20 to 40 years of age is considered the best period in life, while the period of 70 to 80 years of age is considered as the worst period in life followed by childhood.

## Stability of affect

*H:* With respect to the past it seems that negative events are more stable than positive events.

*T:* For the future it turns out that positive events are more stable for women than for men, while negative events are more stable for men than for women.

*H:* Memories from the bump period are mostly positive memories. Negative memories from this period, however, are relatively more stable than positive memories.

*H:* More events actually happen than respondents expect to happen in the near future and most of these events are negative events.

## Content of life

*P:* The general pattern of the life course shows that childhood and adolescence are characterized by School, young adulthood by Relations, middle adulthood by Work, and older adulthood by Health and Death.

*H:* Events within the categories Relations and School are mentioned most frequently. Events within the subcategories Physical Health, Commitment, Birth Child and Starting School are mentioned most frequently.

*P:* The content of autobiographical memories and expectations is dependent of age and gender.

*H:* Younger respondents mention more events within the category Growth than older respondents.

*P:* Men mention more events in the category Work while women mention more events in the categories Health and Birth. Men are more dependent of parents and partner than women. The life course of women shows greater variety than the life course of men especially as they get older.

*P:* The past life story consists of personal memories while the future life story is more generic and mainly normative.

## Stability of content

H: Events in the life story within the category Relations are most stable followed by School, Death and Other, while events concerning Growth are least stable. Events within the subcategories Relations Others, Travel, Problems Work, Death Family, End Relations, Birth Family, War and Rest, which are mainly accompanied by a negative affect, are most stable.

H: Memories from the bump period are mostly positive memories such as Begin Relations, Commitment, Birth Child, Finishing School and Beginning Work. Negative memories from this period, however, are relatively more stable than positive memories.

Generally, it can be concluded that a start has been made with the exploration of the dynamics of autobiographical memory. The contours of (patterns of) stability and change of autobiographical memory over the lifespan have been marked. Since there are almost no empirical data concerning the development of AM over the adult lifespan the results of this LIM-study can serve as a starting point with which results of future studies can be compared. What is more, examining AM in a lifespan perspective provides a good deal of information about the subjective human life course which can be used in everyday life as well as for policy developments in different areas, for instance with respect to health care and life course arrangements. The LIM-data set offers a variety of opportunities to continue the study of AM and raises quite a number of interesting questions concerning the great themes of life.

# References

Abeles, R.P. (1987). *Lifespan perspectives and social psychology.* Hillsdale: Lawrence Erlbaum Associates.

Aldwin, C.M., & Levenson, M.R. (2001). Stress, coping, and health at midlife: A developmental perspective. In M.E. Lachman (Ed). (2001), *Handbook of midlife development* (pp. 188–214). New York: John Wiley & Sons.

Allport, G.W. (1937). *Personality: A psychological interpretation.* New York: Holt, Rinehart & Winston.

Anderson, S.J., Cohen, G. & Taylor, S. (2000). Rewriting the past: some factors affecting the variability of personal memories. *Applied Cognitive Psychology, 14,* 435–454.

d'Argembeau, A., Comblain, C., & Van der Linden, M. (2003). Phenomenal characteristics of autobiographical memories for positive, negative and neutral events. *Applied Cognitive Psychology, 17,* 281–294.

Assink, M. (1996). *LIM|Levenslijn: Structuuranalyse* [LIM|Life-line: Structural analysis] (MA thesis). Amsterdam, The Netherlands: University of Amsterdam.

Assink, M.H.J., & Schroots, J.J.F. (2002). The distribution of affect over the lifespan. *Hallym International Journal of Aging, 4,* 99–117.

Back, K.W. (1982). Types of life course and gerontology. *Academic Psychology Bulletin, 4,* 9–16.

Back, K.W., & Bourque, L. (1970). Life graphs: Aging and cohort effect. *Journal of Gerontology, 25,* 249–255.

Baddeley, A. (1992). What is autobiographical memory? In M.A. Conway, D.C. Rubin, H. Spinnler, & W.A. Wagenaar (Eds.), *Theoretical perspectives on autobiographical memory* (pp. 13–29). NATO ASI Series D: Behavioural and Social Sciences, Vol. 65. Dordrecht, The Netherlands: Kluwer Academic.

Baddeley, A.D. (1999). *Essentials of human memory.* East Sussex: Psychology Press.

Baltes, P.B. (1968). Longitudinal and cross-sectional sequences in the study of age and generation effects. *Human Development, 11,* 145–171.

Baltes, P.B., & Nesselroade, J.R. (1979). History and rationale of longitudinal research. In J.R. Nesselrade & P.B. Baltes (Eds.), *Longitudinal research in the study of behavior and development.* New York: Academic Press.

Baltes, P.B., Reese, H.W., & Lipsitt, L.P. (1980). Lifespan developmental psychology. *Annual Review Psychology, 31,* 65–110.

Baltes, P. B., Reese, H. W., & Nesselroade, J. R. (1988). *Introduction to research methods, lifespan developmental psychology.* Hillsdale, NJ: Lawrence Erlbaum Associates, Inc.

Baum, S.K., & Stewart, R.B. (1990). Sources of meaning through the lifespan. *Psychological Reports, 67,* 3–14.

Baumeister, R.F., Bratslavsky, E., Finkenauer, C., & Vohs, K.D. (2001). Bad is stronger than good. *Review of General Psychology, 5,* 323–370.

Banaji, M.R., & Crowder, R.G. (1989). The bankruptcy of everyday memory. *American Psychologist, 44,* 1185–1193.

Bartlett, F. (1932). *Remembering.* Cambridge: Cambridge University Press.

Bee, H. (1995). *Lifespan development.* New York: Harper Collins College Publishers.

Beets, G., Dourleijn, E., Liefbroer, A. & Henkens, K. (2000). *De timing van het eerste kind in Nederland en Europa* [Timing of birth first child in The Netherlands and Europe]. 's-Gravenhage, The Netherlands: Ministerie van Sociale Zaken en Werkgelegenheid.

Berntsen, D. & Rubin, D.C. (2002). Emotionally charged autobiographical memories across the lifespan: the recall of happy, sad, traumatic, and involuntary memories. *Psychology and Aging, 17,* 636–652.

Birren, J.E., & Deutchmann, D.E. (1991). *Guiding autobiography groups for older adults; exploring the fabric of life.* Baltimore: Johns Hopkins University Press.

Birren, J.E. & Hedlund, B. (1987). Contributions of autobiography to developmental psychology. In N. Eisenberg (Ed.), *Contemporary topics in developmental psychology.* New York: John Wiley & Sons.

Birren, J.E., & Schroots, J.J.F. (2001). The history of geropsychology. In J.E. Birren & K.W. Schaie (Eds.), *Handbook of the psychology of aging* (5th ed.) (pp. 3–52). San Diego: Academic Press.

Birren, J.E., & Schroots, J.J.F. (2006). Autobiographical memory and the narrative self over the lifespan. In J.E. Birren & K.W. Schaie (Eds.), *Handbook of the psychology of aging* (6th ed.) (pp. 477–498). San Diego: Academic Press.

Blonsky, P. (1929). Das Problem der ersten Kindheitserinnerung und seine Bedeutung. *Archiv für die gesamte Psychologie, 71,* 369–390.

Bluck, S. (2001). Autobiographical memories: A building block of life narratives. In G. Kenyon, P. Clark & B. de Vries (Eds.), *Narrative gerontology: Theory, research, and practice* (pp. 67–89). New York: Springer.

Bluck, S., & Habermas, T. (2000). The life story schema. *Motivation and Emotion, 24,* 121–147.

Bluck, S., & Habermas, T. (2001). Extending the study of autobiographical memory: Thinking back about life across the lifespan. *Review of General Psychology, 5,* 135–147.

Bohlmeijer, E., Smit, F., & Cuijpers, P. (2003). Effects of reminiscence and life review on late-life depression: a meta-analysis. *International Journal of Geriatric Psychiatry, 18,* 1088–1094.

Bourque, L.B., & Back, K.W. (1977). Life graphs and life events. Journal of Gerontology, 32, 669–674.

Brewer, W.F. (1986). What is autobiographical memory? In D.C. Rubin (Ed.), *Autobiographical memory* (pp. 25–49). Cambridge, UK: Cambridge University Press.

Brewer, W.F. (1995). What is recollective memory? In D.C. Rubin (Ed.), *Remembering our past: Studies in autobiographical memory* (pp. 19–66). Cambridge, UK: Cambridge University Press.

Brim, O.G., & Ryff, C.D. (1980). On the properties of life events. In P.B. Baltes & O.G. Brim (Eds.), *Lifespan development and behavior* (Vol. 3). New York: Academic Press.

Broadbent, D.E. (1958). *Perception and communication.* New York: Pergamon Press.

Brugman, G.M.M. (2000). *Wisdom: Source of narrative coherence and eudaimonia: A lifespan perspective.* Delft, The Netherlands: Eburon.

Bühler, C. (1933). *Der Menschliche Lebenslauf als Psychologisches Problem.* Leipzig: Hirzel.

Burt, C.D.B., Kemp, S., & Conway, M.A. (2003). Themes, events, and episodes in autobiographical memory. Memory and Cognition, 31, 317–325.

Butler, R. (1963). The life review: An interpretation of reminiscence in the aged. *Psychiatry, 26,* 65–76.

Carstensen, L.L., Isaacowitz, D.M. & Charles S.T. (1999). Taking time seriously: A theory of socioemotional selectivity. *American Psychologist, 54,* 165–181.

Chiriboga, D.A. (1984). Social stressors as antecedents of change. *Journal of Gerontology, 39,* 468–477.

Christianson, S. & Safer, M.A. (1996). Emotional events and emotions in autobiographical memories. In D.C. Rubin (Ed.), *Remembering our past: Studies in autobiographical memory* (pp. 218–243). Cambridge, UK: University Press.

Cochrane, R., & Robertson, A. (1973). The life events inventory: A measure of the relative severity of psychosocial stressors. *Journal of Psychosomatic research, 17,* 135–139.

Collins Cobuild English Dictionary (1995). The University of Birmingham: Harper Collins Publishers.

Conway, M.A., & Fthenaki, A. (2000). Disruption and loss of autobiographical memory. In L. Cermak (Ed.), *Handbook of neuropsychology: Memory and its disorders* (2nd ed., pp. 257–288). Amsterdam, The Netherlands: Elsevier.

Conway, M.A., & Haque, S. (1999). Overshadowing the reminiscence bump: Memories of a struggle for independence. *Journal of Adult Development, 6,* 35–44.

Conway, M.A., & Holmes, A. (2004). Psychosocial stages and the accessibility of autobiographical memories across the life cycle. *Journal of Personality, 72,* 461–480.

Conway, M.A., & Pleydell-Pearce, C.W. (2000). The construction of autobiographical memories in the self-memory system. Psychological Review, 107, 261–288.

Conway, M.A., & Tacchi, P.C. (1996). Motivated confabulation. *Neurocase, 2,* 325–339.

Crovitz, H.F., & Schiffman, H. (1974). Frequency of episodic memories as a function of their age. *Bulletin of the Psychonomic Society, 4,* 517–518.

Conway, M. A., Wang, Q., Hanyu, K., & Haque, S. (2005). A cross-cultural investigation of autobiographical memory: On the universality and cultural variation of the "Reminiscence Bump." *Journal of Cross-Cultural Psychology, 36,* 739–749.

Danish, S.J., Smyer, M.A., & Nowak, C. (1980). Developmental intervention: Enhancing life-event processes. In P.B. Baltes & O.G. Brim (Eds*.), Lifespan development and behavior* (Vol. 3). New York: Academic Press.

Davis, P.J. (1999). Gender differences in autobiographical memory for childhood emotional experiences. *Journal of Personality and Social Psychology, 76,* 498–510.

Deeg, D.J.H. (1989). *Experiences from longitudinal studies of aging: Conceptualization, organization, and output.* Nijmegen, The Netherlands: Netherlands Institute of Gerontology.

Deeg, D.J.H. (2002). Volksgezondheid en epidemiologie [Public health and epidemiology]. In J.J.F. Schroots (Red.), *Handboek psychologie van de volwassen ontwikkeling & veroudering* [Handbook of adult development and aging] (pp. 433–454). Assen, The Netherlands: Koninklijke Van Gorcum.

Draaisma, D. (2001). *Waarom het leven sneller gaat als je ouder wordt: Over het autobiografisch geheugen.* Groningen: Historische Uitgeverij [translated by Arnold Pomerans and Erica Pomerans in 2004: Why life speeds up as you get older: How memory shapes our past. Cambridge, UK: Cambridge University Press].

Drenth, P.J.D., & Heller, F. (2004). The dangers of resource myopia in work and organisational psychology: A plea for broadening and integration. *Applied Psychology: An International Review, 53,* 599–613.

Drenth, P.J.D. & Sijtsma, K. (2006). *Testtheorie. Inleiding in de theorie van de psychologische test en zijn toepassingen* [Testtheory. Introduction in the theory of psychological tests and its applictions].   Houten/Antwerpen: Bohn Stafleu Van Loghum.

Ebbinghaus, H.E. (1964). *Memory: A contribution to experimental psychology.* New York: Dover (Original work published 1885).

Elder, G.H., Jr. (1998). The life course and human development. In R.M. Lerner (Ed.), *Handbook of child psychology: Vol. 1. Theoretical models of human development* (pp. 939–991). New York: John Wiley & Sons.

Elnick, A.B., Margrett, J.A., Fitzgerald, J.M., & Labouvie-Vief, G. (1999). Benchmark memories in adulthood: Central domains and predictors of their frequency. *Journal of Adult Development, 6,* 45–59.

Erikson, E.H. (1950). *Childhood and society.* New York: W.W. Norton.

Erikson, E.H. (1958). *Young man Luther: A study in psychoanalysis and history.* New York: Norton.

Erikson, E.H. (1969). *Ghandi's truth: On the origins of militant nonviolence.* New York: Norton.

Faltermaier, T. (1997). Why public health research needs qualitative approaches; Subjects and methods in change. *European Journal of Health Psychology, 7,* 357–363.

Ferraro, K.F., & Kelley-Moore, J.A. (2003). A half century of longitudinal methods in social gerontology: Evidence of change in the journal. *Journal of Gerontology: 58B,* S264–S270.

Fingerman, K.L., & Perlmutter, M. (1995). Future time perspective and life events across adulthood. *The Journal of General Psychology, 122,* 95–111.

Fitzgerald, J.M. (1988). Vivid memories and the reminiscence phenomenon: The role of a self narrative. *Human Development, 31,* 261–273.

Fitzgerald, J.M. (1992). Autobiographical memory and conceptualization of the self. In M.A. Conway, D.C. Rubin, H. Spinnler, & W.A. Wagenaar (Eds.), *Theoretical perspectives on autobiographical memory* (pp. 99–114). Boston: Kluwer Academic.

Field, D. (1997). Looking back, what period of your life brought you the most satisfaction. *International Journal of Aging & Human Development, 45,* 169–194.

Fischer, C.T. (1996). A humanistic and human science approach to emotion. In C. Magai & S.H. McFadden (Eds.), *Handbook of Emotion, Adult Development, and Aging* (pp. 67–82). San Diego: Academic Press.

Fitzgerald, J.M. (1995). Intersecting meanings of reminiscence in adult development and aging. In D.C. Rubin (Ed.), *Remembering our past: Studies in autobiographical memory* (pp. 360–383). Cambridge, UK: Cambridge University Press.

Fleeson, W., & Heckhausen, J. (1997). More or less of "me" in past, present and future: Perceived lifetime personality during adulthood. *Psychology and Aging, 12,* 125–136.

Frankl, V.E. (1978). *The unheared cry for meaning.* New York: Simon and Schuster.

Frenkel, E. (1936). Studies in biographical psychology. *Character and Personality, 5,* 1–35.

Frijda, N.H. (1988). The laws of emotion. *American Psychologist, 43,* 349–358.

Fromholt, P. & Larsen, S.F. (1992). Autobiographical memory and life-history narratives in ageing and dementia (Alzheimer type). In M.A. Conway, D.C. Rubin, H. Spinnler & W.A. Wagenaar (Eds.), *Theoretical perspectives on autobiographical memory* (pp. 413–426). Dordrecht, The Netherlands: Kluwer Academic Publishers.

Fromholt, P., Larsen, P. & Larsen, S.F. (1995). Effects of late-onset depression and recovery on autobiographical memory. *Journal of Gerontology: Psychological Sciences, 50,* 74–81.

Fromholt, P., Mortensen, D.B., Torpdahl, P., Bender, L. Larsen, P. & Rubin, D.C. (2003). Life-narrative and word-cued autobiographical memories in centenarians: Comparisons with 80-year-old control, depressed, and dementia groups. *Memory, 11,* 81–88.

Galton, F. (1879). Psychometric experiments. *Brain, 2,* 149–162.

Gergen, M.M. (1988). Narrative structures in social explantion. In C. Antaki (Ed.), *Analysing everyday explanation: A Casebook of Methods* (pp. 94–112). London: SAGE Publications.

Gergen, K.J., & Gergen, M.M. (1987). The self in temporal perspective. In R.P. Abeles (Ed.), *Lifespan perspectives and social psychology* (pp. 121–137). Hillsdale: Lawrence Erlbaum Associates.

Glickman, L., Hubbard, M., Liveright, T. & Valciukas, J.A. (1990). Fall-off in reporting life events: Effects of life change, desirability, and anticipation. *Behavioral Medicine, Spring,* 31–38.

Greenwald, A.G. (1980). The totalitarian ego: Fabrication and revision of personal history. *American Psychologist, 35,* 603–618.

Grob, A., Krings, F., & Bangerter, A. (2001). Life markers in biographical narratives of people from three cohorts: A lifespan perspective in its historical context. *Human Development, 44,* 171–190.

Hall, G.S (1922). *Senescence: The last half of life.* New York: D. Appleton.

Hawking, S. (1988). *A brief history of time.* New York: Bantam.

Headey, B. & Wearing, A. (1992). *Understanding Happiness: A theory of subjective well-being.* Melbourne: Longman Cheshire.

Hentschel, U., Sumbadze, N., & Shubladze, S. (2000). The effect of the general I-E locus of control conviction on remembering and planning one's life: Individual differences in life events reports of Georgian respondents. *Social Behavior and Personality, 28,* 443–454.

Hermans, H.J.M. (1992). Telling and retelling one's self-narrative: A contextual approach to lifespan development. *Human Development, 35*, 361–375.

Hofer, S.M., & Sliwinski, M.J. (2006). Design and analysis of longitudinal studies on aging. In J.E. Birren & K.W. Schaie (Eds.), *Handbook of the psychology of aging* (6th ed.) (pp. 15–37). San Diego: Academic Press.

Holbrook, M.B., & Schindler, R.M. (1989). Some exploratory findings on the development of musical tastes. *Journal of Consumer Research, 16*, 119–124.

Holmes, A., & Conway, M.A. (1999). Generation identity and the reminiscence bump: Memory for public and private events. *Journal of Adult Development, 6*, 21–34.

Holmes, T.H., & Rahe, R.H. (1967). The Social Readjustment Rating Scale. Journal of Psychosomatic Research, 14, 121–132.

Holsti, O.R. (1968). Content analysis. In G. Linzey, & E. Aronson (Eds.), *The handbook of social psychology: Research methods* (pp. 596–692). Massachusetts: Addison-Wesley Publishing Company.

Hooker, K. (1999). Possible selves in adulthood: Incorporating teleonomic relevance into studies of the self. In T.M. Hess & F. Blanchard-Fields (Eds.), *Social cognition and aging* (pp. 97–122). San Diego: Academic Press.

Hooker, K. (2002). New directions for research in personality and aging: A comprehensive model for linking levels, structures, and processes. *Journal of Research in Personality, 36,* 318–334.

Howe, M.L., & Courage, M.L. (1997). The emergence and early development of autobiographical memory. *Psychological Review, 104*, 499–523.

Hoyle, R.H., Harris, M.J., & Judd, C.M. (2002). *Research methods in social relations* (7th ed.). South Melbourne, Vic.: Wadsworth/Thomson Learning.

Jansari, A. & Parkin, A.J. (1996). Things that go bump in your life: Explaining the reminiscence bump in autobiographical memory. *Psychology and Aging, 11*, 85–91.

Janssen, S. M. J., Chessa, A. G., & Murre, J. M. J. (2005). The reminiscence bump in autobiographical memory: Effects of age, gender, education, and culture. *Memory, 13,* 658–668.

Josselson, R. (2000). Stability and change in early memories over 22 years: Themes, variations, and cadenzas. *Bulletin of the Menninger Clinic, 64*, 462–482.

Karney, B., & Coombes, R.H. (2000). Memory bias in long-term close relationships: Consistency or improvement? *Personality and Social Psychology Bulletin, 26*, 959–970.

Kelly, J.R., & McGrath, J.E. (1988). *On time and method.* Newbury Park, CA: Sage.

Kenyon, G., Clark, P., & de Vries, B. (Eds.) (2001). *Narrative gerontology: Theory, research, and practice.* New York: Springer Publishing Company.

Kenyon, G.M., & Randall, W.L. (1999). Introduction: Narrative gerontology. *Journal of Aging Studies, 13*, 1–5.

Keys, C.L.M., & Ryff, C.D. (1999). Psychological well-being in midlife. In S.L. Willis & J.D. Reid (Eds.), *Life in the middle: Psychological and social development in middle age* (pp. 161–180). San Diego: Academic Press.

Kim, J.E., & Moen P. (2001). Moving into retirement: Preparation and transitions in late midlife. In M.E. Lachman (Ed.) (2001), *Handbook of midlife development* (pp. 487–527). New York: John Wiley & Sons.

Kluckhohn, C. & Murray, H.A. (1953). Personality formation: The determinants. In C. Kluckhohn, H.A. Murray & D. Schneider (Eds.), *Personality in nature, society and culture.* New York: Knopf.

Kohli, M. (1986). Social organization and subjective construction of the life course. In A.B. Sørenssen, F.E. Weinert & L.R. Sherrod (Eds.), *Human development and the life course: Multidisciplinary perspectives* (pp. 271–292). Hillsdale, NJ: Erlbaum

Kovach, C.R. (1995). A qualitative look at reminiscing: Using the autobiographical memory coding tool. In B.K. Haight, & J.D. Webster (Eds.), *The art and science of reminiscing: Theory, research, methods and applications* (pp. 103–122). Washington DC: Taylor and Francis.

Kunst, L. (2004). Structurele en gerodynamische aspecten van het LIM | Levensverhaal. [Structural and gerodynamical aspects of the LIM | Life story] (MA thesis). Amsterdam, The Netherlands: Free University, Department of Psychology.

Lange, J. de, & Staa, A.L. van (2004). Transities in ziekte en zorg: op zoek naar een nieuw evenwicht [Transitions in disease and care: searching for a new balance]. *Verpleegkunde, 19*, 142–150.

Levine, L.J. (1997). Reconstructing memory for emotions. *Journal of Experimental Psychology: General, 126*, 165–177.

Levinson, D.L. (1986). A conception of adult development. *American Psychologist*, 42, 3–13.

Levinson, D.L. (1996). *The seasons of a woman's life.* New York: Alfred Knopf.

Linde, C. (1993). *Life stories.* Oxford, UK: Oxford University Press.

Lowenthal, M.F., Thurnher, M., & Chiriboga, D. (1975). *Four stages of life.* San Francisco: Jossey-Bass Publishers.

Luborsky, M.R. (1990), 'Alchemists' visions: Cultural norms in eliciting and analyzing life history narratives'. *Journal of Aging Studies, 4,* 17-29.

Luborsky, M.R. (1998). Creative challenges and the construction of meaningful life narratives. In C. Adams-Price (Ed.), Creativity and successful aging: Theoretical and empirical approaches (pp. 311–337). New York: Springer Publishing.

Mackavey, W.R., Malley, J.E., & Stewart, A.J. (1991). Remembering autobiographically consequential experiences: Content analysis of psychologists' accounts of their lives. *Psychology and Aging, 6,* 50–59.

Markus, H., & Nurius, P. (1986). Possible selves. *American Psychologist, 41,* 954–969.

Martin, P., & Smyer, M.A. (1990). The experience of micro- and macroevents: A lifespan analysis. *Research on Aging, 12,* 294–310.

Maylor, E. A., Darby, R. J., Logie, R. H., Della Sala, S., & Smith, G. (2002). Prospective memory across the lifespan. In P. Graf & N. Ohta (Eds), *Lifespan development of human memory* (pp. 235–256). Cambridge, USA: The MIT Press.

McAdams, D.P. (1985). *Power, intimacy, and the life story: Personological inquiries into identity.* New York: William Morrow.

McAdams, D.P. (1988). Biography, narrative, and lives: An introduction. *Journal of Personality, 56,* 1–18.

McAdams, D.P. (1996). Personality, modernity, and the stories self: A contemporary framework for studying persons. *Psychological Inquiry, 7,* 295–321.

McAdams, D.P. (1997). *Stories we live by: Personal myths and the making of the self.* New York: Guilford Press.

McAdams, D.P. (1999). Personal narratives and the life story. In L.A. Pervin & O.P. John (Eds.), *Handbook of personality, theory and research* (pp. 478–500). New York: The Guilford Press.

McAdams, D.P. (2000). *The person: an integrated introduction to personality psychology* (3th ed.). Fort Worth: Harcourt College Publishers.

McAdams, D.P. (2001). The psychology of life stories. *Review of General Psychology, 5,* 100–122.

McAdams, D.P., & de St. Aubin, E. de (Eds.) (1998). *Generativity and adult development: How and why we care for the next generation.* Washington, DC: American Psychological Association.

McAdams, D.P., Diamond, A., St. Aubin, E. de, & Mansfield, E. (1997). Stories of commitment: The psychosocial construction of generative lives. *Journal of Personality and Social Psychology, 72,* 678–694.

McAdams, D.P., Anyidoho, N.A., Brown, C., Huang, Y.T., Kaplan, B., & Machado M.A. (2004). Traits and stories: Links between dispositional and narrative features of personality. *Journal of Personality, 74,* 761–784.

McAdams, D.P., Bauer, J.J., Sakaeda, A.R., Anyidoho, N.A., Machado, M. A., Magrino-Failla, K., White, K.W., & Pals, J.L. (2006). Continuity and change in the life story: A longitudinal study of autobiographical memories in emerging adulthood. *Journal of Personality, 74,* 1371–1400.

McCrae, R.R., & Costa, P.T., Jr. (1990). *Personality in adulthood.* New York: Guilford Press.

Mead, G.H. (1964). The nature of the past. In A.J. Reck (Ed*.), Selected writings: George Herbert Mead* (pp. 345–354). Chicago: University of Chicago Press.

Mehlsen, M., Platz, M., & Fromholt, P. (2003). Life satisfaction across the life course: Evaluations of the most and least satisfying decades of life. *International Journal of Aging and Human Development, 57,* 217–236.

Mirowsky, J., & Ross, C.E. (1999). Well-being across the life course. In A.V. Horwitz & T.L. Scheid (Eds.), *A handbook for the study of mental health* (pp. 328–347). Cambridge, UK: Cambridge University Press

Mitchell, T.R., Thompson, L., Peterson, E. & Cronk, R. (1997). Temporal adjustments in the evaluation of events: The "Rosy View". *Journal of Experimental Social Psychology, 33,* 421–448.

Moen, P. (1996). Gender, age and the life course. In R.H. Binstock, & L.K. George (Eds.), *Handbook of Aging and the Social Sciences* (4th ed.) (pp. 171–187). San Diego: Academic Press.

Moen, P. & Wethington, E. (1999). Midlife development in a life course context. In S.L. Willis & J.D. Reid (Eds*.), Life in the middle: Psychological and social development in middle age* (pp. 3–23). San Diego: Academic Press.

Murray, H.A. (1938). *Explorations in personality.* New York: Oxford University Press.

Musgrove, P. (1985). Why everything takes 2.71828… time as long as expected. *The American Economic Review, 75,* 250–252.

Neugarten, B.L. (1970). Dynamics of transition to old age. *Journal of Geriatric Psychiatry, 4,* 71–87.

Neugarten, B.L. (1977). Personality and aging. In J.E. Birren & K.W. Schaie (Eds.) *Handbook of the psychology of aging* (pp. 626–649). New York: Van Nostrand-Reinhold.

Neugarten, B.L. (1979). Time, age, and the life cycle. *American Journal of Psychiatry, 136,* 887–894.

Newby-Clark, I.R., & Ross, M. (2003). Conceiving the past and future. *Personality and Social Psychology Bulletin, 29,* 807–818.

Peterson, B.E., & Stewart, A.J. (1990). Using personal and fictional documents to assess psychosocial development: The case study of Vera Brittain's generativity. *Psychology and Aging, 5,* 400–411.

Peterson, C., Grant, V.V. & Boland, L.E. (2005). Childhood amnesia in children and adolescents: Their earliest memories. *Memory, 13,* 622–637.

Phinney, C., Chiodo, L., & Perlmutter, M. (1988). *Major Life Events Inventory.* Ann Arbor, MI: Institute of Gerontology.

Pillemer, D.B. (2003). Directive functions of autobiographical memory: The guiding power of the specific episode. *Memory, 11,* 193–202.

Putney, N.M., & Bengtson, V.L. (2001). Families, intergenerational relationships, and kinkeeping in midlife. In M.E. Lachman (Ed), *Handbook of midlife development* (pp. 528–570). New York: John Wiley & Sons.

Rappaport, H., Enrich, K., & Wilson, A. (1985). Relation between ego identity and temporal perspective. *Journal of Personality and Social Psychology, 48,* 1609–1620.

Reese, H., & Smyer, M.A. (1983). The dimensionalization of life events. In J. Callahan & K.A. McCluskey (Eds.), *Lifespan developmental psychology: Nonnormative life events* (pp. 1–34). New York: Academic Press.

Robinson, J.A. (1986). Autobiographical memory : A historical prologue. In D.C. Rubin (Ed.), *Autobiographical memory* (pp. 19–24). Cambridge, UK: Cambridge University Press.

Robinson, J.A. & Taylor, L.R. (1998). Autobiographical memory and self-narratives: A tale of two stories. In C.P. Thompson, D.J. Herrmann, D. Bruce, J. Don Read, D.G. Payne & M.P. Toglia (Eds.), *Autobiographical memory; Theoretical and applied perspectives* (pp. 125–143). London: Lawrence Erlbaum Associates.

Rönkä, A., Oravala, S., & Pulkkinen, L. (2003). Turning points in adults' lives: The effects of gender and the amount of choice. *Journal of Adult Development, 10,* 203–215.

Rubin, D.C. (Ed.) (1986). *Autobiographical memory.* Cambridge, UK: Cambridge University Press.

Rubin, D.C. (1995). *Remembering our past: Studies in autobiographical memory.* Cambridge, UK: Cambridge University Press.

Rubin, D.C. (2002). Autobiographical memory across the lifespan. In P. Graf & N. Ohta (Eds), *Lifespan development of human memory* (pp. 159–184). Cambridge, USA: The MIT Press.

Rubin, D.C., & Berntsen, D. (2003). Life scripts help to maintain autobiographical memories of highly positive, but not highly negative events. *Memory & Cognition, 31,* 1–14.

Rubin, D.C., & Schulkind, M.D. (1997). Distribution of important and word-cued autobiographical memories in 20-, 35-, and 70-year old adults. *Psychology and Aging, 12,* 524–535.

Rubin, D.C., Rahhal, T.A. & Poon, L.W. (1998). Things learned in early adulthood are remembered best. *Memory & Cognition, 26,* 3–19.

Rubin, D.C., Schulkind, M.D., & Rahhal, T.A. (1999). A study of gender differences in autobiographical memory: Broken down by age and sex. *Journal of Adult Development, 6,* 61–71.

Rubin, C.R., Schrauf, R.W. & Greenberg, D.L. (2004). Stability in autobiographical memories. *Memory, 12,* 715–721.

Runyan, W.M. (1983). Idiographic goals and methods in the study of lives. *Journal of Personality, 51,* 413–437.

Saldaña, J. (2003). *Longitudinal qualitative research: Analyzing change through time.* Walnut Creek: Altamira.

Sandoval, J. (2002). Moving. In J. Sandoval (Ed.), *Handbook of crisis counseling, intervention, and prevention in the schools* (2nd ed.) (pp. 231–247). Mahwah: Lawrence Erlbaum Associates.

Sarason, I.G., Johnson, J.H., & Siegel, J.M. (1978). Assessing the impact of life changes: Development of the Life Experiences Survey. *Journal of Consulting and Clinical Psychology, 46,* 932–946.

Schachter, D. (2001). *The seven sins of memory: How the mind forgets and remembers.* Boston: Houghton Mifflin Company.

Schaie, K.W. (1965). A general model for the study of developmental problems. *Psychological Bulletin, 64,* 92–107.

Schaie, K.W., & Baltes, P.B (1975). On sequential strategies in developmental research and the Schaie-Baltes controversy: Description or explanation? *Human Development, 18,* 384–390.

Schaie, K.W., & Hofer, S.M. (2001). Longitudinal studies in aging research. In J.E. Birren & K.W. Schaie (Eds.), *Handbook of the psychology of aging* (5th ed.) (pp. 53–77). San Diego: Academic Press.

Scherder, E.J.A., Schroots, J.J.F., & Kerkhof A.J.F.M. (2002). Psychologische behandelmethoden in levensloopperspectief [Psychological methods for treatment in lifespan perspective]. In J.J.F. Schroots (Ed.), *Handboek psychologie van de volwassen ontwikkeling & veroudering* [Handbook of the psychology of adult development & aging] (pp. 375–409). Assen: Koninklijke Van Gorcum.

Schmotkin, D. (1991). The role of time orientation in life satisfaction across the lifespan. *Journal of Gerontology, 46,* 243–251.

Schrauf, R.W., & Rubin, D.C. (2001). Effect of voluntary immigration on the distribution of autobiographical memories over the lifespan. *Applied Cognitive Psychology, 15,* S75–S88.

Schroots, J.J.F. (1982). Ontogenetische psychologie; een eerste kennismaking [Ontogenetic psychology; a first introduction]. *De Psycholoog, 17,* 68–81.

Schroots, J.J.F. (1984). The affective consequences of technological change for older persons. In P.K. Robinson, J. Livingston & J.E. Birren (Eds.), *Aging and technological advances* (pp. 237–247). New York: Plenum Press.

Schroots, J.J.F. (1988). On growing, formative change and aging. In J.E. Birren & V.L. Bengtson (Eds.), *Emergent theories of aging* (pp. 299–329). New York: Springer.

Schroots, J.J.F., (1991). Metaphors of aging and complexity. In G.M. Kenyon, J.E. Birren & J.J.F. Schroots (Eds.), *Metaphors of aging in science and the humanities* (pp. 219–243). New York: Springer Publishing Company.

Schroots, J.J.F. (1995). Gerodynamics: Toward a branching theory of aging. *Canadian Journal on Aging, 14*, 74–81.

Schroots, J.J.F. (1996). The fractal structure of lives: Continuity and discontinuity in autobiography. In J.E. Birren, G.M. Kenyon, J.E. Ruth, J.J.F. Schroots & T. Svensson (Eds.), *Aging and biography: Explorations in adult development* (pp. 117–130). New York: Springer Publishing Company.

Schroots, J.J.F. (2003a). Ageism in science: Fair-play between generations. *Science and Engineering Ethics, 9,* 445–451.

Schroots, J.J.F. (2003b). Life-course dynamics: A research program in progress from The Netherlands. *European Psychologist, 8*, 192–199.

Schroots, J.J.F. (2004). LIM|Levenslijn Interview Methode. Interventie Protocol [LIM|Life-line Interview Method. Intervention Protocol] (Versie 1.0). Amsterdam: Stichting ERGO.

Schroots, J.J.F. (2007). *LIM | Lifeline Interview Method. Manual* (version 2007). Amsterdam: Stichting ERGO.

Schroots, J.J.F. (2008a). *The Janus model of life-course dynamics.* Amsterdam: Stichting ERGO [Utrecht University Press: Igitur].

Schroots, J.J.F. (2008b). The hidden potentials of senior researchers. In H.A. Becker & J.J.F. Schroots (Eds.), *Releasing the potentials of senior scholars & scientists: Emerging productivity in a new ERA.* Amsterdam: Stichting ERGO [Utrecht University Press: Igitur].

Schroots, J.J.F., & Assink, M. (1998). LIM|Levenslijn: Een vergelijkend structuur- onderzoek. [LIM|Life-line: A comparative study of structure]. *Tijdschrift voor Ontwikkelingspsychologie, 24,* 1–23.

Schroots, J.J.F., & Assink, M.H.J. (2004). LIM|Levensverhaal: Een vergelijkende inhoudsanalyse [LIM|Life story: A comparative content analysis]. *Tijdschrift voor Ontwikkelingspsychologie, 25,* 3–42.

Schroots, J.J.F., & Assink, M.H.J. (2005). Portraits of life: Patterns of events over the lifespan. *Journal of Adult Development, 12*, 183–198.

Schroots, J.J.F., & Birren, J.E. (1988). The nature of time: Implications for research on aging. *Comprehensive Gerontology C, 2*, 1–29.

Schroots, J.J.F., & Birren, J.E. (1990). Concepts of time and aging in science. In Birren J.E. & Schaie, K.W. (Eds.), *Handbook of the psychology of aging* (3rd ed.) (pp. 45–64). San Diego, CA: Academic Press.

Schroots, J.J.F., & Birren, J.E. (1993). Theoretical issues and basic questions in the planning of longitudinal studies of health and aging. In J.J.F. Schroots (Ed.), *Aging, health and competence: The next generation of longitudinal research* (pp. 3–34). Amsterdam, The Netherlands: Elsevier.

Schroots, J.J.F., & Birren, J.E. (2002). The study of lives in progress: Approaches to research on life stories. In G.D. Rowles & N.E. Schoenberg (Eds.), *Qualitative gerontology: A contemporary perspective* (pp. 51–56). New York: Springer Publishing Company.

Schroots, J.J.F., & Dijkum, C. van (2004). Autobiographical memory bump: A dynamic lifespan model. *Dynamical Psychology* (http://www.goertzel.org/dynapsyc/2004/autobio.htm).

Schroots, J.J.F., & ten Kate, C.A. (1989). Metaphors, aging and the Life-line Interview Method. In D. Unruh & G. Livings (Eds.), *Current perspectives on aging and the life cycle. Volume 3: Personal history through the life course* (pp. 281–298). London: JAI Press.

Schroots, J.J.F. & van Dongen, L. (1995). Birren's ABC: AutoBiografieCursus [Birren's ABC: AutoBiography-Course]. Assen: Van Gorcum.

Schroots, J.J.F., & Yates, F.E. (1999). On the dynamics of development and aging. In V.L. Bengtson & K.W. Schaie (Eds.), *Handbook of theories of aging* (pp. 417–433). New York: Springer.

Schroots, J.J.F., Birren, J.E., & Kenyon, G.M. (1991). Metaphors and aging: An overview. In G.M. Kenyon, J.E. Birren & J.J.F. Schroots (Eds.), *Metaphors of aging in science and the humanities* (pp. 1–16). New York: Springer.

Schroots, J.J.F., van Dijkum, C., & Assink, M.H.J. (2004). Autobiographical memory across the lifespan. *International Journal of Aging and Human Development, 58, 69–85.*

Schroots, J.J.F., Kunst, L., & Assink, M.H.J. (2006). Op zoek naar de woordstructuur van het LIM | Levensverhaal [In search of the wordstructure of the LIM | Life story]. *Tijdschrift voor Gerontologie en Geriatrie, 37,* 9–18.

Sehulster, J.R. (1996). In my era: Evidence for the perception of a special period of the past. *Memory, 4,* 145–158.

Serrano, J.P., Latorre J.M., Gatz, M., & Montanes, J. (2004). Life review therapy using autobiographical retrieval practice for older adults with depressive symptomatology. *Psychology and Aging, 19,* 272–277.

Settersten, R.A. (1999*). Lives in time and place. The problems and promises of developmental science.* New York: Baywood Publishing Company.

Sijbrandij, M., Olff, M., Reitsma, J.B., Carlier, I.V.E., & Gersons, B.P.R. (2006). Emotional or educational debriefing after psychological trauma: Randomised controlled trial. *British Journal of Psychiatry, 189*, 437–459.

Skowronski, J.J. (2005). In diversity there is strength: An autobiographical memory research sampler. *Social Cognition, 23*, 1–10.

Smith, C.P. (2000). Content analysis and narrative analysis. In H.T. Reis & C.M. Judd (Eds.), *Handbook of research: Methods in social and personality psychology* (pp. 313–335). Cambridge, UK: Cambridge University Press.

Smolenaars, E. (2005). *65 jaar als uiterste houdbaarheidsdatum: een onderzoek naar de leeftijdsgrens van 65 jaar in wet – en regelgeving* [The age of 65 as the final use-by date: A study after the age limit in law and rules]. Utrecht: LBL, expertisecentrum leeftijd en maatschappij.

Staudinger, U.M., Bluck, S. & Herzberg, P.Y. (2003). Looking back and looking ahead: Adult age differences in consistency of diachronous ratings of subjective well-being. *Psychology and Aging, 18*, 13–24.

Sterns, H.L., & Huyck, M.H. (2001). The role of work in midlife. In M.E. Lachman (Ed.), *Handbook of midlife development* (pp. 447–486). New York: John Wiley & Sons.

Stewart, A.J., Franz, C., & Layton, L. (1988). The changing self: Using personal documents to study lives. *Journal of Personality, 56*, 41–74.

Strongman, K.T. (1996). Emotion and memory. In C. Magai & S.H. McFadden (Eds), *Handbook of emotion, adult development, and aging* (pp. 133–147). San Diego: Academic Press.

Sugarman, L. (1986). *Lifespan development: Concepts, theories and interventions.* London: Methuen & Co.

Sugarman, L. (2001). *Lifespan development: Frameworks, accounts and strategies* (2nd ed.). East Sussex: Psychology Press.

Suh, E., Diener, E. & Fujita, F. (1996). Events and subjective well-being: only recent events matter. *Journal of Personality and Social Psychology, 5*, 1091–1102.

Takkinen, S., & Suutama, T. (2004). Life-lines of Finnish people aged 83–87. *International Journal of Aging and Human Development, 59*, 339–362.

Thompson, C.P. (1998). The bounty of everyday memory. In C.P. Thompson, D.J. Herrmann, D. Bruce, J. Don Read, D.G. Payne, & M.P. Toglia (Eds.), *Autobiographical memory: Theoretical and applied perspectives* (pp. 29–44). London: Lawrence Erlbaum Associates.

Thompson, C.P., Skowronski, J.J., Larsen, S.F. & Betz, A.L. (1996). *Autobiographical memory: Remembering what and when.* New Jersey: Lawrence Erlbaum Associates.

Thorne, A., Cutting, L. & Skaw, D. (1998). Young adults' relationship memories. *Narrative Inquiry, 8*, 237–268.

Tulving, E. (1972). Episodic and semantic memory. In E. Tulving & W. Donaldson (Eds.), *Organization of memory* (pp. 381–403). New York: Academic Press.

Tulving, E. (1984). Relations among components and processes of memory. *Behavioral Brain Science, 7*, 257–268.

Tulving, E. (1991). Concepts of human memory. In L.R. Squire, G. Lynch, N.M. Weinberger & J.L. McGaugh (Eds.), *Memory: Organization and locus of change* (pp. 3–32). New York: Oxford University Press.

Tulving, E. (2002). Episodic memory: From mind to brain. *Annual Review of Psychology, 53*, 1–25.

Twisk, J.W.R. (2003). *Applied longitudinal data analysis for epidemiology: A practical guide.* Cambridge, UK: Cambridge University Press.

Vreeswijk, M.F. van, & Wilde, E.J. de (2004). Autobiographical memory specificity, psychopathology, depressed mood and the use of the Autobiographical Memory Test: A meta-analysis. *Behaviour Research and Therapy, 42*, 731–743.

deVries, B. & Watt, D. (1996). A lifetime of events: Age and gender variations in the life story. *International Journal of Aging and Human Development, 42*, 81–102.

deVries, B., Blando, J., Southard, P., & Bubeck, C. (2001). The times of our lives. In G. Kenyon, P. Clark, & B. de Vries (Eds.), *Narrative gerontology: Theory, research, and practice* (pp. 137–158). New York: Springer Publishing Company.

deVries, B., Suedfeld, P., Krell, R., Blando, J.A. & Southard, P. (2005). The Holocaust as a context for telling life stories. *International Journal of Aging & Human Development, 60*, 183–187.

Wagenaar, W.A. (1986). My memory: A study of autobiographical memory over six years. *Cognitive Psychology, 18*, 225–252.

Wagenaar, W. A., & Groeneweg, J. (1990). The memory of concentration camp survivors. *Appied Cognitive Psychology, 4*, 77–87.

Walker, W.R., Skowronski, J.J., & Thompson, C.P. (2003). Life is pleasant – and memory helps to keep it that way! *Review of General Psychology, 7*, 203–210.

Watt, L.M., & Cappeliez, P. (1995). Reminiscence interventions for the treatment of depression in older adults. In B.K. Haight, & J.D. Webster (Eds.), *The art and science of reminiscing: Theory, research, methods and applications* (pp. 221–232). Washington DC: Taylor and Francis.

Webster, J.D., & Haight, B.K. (1995). Memory lane milestones: Progress in reminiscence definition and classification. In B.K. Haight & Webster, J.D., The art and science of reminiscing: Theory, research, methods, and applications, (pp. 273–286). Washington DC: Taylor & Francis.

Wessel, I., Merckelbach, H., & Dekkers, T. (2002). Autobiographical memory specificity, intrusive memory, and general memory skills in Dutch–Indonesian survivors of the World War II era. *Journal of Traumatic Stress, 15*, 227–234.

Whitbourne, S.K., & Dannefer, W.D. (1985–1986). The 'Life drawing' as a measure of time perspective in adulthood. *International Journal of Aging and Human Development, 22*, 147–155.

Whitehead, A.N. (1929). *Process and reality.* New York: Free Press (1969).

Williams, M.A., & Mattingley, J.B. (2006). Do angry men get noticed? *Current Biology, 16*, R402–R404.

Williams, J.M.G., Ellis, N.C., Tyers, C., & Healy, H. (1996). The specificity of autobiographical memory and imageability of the future. *Memory & Cognition, 24*, 116–125.

Willitts, M., Benzeval, M., & Stansfeld, S. (2004). Partnership history and mental health over time. *Journal of Epidemiology and Community Health, 58*, 53–58.

Yang, J.A. & Rehm, L.P. (1993). A study of autobiographical memories in depressed and nondepressed elderly individuals. *International Journal of Aging and Human Development, 36*, 39–55.

Zauberman, G. & Lynch jr, J.G. (2005). Resource slack and propensity to discount delayed investments of time versus money. *Journal of Experimental Psychology: General, 134*, 23–37.

Zautra, A.J., Afflec, G., & Tennen, H. (1994). Assessing life events among older adults. In M.P. Lawton, & J.A. Teresi (Eds.), *Annual Review of Gerontology and Geriatrics, 14*, 324–352 [New York : Springer].

Zuuren, F.J. van (2002). Kwalitatieve methoden [Qualitative methods]. In J.J.F. Schroots (Ed.), *Handboek psychologie van de volwassen ontwikkeling & veroudering* [Handbook of the psychology of adult development & aging] (pp. 77–95). Assen: Koninklijke Van Gorcum.

# Supplement

# LIM | Life-line Interview Method

## Manual
Version 2007

Johannes J.F. Schroots

# Preface

A need exists in practice for an instrument to collect autobiographical information about a client's past and future in a systematical manner. The usual instruments, a questionnaire and an interview, are adequate only to a very limited extent. The easily quantifiable information of a pre-structured auto-biographical questionnaire, on the one hand, does not do justice to the individual's unique qualities, experiences and expectations; whereas, on the other hand, the unique autobiographical information of an open interview blocks any serious attempts to make a quantitative analysis. The new LIM | *Lifeline Interview Method* intends to fill the manifest need for autobiographical information of both a quantative and qualitative nature.

The LIM is based on the well-known metaphor of the course of a person's life as a journey, a river or an alternation of hills and dales. In this method a person is asked to literally draw a map of their life, both past and future, by drawing a line on a simple sheet of paper. The initial result is a wavering Life-line consisting of highs and lows, which partially reflects a human being on their life path, and partially their imagined future. In two subsequent stages the person is asked to define their sketched lifeline, with its highs and lows, in terms of age and events and to provide details: the results is the Life-story.

The first authorised version of the LIM was preceded by a number of experimental versions, which we were able to test thanks to the unrenumerated effort of a great many of our staff. We would like to take this opportunity to express our gratitude to Mss Marian Assink, Titia Buddingh', Sanne Janus, Corine ten Kate, Marlies van Noppen-Schrijer, Tinca Nijdam and Margreet Vogel.

Last, but not least, we thank all respondents who were willing to share their life story and by this contributed to the successful development of the LIM.

October 2007
*Johannes JF Schroots*

# Contents

# Introduction

The LIM is a carefully standardized research instrument. In the construction phase, as well as during subsequent research, a great deal of effort went into uniformizing the interview material, the research context, the intake procedure, the instruction and the details. Through standardization we have tried to keep the interviews as similar in form as possible. To achieve this goal in practical work, the interviewer must carefully follow the rules in this manual.

## Materials (see Annex)
- Drawing board
- LIM paper (grid: 180/296 x 180 mm)
- Models A, B and C
- Life table (men, women)
- Response form
- Pencils
- Pen
- Tape recorder

## Preparing the interview
Become as acquainted with the LIM as you can. Learn your lines – the text in bold – by heart. During the interview itself you will have little or no time to consult the manual. Choose a quiet room to conduct the interview in, one in which you will not be disturbed. Install, if you can, a table or desk that allows you to sit opposite one another. Keep the interview material within hand's reach, but outside the interviewee's (*Itee*) visual field.

## Conducting the interview
It is your job to create conditions in which the *Itee* can be engaged as fully as possible. It is not possible to give detailed instructions, as the interview behavior and the responses to the interview situation will vary from *Itee* to *Itee*. The following points are therefore intended as suggestions only to ensure the interview goes smoothly:
- Sit opposite the *Itee* at the table and introduce the interview as a research into their life-course. Put the *Itee* at their ease, make small talk and introduce the tape recorder. Inform the Itee that you will take notes during the interview and need the recorder in case you have forgotten something after the interview. Stress the fact that the interview is confidential and the research data anonymous. Start the interview immediately after that.
- The idea of Models A, B and C is for the *Itee* to draw their own lifeline spontaneously and without much deliberation. If necessary, the *Itee* is allowed to make corrections to the line with a dotted line, as long as the original lifeline remains visible.
- Praise the *Itee* for their effort only, not for the results of their effort. Never say that a lifeline or an answer is right or wrong. There is no such thing as a wrong lifeline or life story.
- Try to keep the interview on track by referring regularly to the line drawn with the marks and ages. Conduct the past and future interviews directly after each other, without pausing.
- It is always a good idea to have a few open questions ready. For example: *Could you tell me some more about that?* or *Can you explain that?* and *What do you mean by that?*
- It is more than possible that the *Itee* will become emotional as he or she tells their story. Don't brush over it, but don't go into it too deeply either. Take the time to let the *Itee* quiet down; it is they who largely determine the pace of the interview.

— After the interview, give the *Itee* the opportunity to express their feelings. Tell them, if necessary, that it occurs regularly that the interview stirs up things that people want to talk about further. Give them a telephone number for emergencies

## Response form

Use the response form to make a brief record of the interview. The form comprises three columns, which correspond with the three phases of the interview:

— Column 1: Use this column to note the spontaneous remarks the *Itee* makes as they draw their lifeline; also use it for your own observations (first phase);
— Column 2: In the second phase of the interview, the *Itee* is required to put a mark on the lifeline for each event with the corresponding age or year and to explain briefly what happened (line of the past) or what is going to happen (line of the future). Use the second column to write age or year for each event and take down what *Itee* says verbatim;
— Column 3: In the third phase events are discussed in detail and the *Itee* is allowed to tell their story. Use the third column for taking notes. Make a short note for each event to record the *Itee*'s life story.

## Finally

Check your record directly after the interview.

# Instruction: Start

Introduce yourself and explain clearly why you have requested this interview. Introduce the tape recorder and turn it on. Place the models face down on the table in the right order. Emphasize the confidential nature of the interview.

Clasp the LIM paper to the drawing board and place the board in front of the respondent. Take the pencil in your hand and say:

> **In front of you, you see a board with on it a sheet of paper. On the sheet you see several lines** (indicate the lines broadly with the pencil). **This line represents the time you were born. You were 0 years old then. Look, there is a 0 here and another one there** (indicate where). **This line represents your present age.**
>
> **Would you now please write your age here and there** (indicate top and bottom of line)?

Hand the respondent the pencil and wait until they have written their age.

# Instruction: Models

## Model A

Now take model A and fit it exactly on the drawing board.

**First I will show you some models to give you an idea of what you are supposed to do. Look, this is a lifeline that runs from someone's moment of birth** (indicate pointer) **to their present age** (indicate line). **Not much seems to have happened in this life. Everything has remained more or less the same.**

Give the respondent sufficient time to take in the model. Take model B and place it on top of model A.

## Model B

**Here is another example. The drawing of this lifeline shows highs and lows** (indicate). **The lows** (indicate) **are the hard times in life. They are the difficult periods, in which things in life were going wrong. The highs, on the other hand,** (indicate) **represent the good times. They are the periods in which things in life were going right, the times of good fortune and happiness.**

Again, give the respondent enough time to take in the model. Then place model C on top of model B.

## Model C

**This is the last model. Could you tell me what you see here? Go ahead and point to it.**

Allow the respondent to explain, in their own words, what they see in model C. If the respondent has understood the model, then say:

**Indeed, by the looks of it this person has been through a lot in their life. Not only are there many ups and downs, but they are also pretty high and low. The higher an up or the lower a down, the more important the event is in this life.**
**Is everything clear so far?**

If the person does not understand the instructions, then repeat a model and explain it again slowly. Don't make up a new explanation on the spot, that would only cause confusion. If someone keeps repeating they don't understand, ask them to try anyway (*by telling them, for example, that it's not as hard as they think*).

Once it is apparent that the respondent understands, remove the models from view and continue with the instructions.

# Instruction: Past

- **Now I want to ask you to draw your own lifeline, with all its highs and lows. There are no right or wrong lifelines. We are concerned with your own lifeline. So, please start at this mark and end there** (indicate the entire line).
- **Please start now.**

If the respondent spends too much time deliberating, then say: *Please just begin and draw the line spontaneously as it comes to you.* If the respondent wants to divide the horizontal line into sections, as if it were a ruler, then say: *That is not what you are supposed to do. Just draw the line as it comes to you.*

Now take the answer form and note what the respondent says as they draw the line. Wait until the respondent has drawn the line and note the time.

- **Thank you. By the looks of it, several things happened in your life. Could you now point to me where on the line the *first* important event happened?**
- **Would you please draw a mark through the line at that spot?**
- **How old were you then?**
- **Please write your age next to the mark.**
- **Could you now explain briefly what happened then? We'll come back to it later.**

Write date or age on the response form and note the related event.

- **Would you now make a mark at the *next* important event in your life?**
- **How old were you then?**
- **Please write your age next to the mark.**
- **What happened at that time?**

First have the respondent identify all events in this way; don't go into them further yet at this stage. *Tell the respondent that you will come back to it later.* If a person wants to correct the line, *tell them that they're not supposed to that.* If the respondent persists, allow them to correct the line with a dotted line, but only if the original line remains visible. Check if all the highs and lows have been identified. If they haven't, ask the respondent to do so as yet: *Tell them that you still see a high/low here* (indicate) *that the respondent hasn't said anything about yet and ask them to to tell what happened at that time.*

Now go back to the beginning of the line (the time of birth) and say:

- **Now let's go back to the beginning. Could you tell me something about that period?** (period to first event)
- **Can you now tell me something about the first** (second, third, etc.) **event?** Go through the entire lifeline in this manner. Take down the life story in key words on the third section of the response form.
- **Thank you. Is there anything you would like to add?**

## Instruction: Future

- **Now we have looked at the past, let's continue with the future. We all have an idea of approximately how old we will live to be** (pause).
- **Would you mind telling me what age you think you will reach?**

If the respondent hesitates, then ask *what the first thing is that occurs to them*. If the respondent refuses, then take the life expectancy table (men, women) and read out loud: *According to the statistics you will live to be about …… years old.*

- **Would you please write this age above and below this line?** (indicate) **Thank you.**
- **The future is certain to have its highs and lows as well. I would like to see you extend this line to the future, starting from this point** (indicate termination of past line) **to somewhere on this dotted line** (indicate the entire dotted line). **You don't have talk while you draw.**
- **Please start now.**

Wait until the respondent has drawn the line and note the time.

> **Could you now indicate on this line as well when something is going to happen?**
> **Please put a mark in the line there, as before.**
> **How old will you be at that time?**
> **Please write your age near the mark.**
> **What is going to happen then?**

Next, follow the same procedure as you did above. Return to the beginning of the future line and say:

- **Now let's go back to the beginning. Could you tell me something about this period?** (Period to first event)
- **Can you now tell me about the first** (second, etc.) **event? Go over the entire future line in this way.**
- **Thank you.**

Final question:

- **Take a minute to look at your lifeline. What do you think of it?**

Give the respondent sufficient time to express their feelings about the interview.

# Annex:
# Materials

## LIM Paper*

# LIM | Life-line Interview Method

## Response Form

Johannes J.F. Schroots

# Past

Time Past Line ...... minutes ......seconds

| Age/Year | Event | Story |
|----------|-------|-------|
|          |       |       |

From: Assink, M. & Schroots, J.J.F. (2010). *The dynamics of autobiographical memory using the LIM | Life-line Interview Method*. Cambridge, MA and Göttingen: Hogrefe Publishing. © 2010 Hogrefe Publishing. Web: www.hogrefe.com

## Past – Continued

| Age/Year | Event | Story |
|----------|-------|-------|
|          |       |       |
|          |       |       |

From: Assink, M. & Schroots, J.J.F. (2010). *The dynamics of autobiographical memory using the LIM | Life-line Interview Method*. Cambridge, MA and Göttingen: Hogrefe Publishing. © 2010 Hogrefe Publishing. Web: www.hogrefe.com

# Future

Subjective Life Expectancy: .........

Time Future Line: ...... minutes ......seconds

| Age/Year | Event | Story |
|---|---|---|
| | | |

# Model A

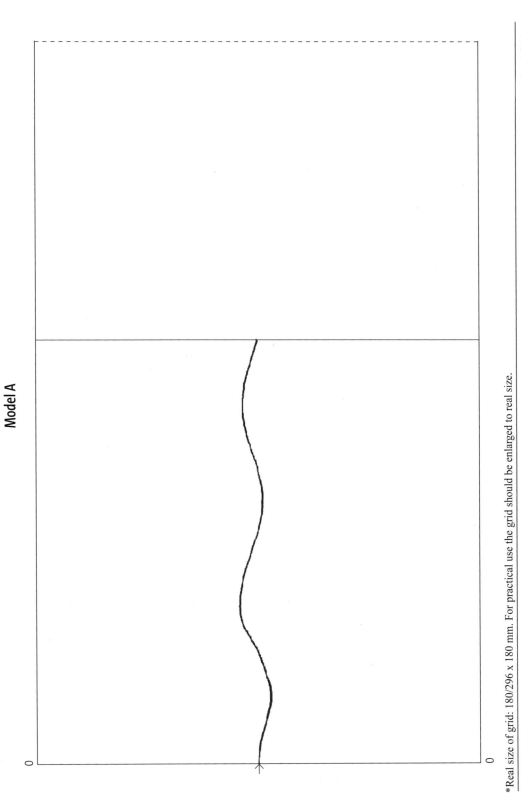

From: Assink, M. & Schroots, J.J.F. (2010). *The dynamics of autobiographical memory using the LIM | Life-line Interview Method*. Cambridge, MA and Göttingen: Hogrefe Publishing.

**Model B**

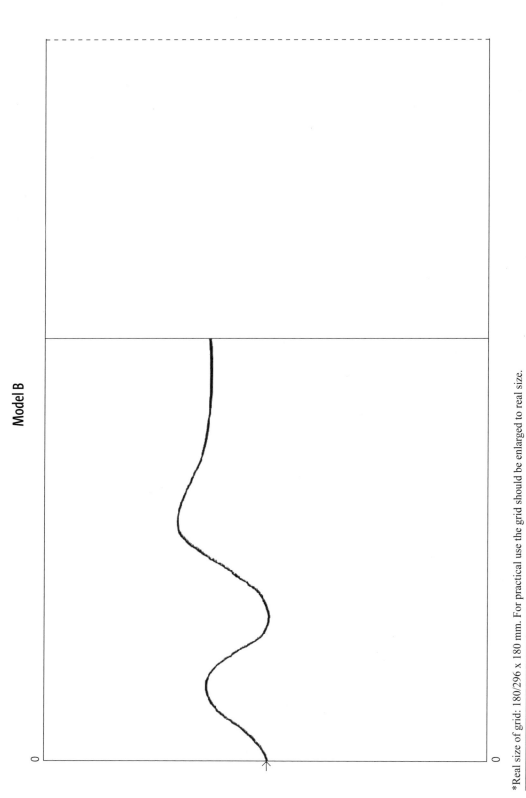

0

0

# Model C

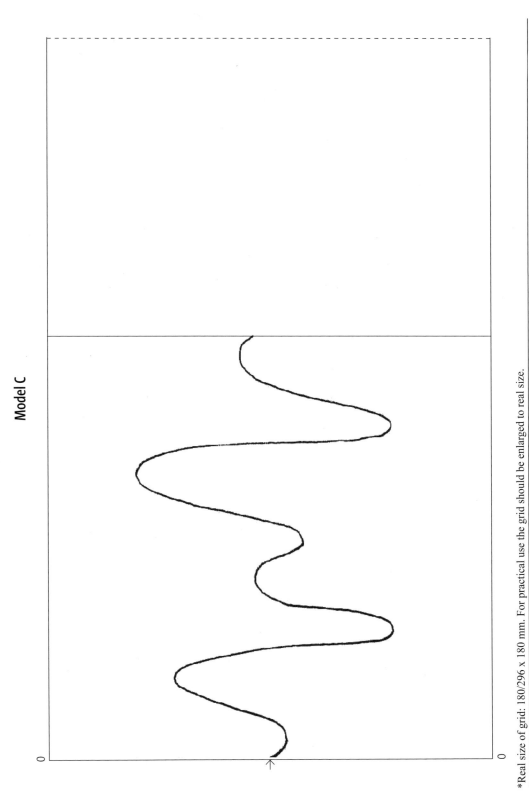

0

0

## Life Expectancy: Men
(CBS 2005, The Netherlands)

| Age | Expected | Age | Expected |
|-----|----------|-----|----------|
| 0 | 77 | 50 | 79 |
| 1 | 77 | 51 | 79 |
| 2 | 77 | 52 | 79 |
| 3 | 77 | 53 | 79 |
| 4 | 77 | 54 | 79 |
| 5 | 77 | 55 | 79 |
| 6 | 77 | 56 | 79 |
| 7 | 77 | 57 | 80 |
| 8 | 77 | 58 | 80 |
| 9 | 77 | 59 | 80 |
| 10 | 77 | 60 | 80 |
| 11 | 77 | 61 | 80 |
| 12 | 77 | 62 | 80 |
| 13 | 77 | 63 | 81 |
| 14 | 77 | 64 | 81 |
| 15 | 77 | 65 | 81 |
| 16 | 77 | 66 | 81 |
| 17 | 77 | 67 | 82 |
| 18 | 77 | 68 | 82 |
| 19 | 77 | 69 | 82 |
| 20 | 77 | 70 | 82 |
| 21 | 77 | 71 | 83 |
| 22 | 77 | 72 | 83 |
| 23 | 77 | 73 | 84 |
| 24 | 77 | 74 | 84 |
| 25 | 78 | 75 | 84 |
| 26 | 78 | 76 | 85 |
| 27 | 78 | 77 | 85 |
| 28 | 78 | 78 | 86 |
| 29 | 78 | 79 | 86 |
| 30 | 78 | 80 | 87 |
| 31 | 78 | 81 | 88 |
| 32 | 78 | 82 | 88 |
| 33 | 78 | 83 | 89 |
| 34 | 78 | 84 | 89 |
| 35 | 78 | 85 | 90 |
| 36 | 78 | 86 | 91 |
| 37 | 78 | 87 | 92 |
| 38 | 78 | 88 | 92 |
| 39 | 78 | 89 | 93 |
| 40 | 78 | 90 | 94 |
| 41 | 78 | 91 | 95 |
| 42 | 78 | 92 | 95 |
| 43 | 78 | 93 | 96 |
| 44 | 78 | 94 | 97 |
| 45 | 78 | 95 | 98 |
| 46 | 78 | 96 | 99 |
| 47 | 78 | 97 | 100 |
| 48 | 79 | 98+ | 101 |
| 49 | 79 | | |

## Life Expectancy: Women
(CBS 2005, The Netherlands)

| Age | Expected | Age | Expected |
|-----|----------|-----|----------|
| 0 | 81 | 50 | 83 |
| 1 | 81 | 51 | 83 |
| 2 | 81 | 52 | 83 |
| 3 | 81 | 53 | 83 |
| 4 | 81 | 54 | 83 |
| 5 | 81 | 55 | 83 |
| 6 | 81 | 56 | 83 |
| 7 | 81 | 57 | 83 |
| 8 | 81 | 58 | 84 |
| 9 | 81 | 59 | 84 |
| 10 | 82 | 60 | 84 |
| 11 | 82 | 61 | 84 |
| 12 | 82 | 62 | 84 |
| 13 | 82 | 63 | 84 |
| 14 | 82 | 64 | 84 |
| 15 | 82 | 65 | 85 |
| 16 | 82 | 66 | 85 |
| 17 | 82 | 67 | 85 |
| 18 | 82 | 68 | 85 |
| 19 | 82 | 69 | 85 |
| 20 | 82 | 70 | 86 |
| 21 | 82 | 71 | 86 |
| 22 | 82 | 72 | 86 |
| 23 | 82 | 73 | 86 |
| 24 | 82 | 74 | 86 |
| 25 | 82 | 75 | 87 |
| 26 | 82 | 76 | 87 |
| 27 | 82 | 77 | 88 |
| 28 | 82 | 78 | 88 |
| 29 | 82 | 79 | 88 |
| 30 | 82 | 80 | 89 |
| 31 | 82 | 81 | 89 |
| 32 | 82 | 82 | 90 |
| 33 | 82 | 83 | 90 |
| 34 | 82 | 84 | 91 |
| 35 | 82 | 85 | 91 |
| 36 | 82 | 86 | 92 |
| 37 | 82 | 87 | 93 |
| 38 | 82 | 88 | 93 |
| 39 | 82 | 89 | 94 |
| 40 | 82 | 90 | 95 |
| 41 | 82 | 91 | 95 |
| 42 | 82 | 92 | 96 |
| 43 | 82 | 93 | 97 |
| 44 | 82 | 94 | 98 |
| 45 | 82 | 95 | 98 |
| 46 | 82 | 96 | 99 |
| 47 | 82 | 97 | 100 |
| 48 | 83 | 98+ | 101 |
| 49 | 83 | | |